MALFUZAT

—————— *of* ——————

The Promised Messiah & Mahdi[as]

Malfuzat — Volume II
Sayings and Discourses of Hazrat Mirza Ghulam Ahmad
The Promised Messiah and Mahdi, on whom be peace,
Founder of the Ahmadiyya Muslim Community

First English translation published in the UK, 2019

Published by:
Islam International Publications Ltd.
Unit 3, Bourne Mills Business Park,
Guildford Road, Farnham, Surrey, GU9 9PS, United Kingdom

For more information please visit:
www.islaminternationalpublications.com
www.alislam.org

© Islam International Publications Ltd.

Translated by Ayyaz Mahmood Khan
Typesetting and Design: Farhan Naseer
Calligraphy: Mubashir Zafri

Printed and bound by CPI Group (UK) Ltd, Croydon, CRO 4YY

ISBN 978-1-84880-991-8

MALFUZAT

Sayings and Discourses of the Promised Messiah and Mahdi^{as}
Founder of the Ahmadiyya Muslim Community

Volume II

A collection from January 1899 to August 1900

Hazrat Mirza Ghulam Ahmad
The Promised Messiah and Mahdi^{as}
Founder of the Ahmadiyya Muslim Community

Published under the auspices of Hazrat Mirza Masroor Ahmad,
Imam and Head of the Worldwide Ahmadiyya Muslim Community,
Fifth Successor to the Promised Messiah^{as},
May Allah be his Helper

ISLAM INTERNATIONAL PUBLICATIONS LIMITED

Contents

1899

6 January 1900

10 January 1900

2 February 1900

14 May 1900

9 July 1900

16 July 1900

Hazrat Mirza Ghulam Ahmad of Qadian
The Promised Messiah & Mahdi
(on whom be peace)

About the Promised Messiah[as]

Hazrat Mirza Ghulam Ahmad, on whom be peace, was born in 1835 in Qadian, India. From his early life, he dedicated himself to prayer, the study of the Holy Quran and other scriptures. He was deeply pained to observe the plight of Islam, which was being attacked from all directions. In order to defend Islam and present its teachings in their pristine purity, he wrote more than ninety books, thousands of letters and participated in many religious debates. He argued that Islam is a living Faith, which can lead humanity to the achievement of moral and spiritual perfection by establishing communion with God.

Hazrat Mirza Ghulam Ahmad, on whom be peace, started experiencing divine dreams, visions and revelations at a young age. In 1889, under divine command, he started accepting initiation into the Ahmadiyya Muslim Community. He continued to receive divine revelations and was thereafter commanded by God to announce that he was the divinely appointed Reformer of the Latter Days, as prophesied by various religions under different titles. He claimed to be the same Promised Messiah and Mahdi whose advent had been prophesied by the Holy Prophet Muhammad, peace and blessings of Allah be upon him. The Ahmadiyya Muslim Community is now established in more than two hundred countries of the world.

After the demise of the Promised Messiah, on whom be peace, in 1908, the institution of *Khilafat* (successorship) was established to continue his mission, in fulfilment of the prophecies made in the Holy Quran and by the Holy Prophet Muhammad, peace and blessings of Allah be upon him. Hazrat Mirza Masroor Ahmad, may Allah be his Helper, is the Fifth Successor to the Promised Messiah, on whom be peace, and the present head of the Ahmadiyya Muslim Community.

A Note About the Translation

References to the Holy Quran contain the name of the *Surah* [i.e. chapter] followed by a chapter:verse citation, e.g. *al-Jumu'ah*, 62:4, and counts *Bismillahir-Rahmanir-Rahim* [In the name of Allah, the Gracious, the Merciful] as the first verse in every chapter it appears.

Explanatory footnotes are clearly marked as being from the Publisher throughout the book.

The name of Muhammad^{sa}, the Holy Prophet of Islam, has been followed by the symbol ^{sa}, which is an abbreviation for the salutation *sallallahu alayhi wa sallam* (peace and blessings of Allah be upon him).

The names of other Prophets and Messengers are followed by the symbol ^{as}, an abbreviation for *alayhis-salam* (on whom be peace).

The names of the companions of the Holy Prophet Muhammad^{sa} or of the Promised Messiah^{as} are followed by the symbol ^{ra}, which is an abbreviation for the salutation *radiyallu anhu/anha/anhum* (may Allah be pleased with him/her/them).

The names of deceased pious Muslims who are not companions of the Holy Prophet Muhammad^{sa} or of the Promised Messiah^{as} are followed by the symbol ^{rh}, which is an abbreviation for *rahmatullahi alayhi/alayha/alayhim* (may Allah have mercy upon him/her/them).

In instances, the actual salutations have been set out in full, but wherever this is not the case, they should nevertheless, be understood as being repeated in full in each case.

Preface

It is by the sheer grace and mercy of Allah Almighty, and the blessings and guidance of Hazrat Khalifatul-Masih V (may Allah be his Helper) that the second volume of *Malfuzat—Sayings & Discourses of the Promised Messiah*as is being published in English. This translation is based on the new ten-volume typed edition of *Malfuzat* prepared and published by Nazarat-e-Isha'at Sadr Anjuman Ahmadiyya in 2016; and the present volume in English spans from January 1899 to August 1900.

A collection of sayings and discourses of the Promised Messiahas was first published in the form of a complete set by Al-Shirkatul Islamiyyah in ten volumes. Subsequently, Nazarat-e-Isha'at published the content of this ten-volume set in five volumes.

Following this, Hazrat Khalifatul-Masih V (may Allah be his Helper) instructed that a computerised typeset edition of *Malfuzat* be prepared. He stated that the books in the five-volume set of *Malfuzat* were heavy and uneasy to handle; therefore, the five-volume *Malfuzat* should be printed in ten volumes again. In light of these instructions, a new typeset edition of *Malfuzat* was prepared and published in ten volumes.

In the preparation of this most recent typeset edition, the original sources from *Al-Hakam* and *Al-Badr* Qadian were studied and every effort was made to include any spoken words of the Promised Messiah, on whom be peace, which had been missed from inclusion previously. Hence, due to this effort there were certain sayings and discourses of the Promised Messiah, which had not previously been included in the collection known as *Malfuzat*; and so they have now been added to this new edition.

In view of the guidance of Hazrat Khalifatul-Masih V (may Allah be his Helper), wherever there are differences in the reports of *Al-Hakam* and *Al-Badr*, these have been recorded in footnotes. The relevant words have been recorded as footnotes in a manner that the context of the respective text is clear. Therefore, in view of this, footnotes have been added in the new edition as required.

In the earlier edition of *Malfuzat* there were certain sayings of the Promised Messiah[as] which had not been placed correctly in terms of chronological order. All such sections have been appropriately rearranged. In certain instances, notes from the Editor had been misplaced; this has been corrected as well.

This English translation is a rendering of pp. 255-513 (or the second half) of volume 1, from the new 2016 edition of *Malfuzat* prepared by Nazarat-e-Isha'at. In accordance with the instructions of Hazrat Khalifatul-Masih V (may Allah be his Helper), this was done so that the size of the English volume could be kept lightweight and as easy to read as possible.

In various sections throughout the Urdu text, it was found that there were misprints or errors in reporting, which had followed through since the old edition of *Malfuzat*, and in fact, even existed in the original sources as recorded by *Al-Hakam*. All such instances were presented with detailed reports to Hazrat Khalifatul-Masih V (may Allah be his Helper), and after his approval, were corrected in the English translation within the main text. No footnotes stating the original misprint and the correction were given in light of guidance from Huzoor-e-Anwar (may Allah be his Helper).

Ayyaz Mahmood Khan was blessed with the good fortune of rendering this English translation from the Urdu. The tireless efforts of Zafir Mahmood Malik are also worthy of mention, who worked with the translator to check the English work against the original source text. The valuable contribution of Amer Safir must also be mentioned who checked a portion of the final translation with the translator. The selfless devotion of Syed Muhammad Tahir Nasser, Syed Muhammad Umar Nasser and Nadia Mahmood must also be highlighted, all of whom edited the final manuscript and offered invaluable improvements to the overall style and readability of the translation. Immense gratitude is also due to Farhan Naseer who designed the layout of the book and prepared it for print.

Additionally, we are grateful to Munavara Ghauri, Syeda Sadaf Nasir Shah, Sadia Rana, Rizwan Khan, Azam Akram and Fatima Amatullah Naseer for assisting in proofreading various sections of the manuscript.

The indexes were prepared with the help of Hassan Ahmad Minhas, Munib Harun Iqbal, Sohaib Ahmad, Junaid Aslam, Subtain Ali Ahmed, Asif Ahmad Rashid, Hashir Riaz Ahmed Butt, Mahir Ahmad, Mubeen Ahmad Doger, Fraz Ahmad, Atta ul Hai, Haris Ahmad, Syed Hashir Hoodh Ahmad, Tahir Ahmad Mian. The verses of the Holy Quran and other Arabic references were checked in the final stages by Hafiz Rahat Cheema. Hafiz Muzaffar Ahmad also assisted in researching difficult passages and Abdul Ghany Jahangeer Khan also provided unrelenting assistance whenever he was called upon.

The Central Arabic Desk also offered their full assistance in various capacities. Throughout the course of this project, Malik Khalid Masood, Nazir Isha'at, offered constant and invaluable support in addressing any queries that were directed to him. From India, if ever any research was required Mamoon Rasheed Tabrez of Qadian, offered his full cooperation.

May Allah the Exalted reward all those who assisted—in any capacity—to bring this work to fruition; may He shower His mercy and grace upon their families and accept their services. *Ameen,* and again, *ameen.*

Publisher

23 June 2019

Introduction

Written for the Five-Volume Set of Malfuzat

Malfuzat refers to the holy and insightful words of the Founder of the Ahmadiyya Muslim Community, Mirza Ghulam Ahmad of Qadian, the Promised Messiah and Mahdi, on whom be peace, which he expressed verbally from time to time in his pure and holy gatherings or before congregations at the Annual Convention, for the purification of his followers and for their spiritual and moral training, thus enabling them to forge a living relationship with God; to teach the knowledge and wisdom of the Holy Quran; to revive the religion of Islam and to establish the shariah of Muhammad[sa].

These blessed sayings and discourses of his Holiness, on whom be peace, are an invaluable source of content that presents decisive verdicts issued by the divinely appointed Arbiter of this age regarding theological debates that had confused the Muslims for 1300 years and also sheds light on other matters of religion; it provides a rebuttal to the allegations levelled against Islam by the Christian priests and the Aryas; it provides evidence for the existence of God and refutes the objections of atheists and western philosophers with relation to life after death, revelation and prophethood; it provides for new converts, who have joined the Ahmadiyya Community, heart-warming advice and guidance of the Promised Messiah[as]; it showcases the unparalleled love that the Promised Messiah[as] possessed for his Master, the Holy Prophet Muhammad, the Seal of the Prophets, peace and blessings of Allah be upon him; it covers the divine claims and teachings of the Promised Messiah[as] and also various incidents from his day to day life; and also sheds light on the life and character of his Holiness and the important milestones in the history of Ahmadiyyat.

It is an immense favour of Allah the Almighty that in this day and age, He has made available such means that these spiritually rejuvenating and faith-inspiring, blessed words of the Imam of the Latter Days have been preserved until the end of time. May Allah Almighty elevate the station of pure-hearted, loyal, unrelenting and revered men such as Hazrat Maulvi Abdul Karim[ra], Hazrat Mufti Muhammad Sadiq[ra] and Sheikh Yaqub Ali Irfani[ra], whom Allah had granted a unique fervour, passion and strength in this regard. Fulfilling their oath of giving precedence to the Faith over worldly affairs, these great men worked tirelessly, day and night, with immense toil and effort to preserve in writing the *Malfuzat* of the Promised Messiah[as], exactly as he had spoken them; and continued to publish these blessed words in *Badr* and *Al-Hakam*, during the lifetime of the Promised Messiah[as].

Efforts to compile *Malfuzat* in book form were undertaken in the past, but it was Hazrat Maulana Jalal-ud-Din Shams[ra] who received the honour of first publishing them in the form of a complete set. Under his supervision, ten volumes of *Malfuzat* were compiled and published in the short time spanning from 1960 to 1967. Albeit, the first volume of *Malfuzat* which comprises the blessed words of the Promised Messiah[as] from 1891 to 1899, was published by Nazarat Talif-o-Tasnif, Sadr Anjuman Ahmadiyya Qadian. This volume was compiled by Chaudhary Ahmad Jaan Sahib, Sheikh Abdul-Qadir Sahib and Maulvi Abdur-Rashid Sahib Zerwi. The second and third volumes were compiled by Chaudhary Ahmad Jaan Sahib. The subsequent parts from volume 4 to volume 10, comprise the blessed words of the Promised Messiah[as] from 15 October 1902 to the date of his demise on 26 May 1908; the honour of collating the content for these volumes was received by Hazrat Maulvi Muhammad Ismaeel Sahib Fazil Diyalgarhi.

The index for the first four volumes was compiled by Hazrat Maulana Jalal-ud-Din Shams[ra] and the index for the remaining six volumes was prepared by Hazrat Maulana Abdul-Latif Bahawalpuri. This set was published in England some years ago. However, in light of the guidance of Hazrat Khalifatul-Masih IV (may Allah be his Helper):

i. The ten-volume *Malfuzat* has been printed in five volumes, and benefits from high quality script and binding.

ii. All verses of the Holy Quran quoted in the text have been referenced.

iii. As required, new subject headings have been added.

iv. For the ease of readers, a new index of subject matter, Quranic verses, names and places have been included.

Wassalam,

Humbly,

Syed Abdul Hayee

Foreword

Written for the Ten-Volume Set of Malfuzat (First Edition)

After we had finished publishing all the books of the Promised Messiah, on whom be peace, we initially planned to begin publishing a new series of the *Ruhani Khaza'in* (Spiritual Treasures) comprising the announcements, letters and blessed words of the Promised Messiah, on whom be peace. However, on the request of our friends and especially on the extreme insistence of Hazrat Sahibzadah Mirza Nasir Ahmad, may Allah protect him, who were of the view that *Malfuzat* ought to be printed quickly, Al-Shirkatul Islamiyyah Limited is now publishing *Malfuzat*.

One reason for our change of plan is the strong feeling of our community that there is a dire need for spiritual training at present. The second reason is—as stated in the foreword to the first edition of *Malfuzat*, Volume 1—that the *Malfuzat* of the Promised Messiah, on whom be peace, is a valuable treasure of extraordinary content that commands the power to teach and train not only us, but also our future generations.

The words of the Promised Messiah, on whom be peace, may be divided into four categories:

Firstly: The books, written treatises, and announcements of the Promised Messiah, on whom be peace, which he wrote himself for publication.

Secondly: Letters of the Promised Messiah, on whom be peace, which he wrote with his own pen and sent to his friends, dear ones and others.

Thirdly: The *Malfuzat* of the Promised Messiah, on whom be peace, referring to those of his words that he spoke in the form of an address or discussion in the presence of a congregation or gathering, or during leisurely moments, etc., and which were noted down by scribes and published in the form of a diary, etc., in the very lifetime of the Promised Messiah, on whom be peace.

Fourthly: Narrations are also a form of *Malfuzat,* but they were not immediately put to writing; in fact, they are collected and recorded from the memory of narrators.

As mentioned in the foreword to the first edition of *Malfuzat,* Volume 1, the reliability and authenticity of the four categories just mentioned ought to be taken in the sequence that they appear above. That is to say, in terms of authenticity, the books of the Promised Messiah[as] stand first, then his letters, followed by his *Malfuzat,* and finally, narrations.

Having said this, as far as the spiritual and moral training of the community is concerned, in a way, *Malfuzat* stands first from among the words of the Promised Messiah[as]. The reason being that the *Malfuzat* of the Promised Messiah, on whom be peace, are those of his words that he spoke directly to his friends and followers. Moreover, these words of his Holiness, on whom be peace, were spoken by him mostly in such settings when he had the education and training of the community in view. Hence, from among the categories mentioned above, *Malfuzat* comprises the greatest treasure as far as moral training and the reformation of one's inner self is concerned. As such, in his book *Fath-e-Islam,* the Promised Messiah, on whom be peace, sheds light on the significance and need of such words in the following manner:

> *There can be no doubt in the fact that these verbal discourses which have taken place in the past or even now, or if I make an address of my own accord at an appropriate time and place—in certain cases—proves more beneficial, effective and swifter in touching people's hearts than reaching them through books. That is why all the Prophets have relied on this method. With the exception of the Word of Allah Almighty, which was recorded in writing with special care and published, whatever else the Prophets preached has always been in the form of discourses and addresses made at the appropriate time. The general practice of Prophets was to find strength from the soul and make addresses like wise lecturers at times of need, in various gatherings and assemblies, in view of their specific circumstances. However, they did not do so like the speakers of today, whose only purpose is to flaunt their wealth of knowledge in their speeches, or who speak to ensnare simple people through their own false logic and sophistries—making those people more worthy of hell than even themselves. On the contrary, Prophets speak with immense simplicity and whatever would gush forth from their own hearts, they would*

fill into the hearts of others.

Their holy words would always fit the occasion perfectly and fulfilled the needs of the time. They would not speak to entertain their addressees or tell them false tales. They find the people ailing, drowned in diverse spiritual afflictions, and give them counsel in order to cure them, or dispel their doubts through conclusive arguments. Their words are few, but house a treasure of vast meaning. Thus, it is this very principle that my humble self keeps in view. As such, the door of dialogue and discourse remains open so that I may speak to my guests and visitors in accordance with the respective capacities, requirements and ailments which afflict them. To view evil as a target towards which one shoots the arrows of one's vital counsel in order to prevent sin and reform the morals of others just as dislocated limbs must be restored is not possible fully unless people are cured face to face. (Ruhani Khaza'in, Volume 3, Fath-e-Islam, pp. 15-17)

Therefore, in view of the education, moral training and reformation of our community, Al-Shirkatul Islamiyyah has changed its initial plan and is now publishing the blessed *Malfuzat* of the Promised Messiah, on whom be peace, earlier than what was previously decided.

About the Present Volume

The text of this volume has been reproduced from *Malfuzat*, Volume 1, published in December of 1936, by the community's central directorate of publications in Qadian. This first edition was arranged and compiled primarily by the efforts of Chaudhary Ahmad Jaan Sahib (Director Finances of Tahrik Jadid), Sheikh Abdul-Qadir Sahib (Maulvi Fazil and currently serving as missionary in Lahore) and Maulvi Abdur-Rashid Sahib (Maulvi Fazil). May Allah grant them the best of rewards. This edition of *Malfuzat* comprises a collection collated from various newspapers and periodicals that spans from 1891 to 1899.

Malfuzat-e-Ahmadiyyah, Part 2, which was compiled by the late Raja Manzur Ilahi (from the Lahore Ahmadiyya Movement) contained extracts from the following sources: *Al-Hakam*, vol. 13, no. 19, pp. 3-4 (under the title 'Before 1873'); *Al-Hakam*, vol. 7, no. 36, pp. 10-11 (under the title 'Near 1879'); *Al-Hakam*, vol. 6, no. 23 (under the title, 'Near the Time of 1879'); *Al-Hakam*, vol. 6, no. 44-45 (under the title 'Before 1879'); *Al-Hakam*, vol. 6, no. 46 and *Al-Hakam*, vol. 7, no. 3 (under the title 'Prior to 1879'); *Akhbar-e-Aam Lahore*, printed on

10 May 1885 (under the title '8 May 1885'); a treatise entitled, *'The Responses to Three Questions by Abdullah James, the Christian'.* Since all of these writings were treatises penned by the Promised Messiah[as] himself, they have not been included in *Malfuzat.* We shall include these sources when the announcements of the Promised Messiah[as] are compiled. As mentioned, *Malfuzat* refers to those words of his Holiness which he expressed verbally and which were then recorded by writers who kept a diary of his words.

May Allah the Exalted make these blessed *Malfuzat* a source of benefit for not only members of the community, but for others as well.

Humbly,
Jalal-ud-Din Shams
Currently in Quetta
20 August 1960

Hence, I loudly proclaim once again, and my friends ought to take heed that they must not disregard my advice and view them as the tales of a story-teller. Everything that I have said to you, I have said with a burning heart and true sympathy, which are inherently a part of my soul. Heed to my words with the ear of your heart and act upon them.

— Hazrat Mirza Ghulam Ahmad of Qadian
The Promised Messiah & Mahdi as

In the name of Allah, the Most Gracious, Ever Merciful
We praise Allah and invoke blessings upon His Noble Messenger[sa];
And upon his servant, the Promised Messiah[as]

Malfuzat of the Promised Messiah[as]

2 January 1899

The Purpose in Writing the Treatise *Kashf-ul-Ghita*

At 8 o'clock in the morning, our Noble Leader, His Holiness[as], went for a walk accompanied by a large number of friends. During the course of his walk, the Promised Messiah[as] said: "Our opponents inflict pain and grief upon me through the use of abusive language in announcements that are full to the brim with falsehood and slander, and on other occasions, they make untrue and utterly false reports to the government and authorities so that they will grow mistrustful of me. If all this was limited and confined to my own person alone, Allah knows full well that I would not have given this the least attention whatsoever. For I am ready to offer myself in the way of Allah Almighty like a sacrificial lamb. However, all these things have a direct effect on our people as a whole. There are some who are weak and cannot bear such suffering. Therefore, I have deemed it appropriate to publish a report of the actual circumstances in full and send it to the government. For if I remain silent, our opponents will continue to hatch conspiracies, and this has a very detrimental effect. Since our hearts are pure and we do not act in a hypocritical or pliant manner like those who are wicked from within, I have complete faith that my treatise *Kashf-ul-Ghita* (The Truth Unveiled), will apprise the esteemed government of my personal background and teachings. This book will also serve as a certificate in the hands of my friends."

5 January 1899

The Reality behind the Mark of Prophethood

After the morning prayer, Maulvi Qutb-ud-Din Sahib, resident of Baddomalhi inquired: "It is narrated that there was a 'mark of prophethood' found between the shoulders on the back of the Messenger of Allah, peace and blessings of Allah be upon him. Some say that this was some sort of a tumour on the skin. What is the actual truth in this respect?"

The Promised Messiah^as said: "The allegation that is raised with respect to the 'mark of prophethood' on the Messenger of Allah, peace and blessings of Allah be upon him, is a matter of secondary importance. I do say, however, with true sincerity and passion, that I believe it does not behove a believer and a true Muslim to refer to a 'mark of prophethood' on the Messenger of Allah, peace and blessings of Allah be upon him, as a tumour and the like. This is disrespectful and insolent behaviour, which leads a person to disbelief. We need not probe into such matters and investigate as to what that 'mark of prophethood' was exactly and the nature of its appearance. For Allah the Exalted put forth countless signs, which were clear and lucid, to confirm the truth of the prophethood of the Messenger, peace and blessings of Allah be upon him. Among these signs, one was the 'mark of prophethood'.

The fact of the matter is that the blessed personage of Allah's Messenger, peace and blessings of Allah be upon him, was to the other Prophets, peace be upon them, as the full moon is to the crescent. The crescent moon is covered by darkness, but when it becomes complete in the form of a full moon, that full moon confirms and establishes the prior existence of the crescent. Hence, know for certain that if the Messenger of Allah, peace and blessings of Allah be upon him, had not appeared, the previous Prophets and various aspects of their prophethood would have remained hidden."

A Favour of the Messenger of Allah upon the Messiah

Now, reflect and do tell me, can man learn about the path that leads to God's Unity by means of the Gospels we have at present? It is indeed astonishing. Do the Prophets of God Almighty come to establish God's Oneness or to have people believe in their own divinity? Therefore, the present-day Gospels have not only lost the way that leads to the Unity of God, but have also destroyed all traces of the prophethood and messengership of Jesus, peace be upon him. God or son of God aside, the Gospels have reduced Jesus[as] to a rank that is even below the Prophets, and have, God forbid, turned him into a man of very immoral standing. However, the holy personage of the Messenger of Allah, peace and blessings of Allah be upon him, appeared and revived his true teaching; in fact, the Holy Prophet[sa] was a healer even for the Messiah himself, whom he brought back from the dead, and upon whom he bestowed a life with which the chosen servants of God and His Prophets are blessed.

The Superiority of Islam

Only that teaching may be deemed perfect which fully develops and nurtures human faculties, rather than one which leans to a certain extreme. Observe the instructions given to us by the teaching of the Gospel and compare them to the teaching given to us by our faculties. Human faculties and the nature of man essentially constitute God's 'book of actions.' How then can His book of words, known as the Book of Allah or God's divine teaching, oppose and contradict His book of actions? In the same manner, if the Messenger of Allah, peace and blessings of Allah be upon him, had not come, allegations would have been levelled against the morals, guidance, miracles and spiritual power of the past Prophets. However, the Holy Prophet[sa] absolved them all by his advent. Therefore, the signs in support of the prophethood of the Holy Prophet[sa] are more brilliant than the sun; they are countless and beyond measure. Hence, raising objections against the prophethood of the Holy Prophet[sa] or the signs of his prophethood is no different from a foolish, blind man saying that it was night even in broad daylight. I say once more that the other religions would have remained in darkness if until now, the Messenger of Allah, peace and blessings of Allah be upon him, had not appeared. Faith would have been destroyed, and the earth would have been ruined by divine curse and chastisement. Islam shines like a lamp that has pulled others out of darkness as well. If one reads the Torah, it becomes difficult to even learn about heaven and hell. If one looks at the Gospel, no traces of God's Unity can be found therein. There is no doubt in the fact that both these books were and are from Allah Almighty, but what light can be attained from them? True radiance and real divine light, which is needed for salvation, is present in Islam alone. Even in the context of God's Unity, wherever you open the Quran, one will find it to be an unsheathed sword which cuts at the root of polytheism. Similarly, all the aspects of prophethood are spoken of so clearly and lucidly in the Holy Quran that no better exposition is possible.

The Essence of the 'Seal of Prophethood'

The pinnacle at which argumentation and divine understanding naturally culminate is to what the term 'Seal of Prophethood' *(khatm-e-nubuwwat)* refers. To raise criticisms after this, like the irreligious, is the work of those who are bereft of faith. All things are characterised by clear facts and one's ability to comprehend them depends on completeness of understanding and enlightenment of vision. With the advent of the Messenger of Allah, peace and blessings of Allah be upon him, faith and divine knowledge reached perfection, and other nations were granted light as well. No other religion was bestowed such a manifestly clear and brilliant shariah. If anyone had received such a law, would it have not wielded the power to influence the Arabs even slightly? The sun which rose from among the Arabs illuminated every people and shined its light on every village. It is the sole pride of the Noble Quran alone that it has the ability to reign supreme over all the other world religions in the matter of God's Unity and prophethood. It is a matter of pride for the Muslims that they have been granted such a book. Those who attack the teachings of Islam and level allegations against its teaching and guidance do so only out of their own benighted nature and lack of faith.

The Permissibility of Polygamy

For example, people object to polygamy and allege that Islam has permitted a man to marry a large number of women. I challenge any brave champion who raises allegations: can you show me where the Quran says that a person must marry more than one woman? It is true, however, and perfectly normal, that in many circumstances an individual is faced with a genuine need to marry more than one wife: for example, if a woman has lost her sight; or has been struck with a serious illness, which has rendered her unable to fulfil her domestic responsibilities and the husband out of sympathy does not wish to divorce her; or if a woman has become afflicted with dangerous ailments of the womb that make it impossible for her to fulfil the natural needs of her husband. Now, if permission to marry a second time had not been given, do tell me, would this not fuel the proliferation of fornication and immorality? Therefore, a religion or shariah which prohibits polygamy most certainly encourages fornication and immorality. However, Islam seeks to cleanse the world of immorality and promiscuity; and therefore, in such circumstances, permits a man to marry more than one wife. In the same vein, when a man is unable to have children, many disputes arise in the family of such a person after his death, and at times, the matter escalates to conflict, even murder and bloodshed. In such a case, it is necessary for such a man to marry more than one wife so that he may have children. In fact, when such circumstances arise, righteous and noble women grant permission themselves. The more one reflects over this matter, the more clear and logical it will appear. Christians have no right to criticise this permission, because those men whom the Christians hold as Prophets and divinely inspired, in fact, even the elders of the Messiah, peace be upon him, married seven hundred wives, while others are reported to have married three hundred. If the Christians respond by saying that these men were sinners and transgressors, they will have a difficult time explaining how the revelations that are attributed to them can be deemed true. There are certain denominations among the Christians who do not deem it permissible to dishonour the Prophets in this manner. The fact is, the Gospel does not even expound this teaching openly; the women of London have been forceful in opposing multiple marriages, and this has resulted in an aversion to the practice. However, look at the outcomes for yourself. In London and Paris, what is chastity and piety worth?

The Battles of Islam Were Defensive

Similarly, their allegations relating to slavery and jihad are also unfounded, because a long chain of similar wars are alluded to in the Torah as well. The wars in Islam were defensive and came to an end in a mere ten years. I confidently say that I can take out and present similar teachings from their own scriptures. I also confidently proclaim that all truths are encompassed by the Holy Quran. If anyone claims that they can present a verity that is not to be found in the Quran, I am prepared to demonstrate that the Quran speaks of that particular point. The Islamic shariah has presented injunctions which accord to the inherent nature of man, and which nurture his faculties in every respect. No allegation can be levelled against the tenets of Islam. However, the objections held by Islam in respect of other religions are ones for which the adherents of those faiths have no answer.

The Face of a Blessed Person and One Who Is Evil

And so, I declare once again that you ought not to view my words with disdain and scorn, for mockery can lead one to disbelief. On the contrary, one ought to possess a sense of respect and fear for the signs of Allah Almighty. Any wise person can provide a thousand responses to such allegations. Do the faces of people not possess signs by which we can distinguish between and recognise a blessed man and one who is evil, or a moral and immoral person? It is narrated in relation to the Messenger of Allah, peace and blessings of Allah be upon him, that a person saw him and said: 'This is not the face of a liar.' Now what sign was present on the face of liars which was not to be found on the face of the Holy Prophet[sa]? There was a distinction on his face that a person of insight could perceive. Who can be so foolish and ignorant that they are unable to distinguish between the face of a righteous and evil person? In the case of a believer, their face and every limb is a source of distinction for them and establishes that they are godly people. So if the 'mark of prophethood' on the back of the Holy Prophet[sa] possessed some similar distinction, do tell me, why this would be so far-fetched? Anything is possible.

One is Only Required to Believe in Matters Relating to Faith

Ultimately, this is a matter of secondary importance. We need not engage ourselves in such discussions. Debates ought to revolve around matters of principle. When a fundamental principle is established, the secondary issues that relate to it are settled themselves. It is necessary for one to believe, not for one to strive in reaching the deeper intricacies and details of beliefs. If an opponent raises objections, we can provide ample refutation. It is necessary to believe in the articles of faith, i.e. to believe in Allah the Exalted and in His attributes, to believe in His angels, divine scriptures, the Prophets, peace be upon them, etc. To accept these things is to adhere to fundamental principles; all other matters are secondary. As far as these fundamental issues are concerned, they are clearly established truths. The teaching of Islam is so coherent that it keeps every human faculty in balance, precisely at its appropriate place, and nurtures it; this is a magnificent miracle of our Prophet, peace and blessings of Allah be upon him. Other teachings are not the same; it is as if they lack certain sensory organs, as it were. As such, all other teachings are deficient or inadequate. Only the teaching of Islam is fully formed. The Unity of God, His attributes, prophethood, lofty morals, the perfection of the inner self, etc., and everything else that man requires have been expounded by Islam so perfectly and lucidly that no lengthy debates are needed in this respect. Other matters that relate to how the Messenger of Allah, peace and blessings of Allah be upon him, ate and what size his morsels were, are debates in which a believer has no need to engage. Salvation does not depend on these matters. Such matters which have been transmitted to us in the form of written narrations ought to be accepted if they are consistent with the true nature of prophethood and do not oppose it, otherwise, they should be interpreted in an appropriate manner. There is no need to engage in lengthy and useless debates on this, that and the other.

The Meaning of the Seal of Prophethood

In the context of the Seal of Prophethood *(khatm-e-nubuwwat)*, I would like to reiterate that the primary meaning of this term implies that all the matters relating to prophethood, instituted by Allah in the beginning with Adam, on whom be peace, were brought to their complete and final end with the Holy Prophet, peace and blessings of Allah be upon him. This is the broad and apparent sense. The second connotation is that the circle of the excellences of prophethood reached its final point of completion with the Holy Prophet, peace and blessings of Allah be upon him.

It is absolutely true that the Quran perfected deficient ideologies and prophethood reached its final end. This is why Islam proved itself to be true to the following:

$$\text{اَلْيَوْمَ اَكْمَلْتُ لَكُمْ دِيْنَكُمْ}^{1}$$

This day have I perfected your religion for you.

In short, these are the signs of prophethood; it is not necessary to debate the deeper intricacies and details of these signs. The principles are clear and manifest, and are well-established truths. A believer need not engage in inconsequential matters. Belief is necessary. If an opponent raises an objection, we can provide a sufficient rebuttal. If an opponent does not desist, we can challenge them to first prove the issues of secondary nature from their own Faith. Therefore, the 'seal of

---

[1] *al-Ma'idah,* 5:4

prophethood' on the Holy Prophet, peace and blessings of Allah be upon him, was one of the signs of his prophethood, and one in which a Muslim believer must believe."[1]

5 January 1899

The Grave and its Relationship with the Soul

Maulvi Qutb-ud-Din Sahib[ra] inquired: "What is the reality of the relationship that we hear about between the soul and the grave?"

The Promised Messiah[as] said: "The fact of the matter is that everything narrated in the Hadith of the Messenger of Allah, peace and blessings of Allah be upon him, about the relationship of souls and graves is absolutely true and correct. The deeper nature and essence of this relationship is another matter, of which knowledge is not necessary. Albeit, it can be said that we are responsible for proving that such a relationship between graves and souls does in fact exist, and that such a phenomenon is not a rational impossibility.

The law of nature demonstrates a parallel in this respect. As we observe, the truth and reality of certain things is ascertained only through the tongue, and in reality the phenomenon in discussion is similar. We can say in broader terms that Allah the Exalted has put in place various methods through which we learn of the deeper reality of things. The properties of certain things are observed through the eye, while other truths are learned of through the ear alone. Moreover, other things are discovered through multiple senses. Further still, how many a truth do we discern through the nucleus of our faculties—the heart. To summarise, Allah the Exalted has designed various methods and means by which to ascertain the truth. For example, if someone were to place a lump of crystallised sugar *(misri)* on their ear, they would not be able to experience its taste, nor would they be able to perceive its colour; similarly, if brought before the eyes, one would not be able to say anything as to its taste. This clearly demonstrates that there are varying faculties and powers by which one attains to the deeper reality of things. Now, if a person desires to experience the taste of something and places it before their eyes, would we say that the edible thing is tasteless? Or if there was a sound and someone tried to hear it using their tongue instead of their ears, would this be possible? The philosophically inclined in this day and age suffer from the illusion

---

[1]   *Al-Hakam*, vol. 3, no. 1, dated 10 January 1899, pp. 6-9

whereby they reject a truth due to their own lack of knowledge. Even in daily matters we observe that all tasks are not done by the same person, rather, different people are assigned varying tasks. A water-carrier will fetch water, a launderer will wash clothes, and a cook will prepare food. Hence, division of labour is a phenomenon we observe even in the system instituted by man himself.

Therefore, always bear in mind that different faculties are responsible for various tasks. Man has been vested with many a great faculty, and diverse duties have been assigned to each for their perfection. The ignorant philosopher seeks to determine all matters on the basis of their own limited reason, even though this is completely inappropriate. Historical matters can only be determined by history itself. Moreover, how can one acquire a knowledge of the properties of things except by true experience. Inductive matters are settled through reason. Similarly, there are individually distinct means in place to acquire a knowledge of various things. Man falls to deception and deprives himself of a deeper knowledge of the reality of things when he attempts to attain a complete knowledge of matters by one avenue alone. I do not deem it necessary to speak on the truthful nature of this principle, because even the least bit of reflection makes this manifestly clear and we observe the truth of these matters in our daily lives. Hence, when the soul separates itself from the body or forges a relationship with it, these phenomena cannot be determined by our faculty of reason alone. For if this was the case, philosophers and thinkers would not have gone astray.

Knowledge of the Soul Is Acquired from the Fountain of Prophethood

In the same manner, the relationship that souls possess with graves is a truth no doubt; however, one cannot learn of it through the use of one's eye. It is the task of one's spiritual eye to perceive this phenomenon. If anyone expects to reach the depth of this matter by mere reason alone, then let any paragon of reason tell us even so much as to whether the soul exists or not. There are a thousand disagreements on this issue alone and countless philosophers who are bent towards atheism reject the existence of the soul altogether. If this was an issue that could be solved by reason alone, why would any difference of opinion exist at all? For when the task of an eye is to see, I cannot accept how it is possible for the eye of one person to visually discern a white-coloured object for what it is, while the very same organ in another person should function to sense the taste of that same white object. My purpose is to show that reason alone cannot even tell us with certainty whether the soul exists or not, let alone give us knowledge about its deeper essence or the nature of its relationships. Philosophers consider the soul to be like a lush, green branch and do not consider the soul to have any external, independent existence of its own. The details that we have come to know about in respect of the soul's existence and its relations etc., are received from the fountain of prophethood. Those who depend on reason alone cannot even make an evidenced claim in this context. If someone were to say that there are certain philosophers who have written specific details relating to the soul, then remember that they have done nothing more than to glean from the fountain of prophethood and then state certain details. Hence, when it is established that knowledge about the soul is received from the fountain of prophethood, the fact that the soul has a relationship with the grave ought to be viewed from the perspective of Prophets. It is the spiritual eye which shows us that the soul has a relationship with the pile of dust in which a person is buried and that one receives a response when one says the following words:

اَلسَّلَامُ عَلَيْكُمْ يَاأَهْلَ الْقُبُورِ

Peace be upon you, O dwellers of these graves.

Hence, an individual who employs the faculties that make it possible to meet the dwellers of graves can see the affinity that souls hold with graves.

Let me give you an example in this regard. If there was a block of salt and a block of sugar placed side by side, what conclusion could one draw by mere reason alone? Indeed, when a person tastes each of them, it can then be concluded by two distinct tastes that one is salt and the other is sugar. If, however, a person had no sense of taste, how could they distinguish between sweet and salty?

My task is only to explain through argumentation. Just as the rising sun would remain unaffected by a blind person who denies it, in the same manner, a senseless man unable to benefit from rational argumentation would not disprove a matter. Likewise, how can a person deprived of the spiritual eye, observe the relationship that souls possess with graves? Hence, just because someone is unable to observe this phenomenon, this does not justify their denial of it. Such knowledge cannot be ascertained by mere rationality and induction alone; this is why Allah the Exalted has given humans a range of faculties. If one faculty alone sufficed for everything, what need would there have been for God to bestow man with such a diverse array of faculties? Certain faculties relate to the eye, others to the ear, some to the tongue and others still to the nose. Man possesses various senses. In order to observe the relationship that souls have with graves, a spiritual faculty and sense is required. Anyone who denies this is mistaken. A vast number of Prophets, on whom be peace, and millions of saints and pious individuals have come and gone in the world; countless people who engaged in spiritual exercises have gone by; and all of them are a living testament to this fact. Whether or not we are able to rationally fathom the reality and causes that lie in these connections between souls and graves, the relationship itself cannot be denied. In short, it is spiritual arguments that settle all of these matters. It is no deficiency on the part of one's ears if they are unable to see, for this task is performed by another faculty. I am a witness to the fact, on the basis of my own experience, that the soul definitely has a relationship with the grave; a person can speak to the dead. The soul also holds a connection with heaven, where it is given a position. I proclaim once again that this is an established truth. There is testimony of this even in Hindu scriptures. This is a well-accepted concept, except in the view of those who deny the life of the soul. As for the matter of where this link exists and the nature of this relationship, this is something that the spiritual eye will unravel itself. Geologists are able to tell us where a certain metal is located or where a certain mine exists. These experts possess a sense that enables them to detect such things immediately. Similarly, it is a proven truth that souls certainly have a relationship with graves, and this is to such an extent that those who experience visions, through concentration, can even speak to the dead. Nonetheless, as far as doubts and allegations are concerned, this simply has no end."[1]

The Blessings of Prayer

The Promised Messiah[as] states: "If prayer did not exist, man would have no means by which to attain perfect certainty in cognisance of the Divine. It is through prayer that a person is blessed with revelation. It is through prayer that one engages in converse with God Almighty. With constant supplication, when man reaches the state of the inner-self being annihilated in God *(fana)* through belief in God's Unity, and with love, sincerity and purity, it is then that the Living God, Who is Hidden from the people, manifests Himself to such a one."

---

[1]   *Al-Hakam*, vol. 3, no. 3, dated 23 January 1899, pp. 2-3

Blessed is the One Who Understands

The Promised Messiah[as] states: "Reconcile with God. Adopt true self-restraint. The heaven inspires awe by sending down calamities and the earth warns us with the emergence of epidemics. Blessed is one who understands."[1]

26 January 1899

The Editor of *Al-Hakam* states that His Holiness[as] was on his way to Dhariwal in order to pursue a case of security for keeping the peace[2] brought against him due to Maulvi Muhammad Husain Sahib of Batala. Arrangements for the stay of the party were made at Leel, a small village near Dhariwal. However, on his way to Leel, the Promised Messiah[as] stopped at Khunda. When the Promised Messiah[as] reached Khunda he decided to stay there and called Hazrat Khalifatul-Masih I[ra], who had already reached Leel, to turn back and join him in Khunda as well. When Hazrat Khalifatul-Masih I[ra] arrived in Khunda, the Promised Messiah[as] said: "There is wisdom in everything that Allah the Exalted does. There was news that Muhammad Husain was planning to stay there as well. Therefore, it is good that we did not stay there. It is best to stay away from such people."

Editor's Note: His Holiness[as] set out for the journey from Qadian by carriage but Hazrat Maulana Nur-ud-Din Sahib[ra] departed first from Qadian with a few friends to catch a train and then make the same journey onwards from Batala. It was decided that both parties would depart from Qadian and finally meet at Leel, where arrangements for the stay had been made. However, when the Promised Messiah[as] arrived in Khunda, Rani Ishar Kaur of Dham (the widowed daughter-in-law of Sardar Jaimal Singh) sent word with one of her representatives to the Promised Messiah[as] requesting him to stay in Khunda as her guest. The Promised Messiah[as] accepted her request and so he decided to lodge in Khunda instead. The party who was travelling onwards by train could not be informed of this change in plan, and so they arrived at Leel. However, the Promised Messiah[as] called them over and so they came to Khunda as well.

Invitations and Offerings by Non-Muslims

After some time, Rani Ishar Kaur sent her servants with a tray of sugar candy

---

[1] *Al-Hakam*, vol. 3, no. 3, dated 23 January 1899, p. 2

[2] Refer to Section 107 of the Indian Code of Criminal Procedure. [Publisher]

(misri) and a tray of almonds as an offering to the Promised Messiah[as]. She also sent word with her servants that she was honoured by the arrival of the Promised Messiah[as] and that his stay was no different for her than the coming of the late Sardar Jaimal Singh himself. His Holiness responded, with immense simplicity and in the God-given tone that is characteristic of such holy people, by saying: "Very well, as you have invited us, I accept your offering as well."

Consistency

After everyone had finished eating, the Promised Messiah[as] was informed that an elderly white-bearded man wished to say something. The Promised Messiah[as] very graciously assented with a "Yes." The man presented himself to the Promised Messiah[as] and put forth his submission in verse. The Promised Messiah[as] said: "If an individual consistently follows the prescriptions given to them by their physician, the physician is also generous towards such a patient and God Almighty also brings about a positive result."

Fasting Whilst on a Journey

It was inquired of the Promised Messiah[as] what the instruction was in relation to fasting whilst on a journey. The Promised Messiah[as] responded by saying: "As far as the Quran teaches, we learn:

فَمَنۡ كَانَ مِنۡكُمۡ مَّرِيۡضًا اَوۡ عَلٰى سَفَرٍ فَعِدَّةٌ مِّنۡ اَيَّامٍ اُخَرَ[1]

But whoso among you is sick or is on a journey shall
fast the same number of other days.

In other words, a person who is ill or on a journey is not to fast. This is an order. Allah the Exalted has not stated that anyone who is able should fast, and a person who is unable should abstain. In my view, a traveller should not fast. In general, however, since most people do fast whilst on a journey, a person may fast while they are travelling, considering this to be the established practice. However, the commandment of عِدَّةٌ مِّنۡ اَيَّامٍ اُخَرَ *(to fast the same number of other days when fasts are missed in Ramadan)* must be kept in consideration."

On this, Maulvi Nur-ud-Din Sahib[ra] said: "A person ought to fast a few days every month anyway."

---

[1]　*al-Baqarah*, 2:185

Editor's Note: I would like to say, however, that on another occasion, the Promised Messiah^(as) has also said that a person who burdens themselves and fasts while they are on a journey, as if, seeks to please God by force and not through obedience to His command. This is wrong. True faith lies in doing what God commands and refraining from whatever He so commands.[1]

27 January 1899

After the morning prayer, we were given orders to depart. When the Promised Messiah^(as) passed by the factory in Dhariwal, he said: "It would be good to see this factory sometime. It is beneficial to see new things."

One person said: "Your Holiness, I saw this factory once and I was filled with an inexplicable fervour on witnessing the power of God Almighty. I remained restless until I was able to offer four *rak'ats* of Prayer." The Promised Messiah^(as) said: "The fact of the matter is that all things show a manifestation of Allah Almighty. Just observe how many strengths an insect possesses. And then Allah the Exalted is He in Whose hand is every power and strength."

Since the tent of the Promised Messiah^(as) had been erected near a stream, the Promised Messiah^(as) looked at the stream and at the surrounding trees and said: "This is a very good spot."[2]

26 February 1899

Praise for a Lecture of Hazrat Maulvi Abdul-Karim Sahib^(ra)

The Promised Messiah^(as) read a lecture of Hazrat Maulana Abdul-Karim Sahib^(ra) of Sialkot entitled, *'What Reform and Revival was Brought About by Hazrat Mirza Ghulam Ahmad of Qadian?'* and on 26 February 1899, he addressed the congregation in Mubarak Mosque saying: "It is my desire that all of my friends should read this, because it contains many subtle points of wisdom. This also shows the powerful oratory skills with which a certain man from among us is blessed. It is precisely on this pattern that members of our community ought to strive to become speakers."[3]

---

[1]   *Al-Hakam*, vol. 3, no. 4, dated 31 January 1899, pp. 6-7
[2]   *Al-Hakam*, vol. 3, no. 4, dated 31 January 1899, p. 8
[3]   *Al-Hakam*, vol. 10, no. 35, dated 10 October 1906, p. 7

10 March 1899

Courage and High Resolve

On his morning walk, the Promised Messiah[as] said: "A person must not lose hope. Determination is also a high moral quality and a believer is characterised by high resolve. One ought to always be ready to serve and support the Faith, and should never show cowardice. For cowardice is the mark of a hypocrite. A believer is gallant and courageous, but courage does not imply that they lack good judgement. Any action done without appropriate consideration of the prevailing circumstances is recklessness. A believer is free from haste. In fact, a believer remains prepared to serve the Faith with immense sagacity and forbearance, and is never cowardly.

Sometimes a person will act in a manner that displeases God Almighty and thereby arouses His indignation. For example, if a person shoves away a beggar, this is harsh behaviour, which results in the displeasure of God Almighty. In turn, such a one becomes deprived of the opportunity to give something to the beggar. However, if a person acts in a gentle and noble manner, and even if he gives the beggar a cup of water, this results in a removal of the spiritual contraction of the heart *(qabz)*.

Seeking Forgiveness from Allah—The Cure for Spiritual Contraction

Man undergoes a state of both spiritual contraction *(qabz)* and spiritual expansion *(bast)*. In the state of spiritual expansion, one's pleasure and delight in worship heightens, the heart is opened, one's inclination towards God increases, and warmth and comfort is derived from the Prayer. However, on certain occasions, man experiences a state in which this passion and eagerness is lost and the heart becomes constricted. When this state of affairs arises, one should seek forgiveness from Allah profusely, invoke salutations upon the Holy Prophet[sa] abundantly, and offer Prayer again and again. This is the only way to do away with one's state of spiritual contraction of the heart.

True Knowledge

Logic or philosophy is no knowledge; in fact, true knowledge is that which God Almighty bestows by His mere grace. Such knowledge is a means of developing a deeper understanding of Allah the Exalted and develops a fear of God in the heart. In this regard, Allah Almighty states in the Holy Quran:

اِنَّمَا يَخْشَى اللّٰهَ مِنْ عِبَادِهِ الْعُلَمٰٓؤُا[1]

Only those of His servants who possess knowledge fear Allah.

If knowledge does not increase a person in fear of God, then remember that such knowledge is not such as can further him in cognisance of the Divine."[2]

20 April 1899 in the Late Afternoon

Trust in God

The Promised Messiah[as] states: "Trust in God is the hallmark of Islam. A Muslim is one who believes in giving charity and offering prayer. The Christians do not believe in this. Why is this the case? Christians have crafted their own physical god. One of the greatest and most enduring joys of man, which supports him in times of peril, is trust in God. Only Islam teaches, in the true sense, that one must trust in God."[3]

21 April 1899 on the Day of Eid-ul-Adha

Serving One's Mother

The Promised Messiah[as] states: "The first state that speaks for a person's good nature is whether or not they honour their mother. In relation to Awais Qarni[ra], the Messenger of Allah, peace and blessings of Allah be upon him, would often turn his face towards Yemen and say: 'I can smell the fragrance of God coming forth from Yemen.' The Holy Prophet[sa] would also say: 'He is heavily engaged in serving his mother and this is why he cannot come to visit me.' Apparently it seems strange that the Prophet of God, peace and blessings of Allah be upon him, is present in his time but Awais[ra] is unable to see him in person only due to his constant preoccupation in service and obedience to his mother. However, I find that the Messenger of Allah, peace and blessings of Allah be upon him, has instructed his people to convey his greetings of peace particularly to two people alone—Awais[ra] and the Promised Messiah[as]. This is a remarkable distinction which others have

---

[1] *Fatir*, 35:29
[2] *Al-Hakam*, vol. 7, no. 21, dated 10 June 1903, p. 2
[3] *Al-Hakam*, vol. 3, no. 15, dated 26 April 1899, p. 6

not been fortunate enough to receive. It is written that when Hazrat Umar, may Allah be pleased with him, went to visit him, Awais[ra] said: 'I remain engaged in tending to my mother's needs and so the angels graze my camels.' On the one hand, there were people like Awais[ra] who strove so tirelessly in serving their mothers that they were blessed with such acceptance and honour; while on the other hand, there are those who engage in litigation over pennies, and speak of their mothers so disrespectfully that even ignoble and uncivilised peoples from among the scheduled caste[1] do not act so inappropriately. What is our teaching? It is to inform people of the pure guidance of Allah and the Messenger of Allah, peace and blessings of Allah be upon him. If someone claims to have a relationship with me but does not act in accordance with this guidance, then why do they join my community at all? Those who act inappropriately turn others away from the right path. People will raise objections and say that these people are such that they do not even respect their parents.

Those Who Are Not Dutiful to Their Parents

I truthfully proclaim that a person who is not dutiful to their mother and father will never receive goodness and blessing. So mould yourselves with good intentions to act upon the instructions of God and His Messenger with complete obedience and loyalty; for all good lies in this, otherwise, one is free to act as they please. My duty is only to advise you.

Emphasis on Learning Arabic and English

I would also like to advise my community to learn the Arabic language, because without a knowledge of Arabic, one cannot enjoy the Holy Quran. Therefore, you ought to make an effort to learn Arabic little by little, insofar as it is necessary to understand the translation of the Holy Quran. In this day and age, easy methods to learn Arabic have been introduced. When reciting the Holy Quran is compulsory for every Muslim, what excuse does a person have to not endeavour to learn the Arabic language and for one to waste away their entire life learning English and other languages?

Having said that, it should also be borne in mind that since the rule established in this country has taken on the form of a national government, the language of

---

[1]   Historically, in the subcontinent, Hindus belonging to the lowest, socially disadvantaged class were officially referred to as the scheduled caste. [Publisher]

a national government, therefore, also possesses national importance. Therefore, it is imperative that you learn English as well, so that you are able to fully communicate your views and opinions to the government, and so that you are able to offer it benefit and support."

Phonograph

Then, during the course of a discussion on languages, the Promised Messiah[as] said: "After all, what is the phonograph? It is like a printing press that speaks."

Two Kinds of Suffering

The Promised Messiah[as] states: "No suffering touches a person until it is decreed in heaven. Although the Prophets also experience suffering, but in their case, this is in the form of love. There is a hidden lesson to be learned in the conduct and behaviour of this holy community known as the Prophets, peace be upon them. Certain people, however, are struck by grief, but this is the result of their own doing. Allah the Exalted states:

$$\text{مَنْ يَّعْمَلْ مِثْقَالَ ذَرَّةٍ شَرًّا يَّرَهٗ}^{1}$$

Then whoso does an atom's weight of evil will see it.

In short, it is incumbent for one to remain engaged in seeking repentance and forgiveness from God. One should always remain watchful, lest one's sins exceed all bounds and invite the wrath of God Almighty.

Repentance and Seeking Forgiveness from God

When God Almighty graces someone with His glance of mercy, He instils in the hearts of people a love for that person. However, when a person's evil crosses all bounds, as soon as it is decreed that the heaven is averse to such a one, in accordance with the will of Allah Almighty, the hearts of the people too become hardened towards the person in question. Yet, as soon as such a person seeks refuge at the threshold of God, through repentance and by seeking His forgiveness, a hidden mercy begins to develop in their favour and the seed of love for that person is planted in the hearts of others, without anyone knowing. Hence, repentance and

---

[1]   *az-Zilzal*, 99:9

seeking forgiveness from God is a tried and tested means that never fails."[1]

21 April 1899 before Sunset

Breaking the Cross—An Achievement of the Promised Messiah[as]

The Promised Messiah[as] states: "When this book[2] of mine is published, those who raise repeated allegations and ask what has been achieved by my advent will also have their answer. When I hear these sorts of objections, I am astonished. Are things achieved by some magic spell? Do tell me; after all, Noah, peace be upon him, preached his ministry for nine hundred and fifty years, so in the view of such people, what did he achieve? These people will see—and surely God Almighty will show them manifestly—what I have done. Alas! If only these people would reflect over the current state of affairs. Sixteen years from the present century have elapsed and darkness has reached the extreme; so has no one appeared as a Reformer? Such people do not act with even a shred of justice. In raising allegations against me, they ultimately object against God. For in their view, I have come and done nothing and God has sent no one who would. In fact, if the needs of the present time are put to one side for a moment, according to these unwise people, a person to misguide them has come, yet despite this, the real Mahdi has not appeared and was not sent by God. The fourteenth century was supposed to be blessed, but what blessing did it bring when with it an Antichrist has appeared! Siddiq Hasan and Abdul-Hayy, who were claimants, died at the head of the century; otherwise, perhaps these two could have consoled these people. However, God has demonstrated through His grace that this work was not for them to do, but for someone else.

Whenever a Reformer *(Mujaddid)* appears, they do so in view of the need of that time, not to teach people about issues relating to how they should clean themselves after answering the call of nature or ablution. Does God, Who is Wise and Sagacious, not see that the deadly wind of naturalism and philosophy has swept through the land and that thousands of people have perished? The Christians, who worship the cross, have torn hundreds and thousands of souls away from God. Therefore, at the present time, was a Reformer not needed who would 'break the cross' and demonstrate through argumentation and conclusive facts that the religion of the cross is devoid of the light of truth; and that man cannot

---

[1]   *Al-Hakam*, vol. 3, no. 17, dated 12 May 1899, pp. 4-5
[2]   The book *Masih Hindustan Main* or *'Jesus in India'*. [Compiler]

be the inheritor of salvation through belief in a wooden crucifix? Every other day, the Christians go on publishing and distributing leaflets, 50,000 and even 100,000 in number. Like a swarm of locusts, women, children, young and old are engaged in the work of attacking Islam in any way possible. At this time, the onslaught waged against Islam knows no bounds. On the one hand, God has promised:

$$اِنَّالَهُ لَحٰفِظُوْنَ^1$$

Most surely We will be its Guardian.

On the other hand, our foolish critics are so 'wise' that they claim no one has appeared in Islam with the light of divine insight so as to safeguard the Faith; in fact, an Antichrist has appeared instead. Alas! What a pity! Nay, a thousand pities! This was the perfect time for God to manifest the shining hand of His support and succour. I say, in any case, He has done so. God will manifest His lustre. He will shame my opponents and show them what has been achieved at the hand of the one who has come."[2]

21 April 1899

The Veiling of Faults

The Promised Messiah[as] states: "The nature of God Almighty in concealing the faults of man is such that despite Him witnessing the sins and faults of human beings, in view of this divine attribute of His, He continues to veil their evil deeds so long as they do not surpass the bounds of moderation. Man on the other hand, does not even find any real fault in another and begins to raise a clamour. The fact of the matter is that man has little patience, whereas the being of God Almighty is forbearing and merciful. A wrongdoing person will even wrong their own soul. At times, they will lose full sight of the forbearance of God Almighty and as a result, become brazen. It is then that the divine attribute of retribution begins to operate and seizes such a man. The Hindus say that Parmeshwar is averse to *'att'*, i.e. a thing that is beyond the bounds; that is to say, God dislikes a thing that is in transgression of the limits. However, despite all this, God is so Merciful and Generous that even if a person is steeped in such a state, if they fall at the divine threshold with extreme humility and lowliness, He turns to such a one with His

---

1 *al-Hijr*, 15:10
2 *Al-Hakam*, vol. 3, no. 18, dated 19 May 1899, pp. 4-5

glance of mercy. In short, just as Allah the Exalted does not immediately take note of our faults, and saves us from disgrace through the blessing of His attribute of veiling faults, we too should not be quick to open our mouths if we notice a fault in someone else, which if disclosed, could cause them dishonour and disgrace.

The Cure for Negligence is Seeking Forgiveness from God

Certain people are faced with a state of affairs where various factors, such as employment for example, or something or other, result in the better part of their lives being spent in a state of darkness. Neither do they strive to observe the Prayer with regularity, nor do they find the opportunity to listen to the words of Allah and His Messenger[sa]. They do not even think to ponder over the Book of Allah. When a long period of time passes in this dark state, this way of thinking becomes firm-rooted and takes on the form of a second nature. Hence, at such a time, if one does not turn one's attention to repentance and seeking forgiveness from Allah, then know that such a one is truly unfortunate. The best remedy for negligence and indolence is seeking forgiveness from Allah. Even if faced with a trial on account of their previous failings or indolence, let them wake up during the nights to fall in prostration and offer supplications, and promise to make a sincere and holy transformation in the presence of God."

22 April 1899

A Liar Is Never Granted Respite

The Promised Messiah[as] states: "Many years have passed since I published the claim that I am a recipient of revelation and divine converse. However, even if the period spanning from the publication of *Barahin-e-Ahmadiyyah* to the present time is calculated, a period of twenty years has elapsed. One ought to ask our opponents—who call me a liar and assert that I have forged this false claim—that when God Almighty does not grant respite to a deceiver who falsely claims to receive divine revelation or converse, to the extent that even the Messenger of Allah, peace and blessings of Allah be upon him, was addressed by God that 'If you had attributed false statements to Us, We would have seized you by your jugular vein,' then what concession can there be for anyone else? This statement of God clearly demonstrates that anyone who falsely attributes revelation to Allah Almighty can never enjoy respite. Now, I would like to ask that if my community was not established by God Almighty, then do show me an example from the history of any nation, where someone attributed such falsehood against God and was then granted respite.

As far as I am concerned, a clear criterion is available to us. The Messenger of Allah, peace and blessings of Allah be upon him, received revelation for a lengthy period of twenty-three years. Allah the Exalted has granted me an era that is almost equivalent in time to the era of our Truthful and Perfect Prophet, because twenty years have passed since the publication of *Barahin-e-Ahmadiyyah*—which in the view of my unwise critics—is the period in which I began this 'forgery'. The era that I present in relation to myself is similar to that of a man who is accepted as being truthful; in fact, he is the crown of all those who are truthful, yet these cruel people go on saying even now that my claim is a lie. It is unfortunate that they are so blindly absorbed in disproving me that they fail to see the manner in which even the Messenger of Allah, peace and blessings of Allah be upon him, is caught in the crossfire of their denial. For if God were to support a false man for even twenty or twenty-two years, all I can do is stand astonished. In fact, my heart trembles at the thought of what argument such people could then present in favour of the truthfulness of the Messenger of Allah, peace and blessings of Allah be upon him. A Muslim and a true follower of the Messenger of Allah, peace and blessings of Allah be upon him, will never accept—after witnessing a claimant to revelation receive such a long period of respite—that a false claimant and a liar can also receive such a long period of respite. If no other sign or argument in favour of the truth of such a claimant can be found, even still, a true Muslim is bound to give them the benefit of the doubt in view of faith and must not reject such a person, because the period of their claim bears a resemblance to that of the Messenger of Allah, peace and blessings of Allah be upon him.

If a Christian asserts that a false man can enjoy respite, then it is on them to furnish evidence to that effect. But a Muslim cannot make this assertion. Now, our opponents ought to tell us whether a liar, Antichrist and one who forges a lie against Allah can partake of characteristics that serve as argumentation in favour of prophethood? One must accept that this is absolutely impossible. Such people ought to reflect over my claim and then ponder over the time period that constitutes the era which establishes prophethood. Hence, from every aspect, various points to ponder can be found for those who reflect, and a prudent individual can derive benefit from them."[1]

---

[1]   *Al-Hakam*, vol. 3, no. 21, dated 16 June 1899, pp. 1-2

22 June 1899

During the course of discussion yesterday, the Promised Messiah[as] said: "Know for certain that God will never let this servant of His go to waste and will not cause him to die until those objectives for which he has appeared are manifested at his hand. No one's enmity and no prayer against him can harm him in the least."

The Promised Messiah[as] said these words in response to someone who stated that this man who opposes you and claims to be the recipient of revelation[1] now says that the community will be destroyed.

$$كَبُرَتْ كَلِمَةً تَخْرُجُ مِنْ أَفْوَاهِهِمْ اِنْ يَّقُوْلُوْنَ اِلَّا كَذِبًا^2$$

Grievous is the word that comes from their mouths.

Righteousness and Purity

After the aforementioned, the Promised Messiah[as] said in a heartfelt manner: "Yesterday (i.e. on 22 June 1899), I received the revelation many times that your community should become righteous and if you tread the subtle ways of righteousness, then God will be with you."

The Promised Messiah[as] said: "It grieves my heart immensely when I ask myself what I am to do so my community may adopt true righteousness and purity?"

Then, the Promised Messiah[as] said: "I pray so profusely that sometimes whilst engaged in prayer, I am overcome by weakness, and on certain occasions I begin to feel a loss of consciousness and feel like I may even die."

The Promised Messiah[as] also said: "Until a community becomes righteous in the sight of God, it can never receive divine succour."

The Promised Messiah[as] said: "Righteousness is the essence of the teachings found in all divine scriptures—the Torah and the Gospel etc. The Holy Quran has expressed in a single word the greatest means by which one can act according to the will of God Almighty and attain His ultimate pleasure."

The Promised Messiah[as] said: "I also think about selecting certain people from my community who are truly righteous, who give precedence to religion over worldly affairs, and who are devoted to Allah, so that I may assign them certain religious duties. Then, I will not care about those who remain absorbed in grief

---

[1]   Munshi Ilahi Bakhsh, the accountant, writer of the book *Asa-e-Musa* or *'The Staff of Moses'.* [Publisher]

[2]   *al-Kahf,* 18:6

and pain for this world, and who waste away their lives seeking worldly carrion, day and night."

At night, the Promised Messiah[as] said with a sense of extreme pain: "Alas! At this time, I have no one but God. Strangers, and even my own, are bent on disgracing me. They lie in wait to see me afflicted by misfortunes and vicissitudes. Now if God Almighty does not help me, then I have nowhere to go."[1]

25 June 1899

The *Aqiqah* of Sahibzadah Mirza Mubarak Ahmad

The *aqiqah* of Sahibzadah Mubarak Ahmad Sahib was set to take place on Sunday the 25th of June. His Holiness had entrusted the arrangements for this occasion to Munshi Nabi Bakhsh Sahib. On the day, however, since it was raining, a very cold wind was blowing and there was a dark overcast of clouds, these arrangements could not materialise. The Promised Messiah[as] retired to get some rest and our friend who was responsible for organising everything also went to sleep at home. When the morning had advanced, the Promised Messiah[as] came out and remarked that he could see no arrangements for the *aqiqah*. As people from the village had been invited and certain friends had arrived from other places as well, His Holiness felt a sense of worry for the unreasonable inconvenience that the guests were made to suffer. On the other hand, our friend, Nabi Bakhsh Sahib was extremely perturbed and regretful, as he thought to himself: 'What explanation will I give to the Promised Messiah[as]?' Munshi Sahib presented himself before the Promised Messiah[as] and begged for pardon. The Promised Messiah[as]—the generous man and gracious guide that he is—is not harsh or unjustly critical in nature. The Promised Messiah[as] said: "All right, فُعِلَ مَا قُدِّرَ (*What was destined, has come to pass*)." However, our sensitive friend, Munshi Sahib, could not sit at ease. He was writhing at heart, felt regretful, and would try and do whatever he could. Upon witnessing his state of emotion, His Holiness was reminded of a dream that he saw fourteen years ago which alluded to the fact that he would be blessed with a fourth son, whose *aqiqah* would take place on a Monday.

The joy that the Promised Messiah[as] felt due to the fulfilment of this divine indication and due to the wondrous power of God Almighty, dispelled all our feelings of disappointment and frustration at the lack of preparations. The following

---

[1]   *Al-Hakam*, vol. 3, no. 22, dated 23 June 1899, p. 7

day on Monday, when all of us, the servants of the Promised Messiah[as], were sitting in the inner courtyard of his house, and the head of Sahibzadah Mubarak Ahmad Sahib was being shaved, the Promised Messiah[as] passionately related this dream.[1]

30 June 1899

At night, during the course of discussion, there was mention of epidemics. The Promised Messiah[as] said: "The monsoon season generally is a dangerous time. Indian physicians say that anyone who remains safe in these three months is, as if, born again." Then, the Promised Messiah[as] said: "The coming winter also seems frightening." The Promised Messiah[as] went on to say: "Physicians propose countless safeguards and precautions as preventative measures. Although the phenomenon of means and the importance of having recourse to these means is perfectly justified, but I would say, to what extent can a weak human of limited knowledge scrutinise and exercise caution before making use of various foods or water? In my view, there is no better amulet or charm, nor a more effective precaution or medicine, than seeking forgiveness from God. I advise my friends to foster peace and harmony with God, and remain engaged in prayer."

The Meaning of a Hadith

The Promised Messiah[as] said: "I have a very deep longing and offer supplications so that the lives of my friends are prolonged and the prophecy in the Hadith is fulfilled, which states that in the era of the Promised Messiah, death will vanish from the earth for forty years." Then, the Promised Messiah[as] said: "This obviously, cannot imply that the cup of death will be taken away from all living creatures during this time. What this means is that those from among them who are beneficial to humanity and valuable individuals, Allah the Almighty will bless their lives."[2]

Prior to 10 July 1899

Allah Does Not Allow the Divinely Commissioned to Suffer Disgrace

I remember vividly that on the day that the district superintendent came to Qa-

---

[1]   *Al-Hakam*, vol. 3, no. 23, dated 30 June 1899, pp. 6-7
[2]   *Al-Hakam*, vol. 3, no. 23, dated 30 June 1899, p. 5

dian to search the home of the Promised Messiah[as], there was no prior news or knowledge of the impending search, nor could there have been. On that morning, our respected Mir Sahib heard from somewhere that today a warrant would be coming along with handcuffs as well. Mir Sahib was shocked and became extremely anxious. He hurried in to inform the Promised Messiah[as] and as he was overcome by emotion, he expressed the matter at hand with grave difficulty. His Holiness[as] was writing *Nur-ul-Quran* at the time and he was engaged in a very subtle and delicate subject. The Promised Messiah[as] raised his head, smiled, and said: "Mir Sahib! People wear bangles of silver and gold on occasions of worldly joy. I shall deem that I have put on bangles of iron in the way of Allah Almighty." Then, after a pause, the Promised Messiah[as] said: "But this will never happen, because the government of God Almighty has its own ways of wisdom. God does not allow His divinely commissioned vicegerents to be humiliated."[1]

Week Ending on 10 July 1899

Boundless Joy Due to a Glad-Tiding of Religious Nature

The most astonishing and interesting highlight of this week—which increased our faith immensely—was a letter addressed to the Promised Messiah[as]. The letter states with strong evidence and detail that in the region of Jalalabad, Kabul, there is a shrine[2] of Yuz Asaf, the Prophet, and it is renowned in the area that 2000 years ago this Prophet came from Syria; there is also some land dedicated to honour this shrine by the ruling power in Kabul. There is no room here for further details. The Promised Messiah[as] was so overjoyed by this letter that he said: "Allah the Exalted is a Witness and He is All-Knowing—even if someone had brought me millions of rupees, I would never feel as much joy as this letter has given me."

Brothers, is not the pleasure elicited by a religious matter a sign of those who are sent by Allah? Who, in this age, feels such delight when the supremacy of God's Word is established through such matters?

---

[1]   *Al-Hakam*, vol. 3, no. 24, dated 10 July 1899, pp. 1-2

[2]   Hazrat Mufti Muhammad Sadiq Sahib[ra] relates: "When the Promised Messiah[as] was writing his book *Jesus in India* (perhaps in 1899) a friend by the name of Miyan Muhammad Sultan, a tailor from Lahore, mentioned: 'Once I had the opportunity to visit Afghanistan where I was shown a grave, known as the Tomb of Lamak, the Prophet.' The Promised Messiah, on whom be peace and blessings, said: 'Sometimes the place where a saint or Prophet sits is also turned into a tomb and then people seek blessings from it. It is possible that on his way from Palestine to Kashmir, the Messiah of Nazareth travelled through Afghanistan and stayed in this country somewhere for a few days; and then for some reason, he became renowned in that region as Lamak.'" —See *Dhikr-e-Habib,* By Mufti Muhammad Sadiq[ra], pp. 65-66 for more details. [Publisher]

A Dream and Its Interpretation

A sign that was manifested to revive and strengthen our faith was that in the afternoon, the aforementioned letter arrived unexpectedly, while on that same morning, the Promised Messiah[as] saw a dream. The Promised Messiah[as] saw that Her Majesty the Queen, Empress of India, may Allah preserve her, was seated in the home of the Promised Messiah[as]. In the dream, His Holiness[as] addressed my humble self (Abdul-Karim), as I was seated next to him, and said: "Her Majesty the Queen has most graciously come to my house and has remained here for two days. Gratitude ought to be offered to her."

The interpretation of this dream was that the Promised Messiah[as] would soon receive some form of divine help. For the blessed name of Her Majesty the Queen is 'Victoria' which means, 'one who is triumphant and supported with succour.' At this time, since Her Majesty the Queen is the most successful and fortunate of all the sovereigns on the face of the earth, for this reason, her graciously visiting the home of the Promised Messiah[as] was a sign of immense blessing and success for the Promised Messiah[as]. Now observe the knowledge and power of God. In the afternoon (when the letter was received) the dream was fulfilled. Goodness gracious! What greater succour can there be than for such means to reveal themselves, which stand as a shining argument of God against all the Christians of the world?

The Mission of the Promised Messiah[as]

The Promised Messiah[as] said: "I am amazed when I think about the tasks that this so-called Messiah of the Muslims will perform. The division of his time, as other Muslims explain, is that one part of his day, he will spend breaking crosses made of wood, iron, brass, gold and silver, and another portion, he will spend killing swine. Is this all or will he do anything else?"

The Promised Messiah[as] said: "These people do not stop to think about the actual thing that will establish an argument in favour of the truth against millions of Christians. For if the sword is all they have, Muslims ought to realise that the sword can never be a tool for establishing the truth. Can the truth ever be instilled into the hearts of people through harsh measures? Can coercion ever move a person to be captivated by an argument of Allah? This is all the more objectionable because others will say that such people have no real argument in hand and thus resort to violence."

The Promised Messiah[as] said: "People already raise countless allegations unjustly that Islam was spread by the sword, and now the Muslims seek to prove them right. Furthermore, commonly observed miracles and the like are also insufficient to impress the people of Europe and others from among the Christians. For it is written in their books that many false Prophets will appear and they will manifest signs. Now what other argument, if manifested, could move people to bow their heads? It is the sign that God will manifest at my hand."

Three Avenues for One to Contend Against a Man Commissioned by God

This week a letter was received from the claimant of revelation who lives in Lahore, in which he has made one or two prophecies against the Promised Messiah[as] and his community. The Promised Messiah[as] said in this relation: "Allah the Exalted knows how my heart throbs and is overwhelmed with passion for these people on account of my sympathy for them. I am posed with a challenge as to how I should advise such people. They do not come forth to contend against me by any means. There are only three ways. They can either contend against me in the manifestation of signs in light of those shown in the previous age; they can contend against me in showing new signs for the future; or if nothing else, they can at least pray that the one who is more beneficial to the people be blessed with a long life, according to the following divine promise:

$$\text{وَأَمَّا مَا يَنْفَعُ النَّاسَ فَيَمْكُثُ فِي الْأَرْضِ}^1$$

But as to that which benefits men, it stays on the earth.

It shall then become clear who is beloved and chosen in the sight of God."

The Criterion for Divine Revelation

The Promised Messiah[as] said: "It is unfortunate that some arrogantly flaunt small and insignificant fragments of revelation and dreams, and are unable to comprehend the criterion which establishes any revelation as being divine and free from satanic adulteration. The touchstone is that a revelation from God is accompanied by divine succour, knowledge of the unseen that glistens with divine power,

---

[1] *ar-Ra'd*, 13:18

and is reinforced with a powerful prophecy. Otherwise, such 'revelations' are nothing but absurd statements, which can give no benefit to mankind."

The Promised Messiah[as] said: "If an individual seated at a distance from a gathering only partially grasped the words of a magnificent king, and then proceeded to assert that they had heard the words of that king, what benefit would such a transmission be to the rest of the people? The words related by those who enjoy nearness to the King are distinguishable, and when a well-informed person hears them, they will be able to proclaim that such and such person is addressed directly by the King and receives his good wishes."

The Promised Messiah[as] said: "If my revelations too were ordinary and worthless fragments, and if each and every one of them had not contained knowledge of the unseen and prophecies manifesting divine power, I would consider them to be nothing." Then, the Promised Messiah[as] said: "Let someone present even a single prophecy that is comparable to the one I made about Lekhram."

The Promised Messiah[as] said: "My revelations benefit not only the people, but also the religion of Islam. This standard in itself is a very fundamental criterion which proves that my revelations are from Allah." Then, the Promised Messiah[as] said: "The ways in which God Almighty deals and interacts with me, and manifests signs in my favour, are astonishing. Some of these relate to my own person, others relate to my children, some relate to my family, some relate to my friends, some relate to my opponents, while others still relate to mankind at large."

Emphasis on Meeting the Promised Messiah[as] Often

A message was received from a respected friend of this claimant of revelation from Lahore—a Hafiz Sahib—who said that he viewed past signs to be futile and has no interest in listening to any signs of the past. At this, the Promised Messiah, on whom be peace, said: "Alas! Such people do not understand that nothing from God Almighty should be looked upon as being unworthy of recognition. Allah the Exalted addressed a people of the past in the following words:

$$ اَوَلَمْ يَكْفِهِمْ اَنَّا اَنْزَلْنَا عَلَيْكَ الْكِتَٰبَ يُتْلٰى عَلَيْهِمْ ۚ^1 $$

Is it not enough for them that We have sent down to thee the Book which is recited to them?

---

1   *al-Ankabut*, 29:52

Does this not make reference to signs of the past?" The Promised Messiah[as] went on to say: "Now the times are such that our friends ought to visit me again and again, so that their faith and righteousness may increase by witnessing the new and fresh signs that are manifested daily in my favour."[1]

July 1899

The Purpose of the Establishment of the Ahmadiyya Community

A respectable officer recently came to Qadian for some reason. His Holiness[as], our Imam, Mirza Ghulam Ahmad, Chief of Qadian, also invited him. When all the guests had gathered before the food was served, the Promised Messiah[as] addressed the chief guest and the other friends.[2]

The Promised Messiah[as] said: "Whenever you come here to Qadian, do visit my home without any hesitation at all. We are not accustomed to any formality whatsoever. My endeavours are wholly religious and I am completely detached from the world and its relations and affectations. It is as though I am dead to worldly preoccupations. I am devoted to the Faith and my entire mission is religious in nature—as has always been the case with the past saints and holy men of Islam. My mission is no new undertaking; my task is to dispel those beliefs which pose a danger to the people in every respect, and to purge their hearts is our true desire and objective. For example, some foolish people hold the belief that it is permissible to steal the possessions of people belonging to other nations and usurp the wealth of disbelievers. Then, in order to support their inner, base desires, they fabricate numerous Hadith as well. These people also hold as a matter of doctrine that Jesus[as], who was to reappear in the world, would engage in violence and shed blood—although a religion of compulsion is no religion at all. In short, terrifying doctrines of this sort and false ideologies have taken root in the hearts of people, and it is to dispel and replace them with peaceful doctrines that my community has been established. As has always been the case, people of worldly bent have always opposed divine reformers, saints and those who came to teach virtue. So, too, has been the case with me. My opponents have spread false

---

1   *Al-Hakam*, vol. 3, no. 24, dated 10 July 1899, pp. 3-4

2   The honourable Mufti Muhammad Sadiq Sahib[ra] writes: 'This discourse was based on such beneficial and useful words that I immediately noted most sentences in my notebook, as was my habit. Afterwards, I thought it would be appropriate to give our friends an opportunity to benefit from this deep and subtle discourse through the *Al-Hakam* newspaper. Therefore, I have arranged this text as I remember, with the help of the sentences that I noted down at that time.'

information about me purely by way of slander and calumny, to such an extent that in order to cause me grief they even submitted false reports about me to the government, stating that I was a conspirer who harboured intentions of rebellion. It was necessary for the people to act in this manner; for in every era, the ignorant have always behaved as such towards those who wish them well, i.e. the Prophets and their heirs. However, God Almighty has vested man with intelligence and the government officials know the nature of these people very well.

The Wisdom and Justice of Captain Douglas

As such, one ought to observe the wisdom of Captain Douglas. When Maulvi Muhammad Husain Sahib of Batala said in my connection that I claimed to be a king and an announcement was also read out before him, he was able to grasp with remarkable sagacity that all this was a conspiracy and he refused to lend an ear to any of the falsities of my opponents. Without doubt, in *Izala-e-Awham* and other books, my title *'Sultan'* or King has been written, but this is in the context of the heavenly kingdom, for I have nothing to do with worldly kingdoms. Similarly, my appellation *'Hakam'* is also commonly known, and if translated into English, this term would be rendered as 'Governor General.' It had already been foretold in the prophecies of our Messenger, peace and blessings of Allah be upon him, that the Messiah who was to appear would bear these names. All these titles of mine are mentioned in my books, along with elaborations as well, which elucidate that these are terms relating to heavenly realms and which bear no relation with earthly kings. If I intended evil, why would I forbid people from jihad of the sword etc., and hold them back from engaging in barbaric practices?

In short, Captain Douglas astutely reached the depth of these matters and dealt with complete justice, without leaning even slightly towards either one of the two parties involved out of partiality. In standing for justice and supporting the oppressed, he demonstrated an example of such excellence that I sincerely hope all the esteemed officials in our government forever uphold this lofty example of justice—a perfect example of equity which even leaves behind the justice of Nusherwan. How is it possible for anyone to think ill of the peaceful reign of this government and think to conspire against it?

Cruelties Inflicted Against the Muslims During the Sikh Rule

One ought to realise the degree to which Muslims were hurt during the Sikh reign. The Sikhs killed six to seven thousand men just because one cow was incidentally slaughtered on some occasion. The path of virtue was so obstructed that we hear of a man named Kammay Shah who would raise his hands and pray so that he could receive an opportunity to see a manuscript of *Sahih Bukhari* even once. His supplications would eventually bring him to tears, but the prevailing circumstances of the time would leave him without hope. Today, due to the blessings of this government's reign, that very same *Sahih Bukhari* can be procured for four or five rupees. In that era, people had become so distanced from Islam that a Muslim named Khuda Bakhsh had changed his name to Khuda Singh. As a matter of fact, we are so indebted to this government that if we were to leave this place, we could not enjoy the same freedom even in Mecca or Constantinople. How then can I harbour evil motives at heart against this government? If our people believe that I am against this government or that my religious beliefs are false, they ought to organise a gathering and hear my submissions with a calm heart so that they may be satisfied and their misconceptions may be dispelled.

The mouth of a liar gives off a foul odour and a person of insight is able to perceive it. The work of a truthful one is done in a straightforward and honest manner, and the prevailing circumstances support them.

The Need of the Era

One ought to observe how people have strayed from true doctrines. Two hundred million books have been published against Islam and many hundreds of thousands have become Christian. All things have a limit, and after the dry season, even animals in the jungle raise their heads to the sky hoping for rain. Today, after thirteen hundred years of sun and drought, rain has descended from heaven and now no one can stop this rain. Who can stop the rain when the monsoon season arrives? This is an era in which the hearts of people have become immensely distanced from the truth, to the extent that they have even begun to doubt God Himself.

The Significance of Belief in Allah

All actions are directed by one's belief. For example, if someone were to mistake arsenic for bamboo, they would consume many grams of it. However, if the individual was certain that the substance before them was a deadly poison, they would not bring it anywhere near their mouth. In order to embody true virtue, a belief in the existence of God is necessary, for human authorities are not privy to what a person does in their own home or the actions they commit in hiding. Although a person may claim by tongue to be righteous, if they hold contrary beliefs in their heart, they have no fear of being called to account for it by the people. For there is no government on earth whose fear inspires man constantly and equally during the night and day, in darkness and in light, in seclusion and in public, in private and in the open, at home and in the marketplace. Therefore, in order to reform our morals, belief in such a Being is necessary who watches over man in all states and at all times, and who is privy to all the deeds, actions, and secrets of man's heart. For in actuality, only such a person is truly righteous whose outer and inner state are one, and whose heart accords with his image. Such a person walks on earth like an angel. An atheist is not subject to an authority that can move them to attain the best of morals. All outcomes are the result of belief. For example, a person who recognises a snake's burrow will not put their finger in it. When we know that a certain amount of strychnine is deadly, we firmly hold that it has the power to kill, and it is due to this very belief that we will not consume it so that we may be saved from death.

Proof of the Existence of God Almighty

Decree or the phenomenon whereby all things in the universe move and operate according to a specific measure and under a specific law is evidence of the fact that there must be a determining agent or being that establishes these parameters. If a watch had no conscious inventor, how could this device function consistently as per a set system so that we are able to reap its benefits? Similarly, the order observed in the heavenly watch, and in its fixed and fine-tuned system, demonstrates that it has been intelligently designed for a specific purpose and objective, and in order to benefit us all. In this way, through the created, one can learn of the Creator, and through decree, one can learn of the determining Master behind it.

However, more so than this, Allah the Exalted has furnished another means to prove His own existence. Prior to the event, God discloses His decree to His chosen ones and informs them that on such time and on such day He has decreed for such an event to occur. And so, the individual whom God has chosen for this work informs the people in advance and reveals that such and such an incident will occur; and then that occurrence does in fact take place, just as he has foretold. This is such an argument in favour of the existence of God Almighty, which puts any atheist to shame and leaves them speechless.

God Almighty has granted me thousands of such signs, which result in a captivating belief in the existence of Allah Almighty. Such a large number of my community is present here today. Who from among them has not witnessed at least a few signs of this nature? If you wish, many hundreds more could testify to the same. Have not a large number from among the godly and holy and those who are righteous and pious, and who possess intelligence and insight in every respect, and who are well-established in terms of employment, been satisfied? Have these people not witnessed such things which could never be within the power of man to achieve? If these people are questioned, each and every one of them will declare themselves to be the first of those who bear witness in this respect. Is it possible for people from all walks of life, which include the erudite, scholars, physicians, doctors, merchants, saints, spiritual leaders, lawyers and respected officials, to proclaim that they have witnessed so many heavenly signs with their own eyes if they were first not fully satisfied themselves? And when such people do actually declare what I have said—and anyone who denies this fact is free to confirm it—then in view of this collective testimony, one ought to reflect over the conclusion that a seeker of truth will arrive upon, if in fact, they are truly a seeker of the truth. At the very least, an uninformed person can appreciate without a shadow of doubt that if this group of people composed of the well-educated, wise, and well to do, and those who do not depend on anyone financially, by the grace of Allah, were not perfectly certain about my claim, and if they were not fully satisfied in respect of me, why would they leave their homes, and bear the separation of their loved ones, to live with me here in straitened circumstances as wayfarers? Why are they forever devoted and fondly ready to support my community financially in accordance with their individual circumstances?

All things have an appointed time. Spring arrives at its appointed time and so does the monsoon season. There is no one who can thwart the plans of God."[1]

---

[1]   *Al-Hakam*, vol. 3, no. 26, dated 24 July 1899, pp. 5-7

1 August 1899

A Dialogue with a Hindu Sadhu on Cognisance of the Divine

On 1 August 1899 after the *Maghrib* Prayer, a Hindu ascetic (sadhu), from a well-known class of people, came to visit His Holiness and had a discussion with the Promised Messiah[as]. The following is a summary or abridgement penned in my own words according to memory. —*Editor Al-Hakam*

Promised Messiah[as]**:** Is your practice of meditation according to the tenets of the Sanatan Dharam or the principles of the Arya Samaj?

Ascetic: According to the Sanatan Dharam.

Promised Messiah[as]**:** The Arya Samaj are a sect with words but no action.

Ascetic: Absolutely. These people do not believe in the need for a spiritual teacher (guru). In fact, they do not even believe in Dyanand to be a spiritual guide. They simply say that he has showed them a path and now everyone ought to follow that way.

Promised Messiah[as]**:** Your meditation is full of very strenuous exercises.

Ascetic: Yes, indeed.

Promised Messiah[as]**:** After this exercise, do you develop some sort of strength or power, which causes one to perceive that love which the individual engaged in meditation, possesses for God? For love cannot be perceived or seen to exist until a perfect expression is made from both sides. On the one hand, man must be ready to bear all sorts of grief and pain in the fervour of love, while on the other hand, God *(Parmeshwar)* endows a lustre or light *(parkash)* to such a person, which distinguishes them from others in general.

Ascetic: Yes, a person does manage to develop a certain degree of strength and power.

Promised Messiah[as]**:** Please, do relate something in the context of this power and strength. Not something that you have heard of, but something that you have witnessed yourself, either in your guru or in his guru. You see, things that we have heard about do not possess the same effect, no matter how true they may be, and people consider them to be nothing more than tales and stories. For example, someone may say that there is a certain country where humans fly. Now there can be no doubt that we will be reluctant in believing this because we have neither seen humans flying, nor have we taken flight ourselves. Therefore, in order to increase the strength of our faith and certainty, matters of hearsay are of no benefit. On the contrary, new and fresh observations that we witness before our eyes, and even more so, things that we experience personally, do have an effect. So, the reason I ask this question is so that you will kindly tell me something of the nature that I just mentioned, which you have observed or heard personally from those who engage in this meditative exercise.

Ascetic: Our spiritual leader (guru) did possess certain qualities whereby he could discern the thoughts of others, and when he said something, it would occur. His guru also possessed many such qualities, but I have not seen him. But it is one and the same, because our guru's teacher passed away some eighty years ago, and those who saw him are still alive.

Promised Messiah[as]*:* Have you also performed meditative exercises?

Ascetic: Yes, I have also undertaken such exercises.

Promised Messiah[as]*:* What have you done exactly?

Ascetic: Initially, I would engage in retreats. A single retreat lasts for eight months.

Promised Messiah[as]*:* What would you eat during that time?

Ascetic: In the beginning, I would have rice flour. Then, I began having nothing but porridge—I would boil barley in water and when the mixture would be reduced to half a vessel, I would then keep it aside. The next morning I would have about a litre of that porridge and urinate immediately thereafter. Then, I would eat nothing.

Promised Messiah[as]*:* This did not contain iron etc., did it?

Ascetic: No.

Promised Messiah[as]*:* During this period of spiritual exercise and meditation, did you witness any astonishing or remarkable sights or visions?

Ascetic: Yes, at times I would see a light that would enter my body. Then, I would also see people coming and going from afar.

After this, there were a few minutes of silence, which was finally broken by the following question posed by the Hindu ascetic. —Editor Al-Hakam

Ascetic: Do you believe Parmeshwar (God) to be *aakar* or *nir-aakar*?

At this point, Hazrat Maulvi Nur-ud-Din Sahib explained for the benefit of the audience that aakar means, 'one that can be made into an idol' and nir-aakar means, 'a God who does not require a sculpted form.'

The God of Islam

To this, the Promised Messiah[as] responded: "In order to worship the God that we believe in, we neither require such meditation and exercises, nor are we in need of any idol. In our religion, there is no need whatsoever to bear such difficulties in order to attain the nearness of God Almighty and witness the displays of His power. In fact, those who truly love God and are devoted to Him, can find Him in no time at all, in a very easy manner, and I have experienced this myself. If man moves a single step in God's direction, He moves two steps; if man walks swiftly towards Him, God races towards man and fills his heart with light.

The Wisdom in God Remaining Hidden

In my opinion, those who make idols of God have not understood the wisdom and secret behind God Almighty keeping Himself in a state of apparent hiding. God Almighty being hidden is the very fact that opens the pathways for all of man's quests, searches and investigations. All the knowledge and insight that has ever been revealed to man, though present all along, at some point in time, was hidden. It was the strength of man's struggle and effort that showed its lustre and achieved the ultimate end.

The love of a true lover does not waver by the absence of their beloved, or if their beloved cannot be seen physically. In fact, physical separation results in a kind of longing, which increases the lover in their passion. How then, can someone who searches for God through an idol claim to be a true and sincere lover, when, without the aid of an idol, a person is unable to direct their full attention towards that pure and perfectly beautiful Being? A person ought to test their love themselves. If like the passionate lover, who while sitting and standing, and in every state, whether awake or asleep, can see nothing but the countenance of his Beloved and his full attention is forever inclined to Him, then he should know that he does truly love God Almighty, and most definitely, the light and love of God is present within him. However, if intermediary agencies and external ties and obstructions can divert a person's attention from God, and if one's heart can lose sight of Him for even a moment, then I honestly say that such a person is not a lover of God Almighty and does not love Him; this is why they are deprived of the light and radiance that is granted to true lovers of God.

It is here where most people have stumbled and have rejected God. The foolish did not correctly adjudge their own love; and began to think ill of God, without first taking stock of their own devotion. Therefore, in my opinion, God Almighty is apparently hidden so that the goodness and rectitude in our nature can come forth and develop further, and so that our spiritual powers may be refined and polished, in order to fill us with divine light.

I publish repeated announcements and invite people to experience this for themselves. Some people call me a businessman. Everyone has their own idea and speaks accordingly. However, despite hearing all these differing voices, for what purpose do I publish announcements in all the parts of the world where people reside, be it in Europe or America etc.?

My Purpose

I have no purpose other than to guide people towards that God Whom I myself have witnessed. I do not desire to show God by way of hearsay or tales of the past. In fact, I call upon people to accept God Almighty by presenting to the world my own being and my own person. This is a simple matter. God Almighty moves towards a person with greater speed and swiftness than they advance towards Him. When we observe even on earth that the beloved of an honourable man is afforded respect and honour, how could someone who enjoys the nearness of God Almighty possess no signs to exhibit the omnipotence of God Almighty and His boundless powers?

The Rank of Those Who Enjoy Nearness in the Royal Court of God

Remember that the jealousy of God Almighty never leaves such a person in a state where they are disgraced and ruined. On the contrary, as God Himself is One and without partner, He makes such a person one who is without partner among the people on earth. No one on the face of the earth can contest with such a person. Such a one is attacked on all fronts and every attacker—oblivious to the strength of such people—surmises that they will destroy them. Ultimately, such opponents realise that the manner in which the people who they oppose are saved is the work of a higher force that is above and beyond human power. In fact, if such people knew this from the very beginning, they would not have waged these attacks in the first place.

As such, those who bask in the nearness of God Almighty, and who serve as a sign of His existence and Being, are apparently such that every opponent, in their own view, believes that they will not be able to escape them. This is because the schemes that they hatch and the sum total of their efforts lead them to this belief. However, when a holy person safely emerges from all this with honour and dignity, an opponent is taken aback for a moment and realises that if this were a human affair, this person could not have come out unscathed; so if this person has remained safe and sound, this is not the work of man, but the work of God.

Therefore, this sheds light on the underlying reason behind the attacks made against those who enjoy nearness in the royal court of God. Those who are ignorant in the field of divine knowledge and insight consider such opposition to be a means of disgrace. But what would make them know that this very 'disgrace' is a means of honour and distinction for the people of God, which proves to be a sign in favour of the existence of Allah the Exalted and establishes His Being. This is why such people are referred to as the 'Signs of God'.

In short, my desire in the countless announcements that I publish is to inform the people of the God that I have found and seen, and to show them the closest and quickest way by which they can become a godly person. Therefore, in my opinion, stories and tales cannot serve to advance one in divine knowledge and insight, until man practically sees for himself; and this is not possible in any other way except by following the path that I have shown. Moreover, on this path, such difficulties and hardships are not required. Here, it is the heart that does the work. God Almighty looks at the heart. When there is love and passion in the heart, what use is an idol? The worship of idols can never bring a person true and certain results.

God Almighty Sees Our Sincerity and Love

The sight of God Almighty focuses on a point in the heart of a sincere person. God sees this and knows that the person in question will bear every difficulty and struggle happily for His sake. It is not necessary for a man to undertake strenuous exercises and always be present. I observe that the sweeper who comes to my house undertakes immense toil, and that even our very honourable and sincere friends could not do the work that he does. Now would I view my sincere friends as unworthy on account of this, and look at the sweeper as being worthy of more esteem and honour? We have certain friends who come to visit us after extended periods of time and it is not possible for them to sit in our company often, but I know full well that their hearts are moulded in such a way, and their dispositions have been vested with such sincerity and love, that when the time comes, they will offer great services in our cause.

The same principle is to be found in the law of nature as well. The more something is raised in station, the lesser its toil and labour. Just take the example of process servers. They are handed a heap of documents and are ordered to comply and report back within one week. Come rain or shine, be it winter, or even if village roads are damaged and difficult to traverse, no excuse is accepted. And after all this, if you ask them their wage, they receive a meagre five rupees. However, the circumstances of high-ranking officials is at a stark variance.

Asceticism Does Not Lead to Perfect Knowledge of the Divine

This law of nature clearly demonstrates that the divine law deals with the beloved of God Almighty in the same manner. Engaging in dangerous meditations, and rendering one's limbs and faculties lifeless through various exercises, is absolutely absurd and futile. This is why our Perfect Guide, on whom be peace and blessings, has said:

$$لَا رَهْبَانِيَّةَ فِى الْإِسْلَامِ$$

There is no asceticism in Islam.

That is to say, the fundamental quality of Islam may be described as such:

گردن نہادن برحکم خدا و موافقت تامہ بمقادیر الہیہ

To bow one's head before the command of God and
fully accept the decrees of the Divine.

When a person develops this quality, there is no need for asceticism. In other words, such exercises and meditations are not required."

After this, the Hindu ascetic left and food was served. The Promised Messiah[as] said: "This is why Islam has not prescribed asceticism. For asceticism does not lead to perfect knowledge of the Divine."[1]

Prior to 10 August 1899

Appeasing the World

Hazrat Maulvi Abdul-Karim Sahib[ra] writes: "I have heard countless times from the blessed tongue of my beloved Master and Guide, the Chief of the Saints, the Jesus promised to appear in this age, peace be upon him, the following: 'I possess the ability to deliver addresses and publish such writings which are articulated in a way that "makes peace with all," as the common saying goes, so that all nations, despite their differences, are pleased; so that no one from among the authorities or the common people are able to find a single point of objection in them. However, how can I bear to suffer the rejection of my God just to please this lowly world?'"[2]

Week ending 11 August 1899

The Reality of Prayer

There were certain people who would write to the Promised Messiah[as] for prayers, and they would receive a written response to the effect that a prayer has been made for them. However, after this, they would write back saying: "There has been no benefit. There are only two cases: either you have not prayed or if you have, you have not done so with full attention."

One day, Hazrat Maulvi Abdul-Karim Sahib[ra] submitted this matter to the Promised Messiah, on whom be peace and blessings, who said: "It appears that there is a dire need to write about the subject of prayer once again. It seems that previous explanations have been insufficient. Prayer is a very delicate matter. One condition is that a firm connection must exist between the person who makes a request for prayer and the supplicant to whom the request is made. This is to the extent that the former's grief becomes the latter's grief, and his joy becomes the other's joy. Just as the cries of an infant make its mother unbearably restless, and milk begins to flow forth in her bosom, in the same way, the plight of the one who

---

[1] *Al-Hakam*, vol. 3, no. 28, dated 10 August 1899, p. 2, taken from a letter of Maulana Abdul-Karim Sahib[ra].

[2] *Al-Hakam*, vol. 3, no. 28, dated 10 August 1899, p. 2, taken from a letter of Maulana Abdul-Karim Sahib[ra].

makes a request for prayer and their cry for help must move the person to whom a request is made, so that the latter is wholly overcome by emotion and supplicates with a sense of resolve."

Even Attention and Emotion in Prayer Descend from God Almighty

The Promised Messiah[as] said: "The fact of the matter is that all these things are conferred as a gift from God Almighty and are not of man's own effort. Even attention in prayer and emotion descend from God, when God wills for the path of success to be cleared for a certain person. However, in the system of apparent means, it is necessary for a supplicant to be moved by a strong catalyst. This is only possible when the one submitting a request for prayer transforms themselves in such a way that the supplicant to whom they have made a request is inclined towards them with a sense of restlessness."

Prayer and Service to the Faith

The Promised Messiah[as] said: "The sort of person who attracts my attention, and for whom I feel an inclination to pray is only of one sort. When I come to know that a certain person is engaged in serving the Faith, and their person is beneficial to God, the Messenger of God, the Book of God and the servants of God, the pain and anguish that such a person feels is actually my own."

The Promised Messiah[as] said: "Our friends ought to make a firm resolve in their hearts that they will serve the Faith. A person ought to serve in whichever manner or way that is possible for them." Then, the Promised Messiah[as] said: "I truthfully say that valuable and worthy in the sight of God is the one who is a servant of the Faith and beneficial to mankind. Otherwise, God does not care if such people die like dogs and sheep."

The Bond Between God Almighty and Man

One day, the Promised Messiah, on whom be peace, said: "Two friends can only carry on as such when on certain occasions the former listens to the latter and vice versa. If one friend demands to get his way every time, this will spoil the relationship. So, too, should be the case in the bond between man and God. At times, Allah Almighty accepts the servant's desire and opens to them the door of His grace, and on other occasions, the servant must submit to the divine decrees of fate and destiny. In truth, it is God Almighty who possesses the right to try His servants, and these trials from God are for man's benefit. God makes those who prove to be sincere even after they are tried, the inheritors of divine bounty—this is how God's law of nature operates."

Preoccupation in Worldly Affairs Results in a Loss in the Hereafter

A young man presented himself before the Promised Messiah, on whom be peace, and began to relate his story of the worldly misfortunes with which he was confronted, as well as his countless woes and sorrows. The Promised Messiah[as] advised him at length and said: "To become fully engrossed in such matters causes a person to be deprived in the hereafter. A believer must not wail and mourn over their circumstances in this way." Then the young man began to weep loudly and profusely at which the Promised Messiah[as] expressed extreme displeasure and disapproval. He said: "Enough! It is my belief that such weeping leads a person to hell. In my estimation, tears which fall out of grief and sorrow for the world are a fire that burn the very one who sheds them. My heart turns cold when I witness the state of such a person who mourns, longing for this carrion of a world."

The Nature of Exemplary Trust in God

One day in a gathering of the Promised Messiah[as], the discussion turned to trust in God. The Promised Messiah[as] said: "I find that the state of my heart is a strange one. When it is extremely humid and the heat becomes immensely intense, people begin to hope with a sense of certainty that rain will soon follow. Similarly, when I find my casket to be empty, I feel a firm sense of certainty in the grace of God that now it will be replenished, and this is exactly what happens."

Then, the Promised Messiah[as] swore by God Almighty and said: "When my pouch is empty, the sort of joy and pleasure that I experience in trusting God Almighty at such a time is beyond my ability to explain. My state at such a time is extremely comforting and satisfying, in comparison to when my pouch is full."

The Promised Messiah[as] went on to say: "In the days when my father and brother were overwhelmed by a multitude of woes and sorrows on account of lawsuits surrounding various worldly matters, they would often look at my state of affairs with envy and say: 'He is a very fortunate man. No grief comes anywhere near him.'"

The Rank of the Messenger of Allah[sa] and the Two Chiefs

On one occasion, a friend who was truly absorbed in love for the Promised Messiah[as], submitted to him: "Why should we not consider you to be greater in status than the *Shaykhayn*[1] (the Two Chiefs) and closer in rank to the Noble Messenger, peace and blessings of Allah be upon him?" Goodness gracious! On hearing this, His Holiness became pale and an inexplicable anxiety and restlessness overtook him from head to toe. I swear in the name of God, who is Jealous and Holy, that this particular instance increased my faith in the Promised Messiah[as] even more. The Promised Messiah[as] delivered an all-encompassing address continuously for six hours. When he began speaking, I looked at my watch, and when he finished, I looked at my watch again. He spoke for six hours. Not a minute less.

To speak on a subject for so long, without rest, was an extraordinary occurrence. In his entire discourse, the Promised Messiah[as] spoke of the virtues and qualities of the Noble Messenger, may the choicest blessings and salutations be upon him, and about his own servitude and subservience to him. He also spoke of the excellences of the honourable *Shaykhayn*, may peace be on both of them. The Promised Messiah[as] said: "It is sufficient for me that I am an admirer of these men and the dust beneath their feet. The partial superiority which God Almighty has conferred upon them can never be attained by anyone until the Day of Resurrection. When will Muhammad, the Messenger of Allah, peace and blessings of Allah be upon him, ever be born again on earth so that one may receive the opportunity to render such service as the honourable *Shaykhayn*, peace be on both of them."[2]

17 August 1899

A few days ago, someone wrote to the Promised Messiah[as] from Bereli inquiring: "Are you the same Promised Messiah foretold in the various Hadith of God's Messenger, peace and blessings of Allah be upon him? Respond by taking an oath on God Almighty." As was the custom, I responded to the person with a few lines from *Tiryaq-ul-Qulub,* a book of the Promised Messiah[as], which could have been a sufficient response. The individual was not satisfied. He wrote to me again and addressed me saying: "I would like Hazrat Mirza Sahib to write on oath, with his

---

[1]   A title of honour which refers to Hazrat Abu Bakr[ra] and Hazrat Umar[ra].

[2]   *Al-Hakam*, vol. 3, no. 29, dated 17 August 1899, pp. 1-5

own hand, as to whether he is the same Promised Messiah who has been mentioned in the Hadith and the Holy Quran." After the evening Prayer, I placed an inkpot, pen and paper before the Promised Messiah[as] and submitted that a certain individual had written such and such request. His Holiness took the paper at once and wrote the following lines:

> Previously, I have already written the following declaration clearly in my books as an oath before the people, but once again, on this document, I swear by God Almighty, in Whose hand is my life, and write that I am the same Promised Messiah who has been foretold by the Messenger of Allah, peace and blessings of Allah be upon him, and who has been mentioned in the authentic Hadith recorded in *Sahih Bukhari*, *Sahih Muslim*, and other books from among the six authentic books of Hadith. وَ كَفَى بِاللهِ شَهِيْدًا (*And Allah is sufficient as a witness*).
>
>
>
> *The writer,*
> *Mirza Ghulam Ahmad*
> *May Allah forgive him and support him*
> *17 August 1899*
>
>

In relating this account, I have two objectives in mind. Firstly, so that the faith of our own community may be increased and so that they too can experience the same joy and pleasure that the fortunate ones present here at the time felt. Those of us present here at the time must wholeheartedly profess that our faith was revived. Secondly, those who reject the Promised Messiah[as] and think ill of him, ought to reflect with a calm heart and contemplate on whether a committed liar and a self-made deceiver can possess the grace and courage to swear in this manner by God, the Possessor of Glory, in such a gathering? Allah is the greatest! Allah is the greatest! Indeed, Allah is the greatest![1]

21 October 1899

The Purpose of the Advent of the Promised Messiah— To Develop a Living Faith in the Living God

Lalah Keshudas, Tehsildar of Batala, coincidentally happened to visit Qadian and so he came to see the Promised Messiah[as]. He submitted to His Holiness that

---

[1] *Al-Hakam*, vol. 3, no. 32, dated 9 September 1899, pp. 4-5

he was very fond of visiting holy men and it was due to this very desire that he had come to visit the Promised Messiah[as]. His Holiness said: "There is no doubt that if you did not possess a love for those filled with goodwill, why would you come to visit me? For why would a worldly man bother to visit someone who sits secluded in a corner away from the rest of the world? This requires an affinity of natures.

The fact of the matter is that when man is a mortal being, when there is no telling when death will arrive, and when life is transitory, how crucial it is for him to become constantly engaged in seeking his own reformation and prosperity. However, I observe that the people of the world are so obsessed in their own preoccupations, that they are not the least concerned or worried for the hereafter. They are becoming so indifferent towards God Almighty, that it is as if He did not exist at all. In these circumstances, when the state of the world is becoming so weak in faith, Allah the Exalted has appointed me and sent me so that I may show them the path which leads to a living belief in the Living God.

As is the general law of God, many people who are deprived of good nature and guidance, who do not fear God and are bereft of a sense of justice, have declared me to be false and have named me a liar. They left no stone unturned in causing me grief and strove to harm me. They issued edicts of disbelief against me so that the Muslims would think ill of me and submitted false reports about me to the government to incite the authorities against me. They brought forth false lawsuits against me, cursed me and conspired to kill me. In short, what did they not do? But my God stands by my side at all times. He informed me in advance of their every scheme and revealed to me the final end of each. Ultimately, everything transpired exactly as God had informed me long ago.

However, there are those who have been blessed with a good nature, fear of God and the light of faith; those who recognised me and who flocked around me to partake of that light, which God has conferred upon me in the form of enlightenment and divine insight. These people include distinguished scholars, graduates, lawyers, doctors, honourable government officials, merchants, landlords and common people as well.

It is unfortunate that our unworthy opponents cannot even bring themselves to at least listen calmly to the truth that I present. For they are empty of such lofty morals. Otherwise, devotion to the truth demands the following:

مرد باید که گیرد اندر گوش گر نوشت ست پند بر دیوار

A man ought to put into his ear;
a piece of advice, even if written on a wall.

The Religion of Truth and God's Unity

In this age, people express a strong aversion when they hear the word 'religion' and to accept the true religion is as if they were entering the jaws of death. A true religion is one to which the 'hidden law' testifies as well. For example, we put forth the concept presented by Islam known as the Unity of God, and claim that this is the true teaching of the Divine. This is because the teaching instilled in the very disposition of man is that of God's Unity. A view of nature also bears testimony to this effect. God Almighty has made His creation individually distinct, but pulls them to a unified centre, which demonstrates that it was unity that was always intended. If one releases a droplet of water, they will see that it is spherical in form. The moon, sun and all the celestial bodies are round, and the spherical form necessitates oneness.

Trinity

On this occasion, I leave aside the discussion of countless gods because this concept is a clearly absurd and senseless belief. For if there were innumerable gods, as some believe, this would create havoc in the world. However, I would like to mention the Trinity. I have demonstrated from the phenomenon observed in nature that God is One. Now, if God were three, as the Christians assert, God forbid, water, flames of fire, and the bodies in heaven and earth ought to have been triangular, so that the universe would bear witness to the Trinity. The light of the heart can never attest to the concept of Trinity. When Christian priests are asked whether people would be judged by belief in Trinity or Unity, in places where the Gospels have not reached, they have openly conceded that such people will be judged on their belief in God's Unity. In fact, Dr Pfander has put this admission to writing in his book. Now, in the presence of this clear testimony, I cannot understand why anyone would advocate belief in the doctrine of Trinity. Not to mention that these three gods are strange indeed, for each of them has different duties. In other words, each God in itself is deficient and incomplete, and each god completes the other.

The Divinity of Christ

Furthermore, do not even speak of the Messiah who is deified. His entire life was spent in suspense and anxiety. This son of Adam had no place to lay his head. He was unable to provide any complete example to follow in the way of morality. The teaching he left behind is so insufficient and inadequate that an individual who acts upon this teaching falls to a very low state. How can someone who cries over his own helplessness grant power and honour to anyone else? How can such a one hear the supplications of others, when his own cries and lamentations made throughout the night went in vain? A person who cried and shrieked *'Eloi, eloi, lama sabachthani,'* meaning, 'O God! O God! Why hast thou forsaken me?' yet he was not heard. And to crown this all off, ultimately, the Jews seized him and hung him on the cross, and in light of their own doctrine, established that he was accursed. Even the Christians themselves consider him to be accursed; their justification is that he took this curse upon himself for their sake.

In actuality, 'curse' is something which blackens a person from within; in turn, a man is distanced from God, and God is distanced from him, as if the individual in question no longer holds a relationship with God whatsoever. This is why Satan is also known as the Accursed. Now what is a Christian left with after they accept this curse and admit that the Messiah was an accursed man? The fact of the matter is that nothing remains if one accepts this curse. The Christians have no choice but to make the best of this bad bargain, as it were. And so, to what extent should one speak of the beliefs held by these people? It is Islam that has brought the truth. Furthermore, God Almighty has appointed me to show the light possessed by Islam to those who truly seek it. The truth is that God exists, and He is One. It is my belief that even if the Gospel, and the Holy Quran, and all the scriptures of the Prophets did not exist in the world, the Unity of God Almighty would still stand proven, because its imprint exists in the very nature of man.

The Sonship of God

To attribute a son to God is equivalent to believing that God Almighty will die. For the purpose of a son is to serve as a memory of the father. Now if the Messiah is the son of God, the question which arises is: will God die? Hence, in their beliefs, Christians have neither given regard to the greatness of God, nor have they done justice to the faculties of man. They subscribe to such concepts which are not supported by heavenly light. There is not a single Christian who can show miracles and prove their own faith with the signs that are characteristic of believers. Islam alone can take pride in the mark of distinction that in every era the religion is reinforced by supporting signs; and God has not left the present era deprived either. I have been sent for this very purpose; so that I may manifest to the world in this era the truthfulness of Islam, through supporting signs, which are the hallmark of Islam. Blessed is the one who comes to me with a sound heart in order to find the truth, and blessed is the one who, upon witnessing the truth, accepts it."[1]

---

[1] *Al-Hakam*, vol. 4, no. 28, dated 9 August 1900, pp. 3-4

An Address of the Promised Messiah[as] at the Farewell Gathering[1]

The Purpose of the Advent of the Promised Messiah[as]

The Promised Messiah[as] states: "Authentic and definitive knowledge has been given to us in the Holy Quran alluding to the fact that Jesus, peace be upon him, was taken down from the cross alive and that he was saved from this calamity. However, it is a pity that over the last one thousand years, where many other afflictions have appeared, this matter too fell into darkness, and unfortunately, the notion became firmly rooted within the Muslims that the Messiah[as] was lifted into the heavens alive and that he will descend from the sky when the Resurrection approaches.

However, in this, the fourteenth century, Allah the Exalted sent me by way of divine appointment so that I may dispel the errors that have taken root within the Muslims internally and manifest the truth of Islam before the world. Furthermore, I have been sent to respond to the allegations that are levelled against Islam externally and clearly demonstrate the reality of the other false religions—particularly the religion of the cross, i.e. the Christian faith. I have been tasked to uproot its erroneous doctrines, which are dangerous and harmful to the people, and which are a hindrance to the nourishment and development of man's spiritual faculties.

The True Facts About Jesus[as] Son of Mary

From among these various beliefs, one concept relates to the Messiah ascending into heaven—a notion, which unfortunately, even some Muslims have begun to advocate. It is this very concept on which Christianity is based, because the foundation on which salvation stands in Christianity is this very cross. The Christians

---

[1]   During the very days in which the Promised Messiah[as] was writing his book *Jesus in India*, it came to light that certain relics of the Messiah of Nazareth[as] had been found in Nasibain (situated in the Arab country of Iraq), which furnished evidence of the Messiah's journey and corroborated the fact that he settled in Kashmir. The Promised Messiah[as] deemed it advisable to dispatch a commission or delegation to personally investigate and examine these relics and the state of affairs, and then for the delegation to return to Qadian from the route on which the Messiah journeyed to Kashmir. In order to see off this delegation and bid them farewell, an event was arranged by the name of *Jalsa Al-Wida* (The Farewell Gathering). Due to certain compelling circumstances, although the dispatch of this delegation was postponed, the event, nonetheless, was held on the 12-14 November 1899, with great excitement and celebration. The present address was delivered by the Promised Messiah[as] on this occasion.

believe that the Messiah died on the cross for them, then he came back to life and ascended into heaven, this being proof of His divinity.

Those Muslims who have supported the Christians erroneously do not believe that the Messiah died on the cross, but they do believe that he was raised to heaven alive. However, the reality which Allah Almighty has disclosed to me is that the Messiah son of Mary was tormented severely at the hands of the Jews of his age, just as the truthful are tormented in their respective times at the hands of foolish opponents. Ultimately, these very same Jews strove to somehow put an end to him and kill him on the cross by way of conspiracy and mischief. It would appear that they succeeded in their designs, because it was ordered that the Messiah son of Mary be put on the cross. However, Allah the Exalted who never allows for His truthful and divinely commissioned servants to be wasted, saved him from the curse that was necessitated by him dying on the cross and gave rise to such means that he was taken down from the cross alive.

There are many arguments to this effect that are found in the very Gospel itself, but I do not intend to mention them on this occasion. By studying the incidents that surround the crucifixion according to the Gospel account, it becomes clearly evident that the Messiah son of Mary was taken down from the cross alive. Then, since he had many enemies in his own land—enemies who were thirsty for his blood—and since he had already stated that 'a Prophet is not without honour but in his own country,' alluding to his migration, Jesus[as] decided to leave his homeland. In order to fulfil the obligation of his ministry, he set out in search of the lost sheep of the house of Israel. Passing through Nasibain, he arrived in Kashmir through Afghanistan, and continued preaching to the Children of Israel who were settled in Kashmir. He reformed these people and ultimately passed away whilst he was among them. This is the fact that has been disclosed to me.

The Significance of This Issue

The fundamental pillar of Christianity crumbles as a result of the aforementioned concept alone. For when the Messiah did not die on the cross, and did not resurrect to ascend into heaven after three days, the base and foundation of the edifice of Christ's divinity and the Atonement is destroyed. Moreover, this also does away with the false notion of the Muslims that Jesus[as] ascended into heaven alive and will physically return in the latter days—a belief which is a grave dishonour to the Messenger of Allah, peace and blessings of Allah be upon him, because no old or new Prophet can appear now whose prophethood does not bear his seal. Furthermore, this also proves the actual and pure teaching of the Holy Quran to be true, because the clear declaration of the Messiah, on whom be peace, فَلَمَّا تَوَفَّيْتَنِي[1] is present in the Holy Quran, and no one can deny this.

The Reason for Emphasising the Death of Jesus[as]

It is for this very reason that I stress the belief relating to the death of Jesus[as], for it is with this very death that the death of Christianity is intertwined. It is for this purpose that I have begun to write the book *Masih Hindustan Mein* (Jesus in India). In order to address the various demands of this book in terms of content, I deemed it appropriate to dispatch a few individuals from my community, whose task it will be to visit the relevant regions and look into the relics that are reported to exist there. Therefore, it is with this objective in mind that I have called this gathering, so that we may offer prayers for these, our friends, before seeing them off, that may they depart on this blessed journey safe and sound and return successful.

The Journey of Jesus[as] to Nasibain After the Crucifixion

Even if the proposed journey were not to have taken place, God Almighty by His mere grace and mercy has still provided such ample testimony and arguments, that I am certain that the pen and tongue of our opponents could not refute them. Nonetheless, however, a believer always strives for progress, and hungers and thirsts to learn as many verities and insights as possible; a believer is never satiated. Hence, it is also my desire to gather as many proofs and arguments as possible in this regard. It is for this very reason that I have decided to send my friends to Nasibain. We have learned that the ruler of Nasibain wrote to the Messiah[as] offering him to come to his land (when the Messiah was suffering at the hands of his own ungrateful people) and after Jesus[as] was delivered from the crucifixion, he reached this land and was saved from his wretched people. The ruler of Nasibain also wrote to Jesus[as]: 'If you come and stay with me, I shall be blessed to serve you. I am ill, please pray for me as well.' Although I came to know of this in an English book, but I have found a similar gist in *Rauda-tus-Safa*, a work of Islamic history as well. Therefore, one is led to believe that the Messiah,

---

[1]   *al-Ma'idah*, 5:118

on whom be peace, definitely travelled to Nasibain, and it was via this route that he journeyed on to India.

Allah the Exalted is the Possessor of all knowledge, but my heart also bears witness that on this trip, God-willing, the truth will become manifest and the true state of affairs will become clear. It is possible that during this expedition, certain writings or inscriptions are unearthed, which shed light on various aspects relating to the journey of the Messiah, on whom be peace. Perhaps we may find the grave of someone from among the disciples, or other discoveries of this nature, which support our objective. Therefore, I have prepared three men from my community to undertake this journey. It is my desire to write an Arabic treatise for them as well, to preach my mission, so that they may distribute it wherever they go on their journey. In this manner, the journey will also prove beneficial in propagating the message of my community.

A Sincere and Loyal Community

I am thankful to God Almighty for granting me a sincere and loyal community. I observe that whenever I call upon them for any task or purpose, they swiftly and passionately come forward, in an attempt to outstrip one another, according to their own strength and ability. I can see that they possess devotion and sincerity. Whenever I make a command, they are ready to obey. The truth is that no nation or community can be moulded until they possess this spirit of fervour, sincerity and devotion in obeying and following their leader.

The Messiah, on whom be peace, was made to suffer difficulties and misfortunes, due to the weakness and unwilling nature of his community—among other things. As such, when Jesus[as] was arrested, one of his greatest disciples, Peter, rejected his Master and Guide; in fact, not only did he reject him, he cursed him three times. Most of the disciples abandoned Christ and fled. In contrast, the example of devotion and loyalty that the companions of the Holy Prophet, peace and blessings of Allah be upon him, demonstrated is unparalleled in the history of the world. They bore all sorts of grief for the Holy Prophet[sa] as though it was nothing; they even left behind their beloved homeland, and gave up their wealth, property and friends. Ultimately, these companions did not even hesitate or express any regret in laying down their lives for the sake of the Holy Prophet[sa]. It was this very loyalty and devotion that ultimately blessed them with prosperity.

Similarly, I can see that Allah the Exalted has endowed my community with an ardour that behoves their rank and status, and they are exemplary in their loyalty and devotion. From the day that I decided to send a delegation to Nasibain, everyone has wished to be chosen for this service and has envied those who have been selected for this purpose. It is their desire that if they were sent instead, this would be their good fortune. Many of our friends presented themselves to embark on this trip. However, before having received these requests, I had already chosen Mirza Khuda Bakhsh Sahib for this mission and had decided that Maulvi Qutb-ud-Din and Miyan Jamal-ud-Din would accompany him. Therefore, I was compelled to turn down these other requests. Nonetheless, I am certain that those who presented themselves for this service with full sincerity and loyalty will not be deprived by Allah the Exalted of their reward, and they will receive their recompense in accordance with their sincerity.

The Greatness of Travelling for the Sake of God Almighty

It is not an easy task to journey to far-off countries and foreign lands. Although it is true that travel has become more convenient in this day and age, but who can know for certain whether they will return from the journey alive. It is not easy to leave behind small children, wives, other relatives and dear ones. These people are open-heartedly leaving behind their businesses and affairs unattended and in a state of danger to undertake this journey, which I believe is worthy of immense spiritual reward. Firstly, they will be worthy of a reward from God because they are setting out on this journey purely to manifest the greatness and Unity of God Almighty; secondly, they will receive a reward on account of the hardships and difficulties that they will have to bear during the course of this trip. Allah the Exalted does not waste a good deed performed by anyone:

$$فَمَنْ يَّعْمَلْ مِثْقَالَ ذَرَّةٍ خَيْرًا يَّرَهُ ^1$$

Then whoso does an atom's weight of good will see it.

Now when he does not allow for even an ounce of goodness performed by anyone to go in vain, can the spiritual reward of such an important journey, which almost resembles a migration, go without recompense from God? Of course not. Devotion and loyalty, however, are necessary. One must shun ostentation and the desire for fame and self-renown. I believe that one cannot bear the trials and

---

1   *az-Zilzal*, 99:8

tribulations of land and sea, and take upon themselves a kind of death, unless they are filled with sincerity. A large number of brothers will continue to pray for these men and I shall also continue to offer prayers for them that may Allah the Exalted make them successful in this mission and return them to us safe and sound. The truth is that even the angels will pray for them and shall accompany them on the way.

The Generosity and Resolve of Our Community

Now, I would also like to express that on this occasion, our community has demonstrated a forbearance and resolve in two forms. Firstly, there is this group of people who will undertake this expedition and have thus subjected themselves to the perils of this journey, and who have prepared themselves to bear those trials and tribulations that will confront them on this path. Secondly, there are those members of the community who have always made financial contributions for my religious objectives and endeavours open-heartedly. I feel no need to elaborate on this, because each and every one in my community, more or less, contributes according to their own ability and strength, and Allah Almighty knows best the sincerity and loyalty with which these people partake in financial contributions.

I know full well that the members of my community have demonstrated the example that was set by the companions of the Holy Prophet[sa] when they were passing through a time of hardship. In my previous announcement, although I have only written the names of a few friends, who demonstrated a model of loyalty and resolve, this does not mean that I am ignorant of others or their worthy services. I am well aware of those who hasten towards me with fervour and sincerity. As I was ill and even now since I am unwell, I was unable to write all of the specific details, nor was such detail possible in a short announcement. Therefore, those people whose names have not been mentioned in the announcement should not grieve. Allah the Exalted knows well the level of their devotion and sincerity.

Financial Sacrifice Must Be For the Sake of Allah Alone

If someone makes a donation or contributes in the way of our religious needs so that their name is published, then remember that such a one desires worldly fame, renown and recognition. However, a person who walks on this path purely for the sake of Allah Almighty, and remains determined to serve the faith, has no need for such things. Worldly renown has no value or worth. Names written in heaven as recognition are of true value. What value is there in names written on paper? They are present at one time and waste away later. However, that which is recorded in heaven is never erased. The effects of this last until the end of time. I have many sincere friends, who are known to very few of you, but they have always stood by my side. For example, there is Mirza Yusuf Baig Sahib, who is a true and genuine friend. I have mentioned him because this is a means of introducing brothers to one another, and this also increases their mutual love. Mirza Sahib has been with me from the time that I lived a life of seclusion. I can see that his heart is replete with love and devotion, and he is constantly filled with a fervour to serve the community. In the same manner, there are many other friends as well and all of them are brimming with the sincerity and fervour of love, each to the extent of their own faith and divine understanding.

There Is Nothing Until One Possesses Strong Faith

Though I am cognisant that people only gradually find the ability to serve by action, there is no doubt that a person's actions strengthen in proportion to a person's strength in faith. This is to such an extent that when a believer's strength in faith matures and develops fully, they reach the station of a Martyr *(Shaheed)* because nothing can stand in their way. Such an individual is not hesitant or reluctant even to sacrifice their dear life.

The Advent of the Holy Prophet[sa] and the Purpose of the Revelation of the Holy Quran

I have mentioned this before as well and it shall be of benefit if I mention this again. I would like to turn your attention to the question of what was the purpose of Allah Almighty in raising Prophets, peace be upon them, and in ultimately sending the Holy Prophet, peace and blessings of Allah be upon him, for the guidance of mankind, and in revealing the Holy Quran? Every individual's actions are fuelled by some purpose. To hold that Allah the Exalted had no real purpose in sending down the Holy Quran or sending the Holy Prophet, peace and blessings of Allah be upon him, is the height of insolence and disrespect. For this, God forbid, attributes a useless action to Allah the Exalted, although His Being is Pure—Holy is He and Exalted is His Majesty.

So bear in mind that in revealing the Holy Quran and sending the Holy Prophet, peace and blessings of Allah be upon him, Allah the Exalted has desired to manifest to the world a magnificent sign of mercy. To this effect, Allah the Exalted states:

$$مَآ اَرۡسَلۡنٰكَ اِلَّا رَحۡمَةً لِّلۡعٰلَمِیۡنَ^1$$

We have sent thee not but as a mercy for all peoples.

Similarly, Allah Almighty states that He sent down the Holy Quran for the following purpose:

$$هُدًی لِّلۡمُتَّقِیۡنَ^2$$

It is a guidance for the righteous.

These are such grand objectives that they are second to none. It is for this very reason that Allah the Exalted willed for all the individual excellences of the past Prophets, peace be upon them, to culminate in the person of Allah's Messenger, peace and blessings of Allah be upon him; and for all the merits and excellences found in the various scriptures to be encapsulated in the Holy Quran; and for all the qualities of the past nations to be gathered in this ummah. Hence, God Almighty desires for us to attain these excellences and so one must not forget that just as God wishes to confer upon us these supreme excellences, He has blessed us with faculties in equal degree. For if we had not been given faculties that accorded in strength, we would never have been able to attain these excellences in any way whatsoever. For example, if someone were to invite a company of people, it would be necessary for them to prepare a quantity of food that suffices those invited; and the size of the house must be able to accommodate them as well. Is it possible that someone would invite one thousand people to a feast, and then build a small hut to seat them all? Of course not! The host will indeed fully consider the number of invitees. In the same manner, the Book of God Almighty is a feast and banquet, for which the whole of the world has been invited. The house that God Almighty has prepared for this invitation is the faculties with which the people have been vested. Nothing can be accomplished without faculties. Now if the teaching of the Holy Quran was presented to an ox, a dog or some other animal, they would not be able to comprehend it, because they do not possess

---

1　　*al-Anbiya*, 21:108
2　　*al-Baqarah*, 2:3

such faculties as can bear the teachings of the Holy Quran. However, Allah the Exalted has granted us those faculties and we can benefit from them.

The Holy Prophet[sa] and His Station as the Seal of the Prophets

Allah the Exalted has blessed us with a Prophet who is the Seal of the Believers, the Seal of the Pious, and the Seal of the Prophets. Similarly, God Almighty revealed upon him a book, which is the Seal of Books—a book which comprehensively encapsulates all others. When it is said that the Messenger of Allah, peace and blessings of Allah be upon him, is the 'Seal of the Prophets' and that prophethood has reached its end in him, this does not imply that prophethood has ended as one brings about the end of someone by strangling them to death. This sort of an 'end' is not worthy of honour. In fact, when it is said that prophethood has come to an end in the Messenger of Allah, peace and blessings of Allah be upon him, this means that the excellences of prophethood have reached their climax in his person. In other words, all the various excellences that were granted to the Prophets, from Adam[as] to Jesus[as] son of Mary—certain qualities to some and different qualities to others—were all combined in the Holy Prophet[sa] and in this way the Holy Prophet[sa] naturally became the Seal of the Prophets. In the same manner, all the teachings, guidance and insights given in various books, came to their final point of completion when they culminated in the Holy Quran, and so the Holy Quran became the 'Seal of the Books'.

We Believe With Full Insight that the Messenger of Allah[sa] Is the Seal of the Prophets

It should also be understood that the allegation which is levelled against my community and I, that we do not believe in the Messenger of Allah, peace and blessings of Allah be upon him, as being the Seal of the Prophets, is a grave calumny against us. Our critics do not believe in the Holy Prophet[sa] as being the Seal of the Prophets even one part out of a hundred thousand, as compared to the strength, certainty, divine understanding and insight with which we believe it, nor do they have it within themselves to do so. They do not grasp the underlying essence and secret in the Seal of Prophethood and the Seal of the Prophets, peace and blessings of Allah be upon him. They have merely heard this term from their forefathers, but they are ignorant of its true essence and do not know what the

Seal of Prophethood means and what it means to believe in this concept. However, Allah the Exalted knows well that we believe with perfect insight that the Holy Prophet, peace and blessings of Allah be upon him, is the Seal of the Prophets. Moreover, God Almighty has disclosed to us the true essence of the Seal of Prophethood in such a way that the intense pleasure which we derive from the sherbet of divine insight that we have been given to drink cannot be understood by anyone other than those who have been satiated by this fountain.

A worldly metaphor that we can give in the context of the Seal of Prophethood could be that the moon begins in the form of a crescent, and on the fourteenth night it becomes complete, at which point it is referred to as the full moon. In the same manner, the excellences of prophethood reached their end or completion in the person of the Holy Prophet, peace and blessings of Allah be upon him. Those who hold the belief that prophethood has forcefully come to an end and that the Holy Prophet, peace and blessings of Allah be upon him, should not even be given superiority over Jonah the son of Matthew, have not understood the underlying reality at all and have no knowledge whatsoever of the merits and excellences of the Holy Prophet, peace and blessings of Allah be upon him.

Despite their own weak understanding and lack of knowledge, they assert that we deny the concept of the Seal of Prophethood. What shall I say to such ailing people, and how shall I express pity for them? If they had not taken on such a state and if they had not become so utterly distanced from Islam, what need was there for my advent? The faith of these people has become extremely frail, and they are unaware of the true meaning and purpose of Islam. If this were not the case, there would be no reason for them to harbour such animosity against the men of God, which leads one to disbelief

The Hallmark of Good Deeds

These people fail to understand this and state: 'What about us is un-Islamic? We proclaim لَا إِلَهَ إِلَّا اللّٰه (*There is none worthy of worship except Allah*) and also observe the Prayers, we fast during the days of Ramadan, and pay the Zakat.' However, I declare that all of these actions of theirs are not good deeds in the true sense. They are a mere shell that is empty of the kernel. For if their actions were good deeds in the deeper sense, why do they not bring about positive results? Good deeds are characterised by the quality of being pure from all forms of corruption and adulteration. But where can such qualities be found in these people? I can never accept that a person be a righteous believer who performs good works, yet he should be an enemy of the godly; yet these people refer to me as being irreligious and an atheist, and have no fear of God.

I have sworn by Allah the Exalted and proclaimed that Allah Almighty has raised me by way of divine appointment. If these people possessed even the slightest regard in their hearts for the greatness of Allah Almighty, they would not reject me. In fact, they would be fearful, lest they became those who denigrate the name of God Almighty. However, this could only be if they possessed a true and outstanding faith in Allah the Exalted, and if they feared the Day of Recompense, and if they acted upon the following verse of the Holy Quran:

$$\text{لَا تَقْفُ مَا لَيْسَ لَكَ بِهِ عِلْمٌ}^{1}$$

And follow not that of which thou hast no knowledge.

Rejecting the Saints of Allah Results in a Loss of Faith

The mindset and strength of faith possessed by those that I have just mentioned is such that they claim that a person who denies a Prophet is a disbeliever, but that rejecting a saint does not necessitate disbelief. They feel there is no harm in denying one man.[2] These people think that rejecting the saints of Allah is inconsequential and they assert that there is no harm in doing so. However, the fact of the matter is that rejecting the saints of Allah results in one losing their faith. A person who reflects on this issue will clearly see the truth; in fact, they will see the truth as clearly as one sees their face in the mirror.

It ought to be borne in mind that one loses their faith in two ways. Firstly, by rejecting the Prophets, on whom be peace, and this is something that no one can deny and is an accepted fact. Secondly, rejecting the saints of Allah and those divinely commissioned by Him results in a loss of faith.

A loss of faith through the rejection of Prophets is a clear matter of which everyone is aware. However, I should still like to elaborate that a denial of the Prophets results in a loss of faith because the Prophets declare that they have been sent from God. Moreover, God states: 'Whatever the Prophets announce are My words, I have sent this Prophet so believe in him, accept My book and act upon

---

1   *Bani Isra'il,* 17:37
2   *Al-Hakam,* vol. 9, no. 9, dated 17 March 1905, pp. 5-6

My commandments.' A person who does not accept the Book of Allah Almighty, and who does not act upon the guidance and injunctions stipulated therein, becomes a disbeliever by denying them. However, the means by which a person loses their faith when they deny the saints of Allah is different. It is mentioned in a Hadith that Allah the Exalted states:

مَنْ عَادَ لِیْ وَلِیًّا فَاٰذَنْتُهٗ لِلْحَرْبِ

Meaning, an individual who harbours enmity towards a friend of Mine, as if becomes prepared to war with Me. It is a matter of principle that when a certain individual loves another, in the manner that one loves their own child, if someone were to say again and again: 'May this child die', and repeats other such hurtful things, and inflicts grief upon the child, how can a parent like such a person? How can a father love the individual who prays against his child and repeats such painful words? In the same manner, the saints of Allah the Exalted are like His children, because they discard the mantle of their adult independence, as it were, and hand themselves over to God in complete submission so that they may be nurtured in the mercy of God's lap. Allah the Exalted is their Guardian and Protector, and is Jealous for them. When an individual—irrespective of how regular they may be in Prayer and fasting—opposes them and becomes adamant in causing them grief, the jealousy of God is incensed and His wrath surges forth against those who oppose them. For such people have sought to inflict grief upon the beloved of God and at that time, neither do the Prayers of such an opponent serve any benefit, nor their fasting. For through the observance of Prayer and fasting, they sought to please God, but now they have displeased Him through another action. How then can such a person receive the pleasure of God when the cause for His displeasure still exists? Foolish people of this nature are uneducated as to the means that arouse God's wrath; in fact, they are conceited and pride themselves over the observance of their Prayers and fasting. As a result, the wrath of God Almighty continues to swell day after day, and instead of attaining His nearness, Allah the Exalted only moves further and further away from them each day, until finally, such a one becomes truly accursed in heaven.

How can one who opposes a person, whose inner self is annihilated in God, and who lays prostrate upon the divine threshold, and who is being nurtured in the lap of God's providence, and who is covered by the mercy of God Almighty, to the extent that his words are as though God speaks, and his friend is the friend of God, and his enemy becomes an enemy of God, ever be a believer? How can one be an enemy of God Almighty and still be a true believer? Such a one loses their faith and incurs the wrath of God. To show hostility towards and inflict grief upon those appointed by God Almighty and the saints of Allah can never bring good fruits. Anyone who surmises that they can rest in peace after inflicting grief and suffering upon the beloved of God is gravely mistaken and only deceives their own soul.

A person who opposes a saint of Allah also loses their faith because a saint *(wali)* enjoys nearness to God; the very word *'wali'* means 'to be near.' These people as if behold God before their eyes, whereas others are separated from God, as if a wall stands between them and God. How can these two classes of people be equal? One from among them has no veil before him; God Almighty has granted him eyes and bestowed upon him insight, and therefore, every word and action of such a one is based on certainty. A person of this nature is not like he who is blind, or one who stumbles here and there and knocks into things. In fact, God descends upon the heart of such a one and He becomes his Guide and Guardian at every step. The darkness of Satan's mischief cannot come anywhere near such a person. As a matter of fact, this darkness is burnt into ashes and then this individual can see everything. All the words of such a person are divine verities and insights. His interpretations of the Hadith are correct, because he is able to hear them himself directly from the Holy Prophet, peace and blessings of Allah be upon him, and those narrations are as if his own, whereas others must quote the same narration through a chain extending 1300 years. Again, what relation do these two classes of people have with one another? The beloved of God possess a treasure that is based entirely on pure insights and divine light, but an individual who opposes him, and rejects everything that he says, and who, as if, becomes determined to deny every point of wisdom that he expounds, goes on denying everything until their wall of faith and understanding begins to crumble. When a certain person speaks of the straight path, and lucidly expounds divine insights and verities, while another rejects him, what will be the ultimate result of this encounter? Obviously that the latter has rejected and will continue to reject the overall beliefs of the Holy Quran. It is by virtue of this that such a person ultimately rejects God Almighty and finally loses his faith.

In short, there is no doubt whatsoever that rejecting the saints of Allah causes one to lose one's faith. As such, one must always refrain from denying the saints of Allah. A major factor behind the misfortune of the Jews and their incurring the wrath of God was due to the fact that they continuously rejected the divinely commissioned ones of God Almighty and His Messengers, and continued to partake in opposing them and causing them grief. Ultimately, this resulted in the wrath of Allah Almighty descending upon them.

Another Aspect of the Holy Prophet[sa] Being the Seal of the Prophets

I return to my earlier discussion and state that another aspect of the Holy Prophet, peace and blessings of Allah be upon him, as the Seal of the Prophets is also that Allah the Exalted, merely by His grace, has instilled this community with extraordinary and exceptional abilities. This is to such an extent that it is also stated in a Hadith:

عُلَمَاءُ أُمَّتِىْ كَأَنْبِيَاءِ بَنِىْ اِسْرَائِيْلَ

The scholars of my community are like the Prophets of the Children of Israel.

Though the scholars of Hadith may have their reservations, the light of my heart testifies to the truth of this Hadith, and I accept its authenticity without any questions or objections whatsoever. No saint has rejected this Hadith by way of anything disclosed to them in visions; in fact, if anything, they have confirmed it. The meaning of this Hadith is that, 'The scholars of my community are like the Prophets from among the Children of Israel.' However, one should not be mislead by the word 'scholars'. Some people are stuck on a word and are unable to grasp the underlying meaning. This is why such people are unable to progress in understanding the commentary of the Holy Quran.

The Definition of a Godly Scholar

A godly scholar is not one who is unmatched in Arabic morphology, syntax and logic. In fact, a godly scholar is one who constantly remains in fear of Allah the Exalted and whose tongue does not engage in vain speech. However, today we are passing through an era when even those whose profession it is to wash corpses before burial call themselves scholars and have taken this title for themselves.[1] Therefore, this word has lost its value immensely and has now taken on a mean-

---

[1] It was customary in the subcontinent to employ people to wash the dead before burial. The reference made here is that even those who washed dead corpses by profession fancied themselves scholars on account of the scant knowledge they possessed of Islamic burial rites. [Publisher]

ing that is against the will and desire of God Almighty. On the contrary, the Holy Quran describes true scholars in the following words:

$$اِنَّمَا يَخْشَى اللّٰهَ مِنْ عِبَادِهِ الْعُلَمٰٓؤُا^1$$

Meaning, the scholars from among the servants of Allah Almighty are those who fear Him. Now, it is crucial to take note that those people who do not possess this quality of fear of God, and being in awe of Him, and who are not righteous, can never, in any way whatsoever, be worthy of this title.

The fact of the matter is that 'scholars' are referred to as *ulama* in the Arabic language. And this is the plural form of *alim*, and in Arabic, *ilm* or 'knowledge' refers to a thing which is certain and categorical; and true knowledge is derived from the Holy Quran. True knowledge can neither be derived from Greek philosophy, nor from the philosophy currently prevalent in England, rather it is attained from the true philosophy of faith. The apex and pinnacle of a believer is that they reach the rank of the *ulama* or scholars, and attain to a station of true certainty, which is the highest level of *ilm* or knowledge.

An individual who is bereft of true and certain knowledge, and who is oblivious to the paths of divine understanding and insight may refer to themselves as scholars all they like, but they are devoid of the merits and qualities of knowledge, and they do not possess the radiance and light that is received from true knowledge. In fact, such people are in a state of utter loss and deprivation; they fill their afterlife with smoke and darkness. It is about these very people that Allah the Exalted states:

$$مَنْ كَانَ فِىْ هٰذِهٖ اَعْمٰى فَهُوَ فِى الْاٰخِرَةِ اَعْمٰى^2$$

In other words, he who is blind in this life shall be raised blind in the hereafter. What knowledge can an individual receive in the next world when he is deprived of knowledge, insight and divine understanding in this world? A person must take with them the eye that perceives Allah the Exalted from this very world. An individual who does not develop such an eye in this world should not expect to behold Allah Almighty in the life to come.

As for those, however, who are bestowed with true divine knowledge and insight, and who receive that knowledge, which is the result of fear of Allah, they are the ones who have been likened to the Israelite Prophets in this Hadith.

---

[1]   *Fatir*, 35:29
[2]   *Bani Isra'il*, 17:73

The Fountainhead of True Knowledge is the Holy Quran

This is so because Allah the Exalted has blessed this community with the Holy Quran, which is the source and fountainhead of true knowledge. An individual who finds the divine verities and insights that are expounded in the Holy Quran—which are attained by true righteousness and fear of Allah—is thereby given such knowledge that makes them the likeness of the Israelite Prophets.

It is perfectly obvious that if a person does not make use of the weapon that is provided to them, this is the person's own fault and not the fault of the weapon itself. This is precisely the state of the world at present. Even though the Muslims were given a matchless blessing in the Holy Quran, which could have saved them from every form of misguidance and could have pulled them out of every form of darkness, they abandoned the Holy Quran and showed no regard for its pure teachings. As a result, they became so utterly distanced from Islam that if now, true Islam is presented before them—as they are utterly ignorant and oblivious to it—they will refer to a true believer as being a disbeliever.[1]

Make Use of Your God-Given Faculties to Become a Saint

There are many people who lead a licentious and dissolute life and they seek the renown, honour, property and wealth of this world. They exhaust their entire life making plans and devising strategies to fulfil such longings and desires. Their yearnings have yet to reach their end when death comes knocking. Now, even people of this nature were given various faculties. If they had made use of these very faculties, they could have attained to the truth. Allah the Exalted was not miserly, but these people failed to employ their own faculties. This is their own misfortune. Fortunate and blessed is the one who employs his faculties.

There are many who, when told to fear God Almighty and to act upon His commandments while abstaining from God's prohibitions, will respond by saying, 'Are we out to become saints?' Such statements constitute disbelief in my view. This is to think ill of God Almighty. Is God Almighty faced with a shortage? After all, these are not limited government jobs which will finish once they are filled. On the contrary, anyone who develops a sincere relationship with God Almighty will benefit from the bounties that were granted to the pious individuals of the past.

---

[1]   *Al-Hakam*, vol. 9, no. 10, dated 24 March 1905, p. 5

بر کریماں کار ہا دشوار نیست

No task is difficult for the valiant.

Allah the Exalted refers to His beloved as saints. Now is it difficult for someone to become a saint in the sight of God Almighty? It is extremely easy. Of course, it is necessary for a person to stand firm in virtue, and tread on the path of God with patience, determination and loyalty, and to not waver in the face of any grief, pain or misfortune. When an individual develops a true relationship with God Almighty and distances themselves from those things which cause His displeasure, and in fact, adopts purity and piety, abstaining from that which is foul, God Almighty also forges a relationship with such a person and grants them His nearness. However, if someone continues to move away from God Almighty and does not make an effort to pull themselves out of impurity, then God Almighty also does not care for such a person, just as He states:

فَلَمَّا زَاغُوْۤا اَزَاغَ اللّٰهُ قُلُوْبَهُمْ ¹

So when they deviated from the right course,
Allah caused their hearts to deviate.

The Ease in Our Spiritual Quest

Our community should not lose hope. The things just mentioned are not severe hardships. I truthfully say that God Almighty has eased our difficulties, because the pathways of our spiritual quest are different from those of others. The state of our spiritual quest does not arch our backs, or require us to lengthen our nails, or stand in water or sit in seclusion for extended periods of time, or freeze our hands in a certain position until they become lifeless, or ruin our physical appearances. By adopting such practices, in their own fancy, there are some who seek to become godly. But I observe that let alone finding God, these people even cease to remain human beings. However, this is not the manner of our spiritual quest. In fact, Islam has prescribed a very easy way and it is the wide and spacious path that is described by Allah the Exalted as follows:

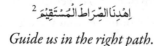

اِهْدِنَا الصِّرَاطَ الْمُسْتَقِيْمَ ²

Guide us in the right path.

---

¹   *as-Saff*, 61:6
²   *al-Fatihah*, 1:6

Now when Allah the Exalted has taught us this supplication, He has not done so without providing us with the relevant means. Instead, on the one hand, where He has taught us this prayer, on the other hand He has also provided the means for its acceptance as well. As such, in the following chapter, He alludes to this acceptance where He states:

$$ذٰلِكَ الْكِتٰبُ لَا رَيْبَ فِيْهِ هُدًى لِّلْمُتَّقِيْنَ ^1$$

This is a perfect Book; there is no doubt in it.

This is a spiritual feast, as it were, with all the necessary arrangements made in advance. Therefore, if a person makes use of the faculties with which they have been endowed, they can most definitely become a saint. I declare with certainty that many people are born in this community who possess immense power and who are replete with light, devotion and loyalty. No one should consider themselves deprived. Has God Almighty published some list of saints, so that one should think that they cannot be among them? God Almighty is remarkably generous. His generosity is a very deep ocean that can never be exhausted. No seeker or searcher has been left deprived. Therefore, you ought to wake during the night and offer supplications and seek God's grace. There are numerous opportunities to offer supplications in the Prayer—the bowing position, while standing and sitting, and in prostration, etc. There are five Prayers that are to be offered in twenty four hours: *Fajr, Zuhr, Asr, Maghrib* and *Isha*. Above and beyond these there is the *Ishraq* Prayer and *Tahajjud*. All of these are opportunities for supplication.

The Actual Purpose and Essence of the Prayer is Supplication

The actual purpose and essence of the Prayer is supplication and supplication is a phenomenon that accords with the law of nature established by God Almighty. You may commonly observe that when a child weeps and cries, and expresses anxiousness, a mother becomes extremely restless as well and gives the child milk. The relationship between divinity *(uluhiyyat)* and servitude *(ubudiyyat)* is similar in nature and cannot be understood by everyone. When a person falls at the gate of God Almighty with extreme humility, lowliness and meekness, and presents his circumstances before God, and requests his needs from Him, the grace that is inherent in divinity surges forth and shows mercy to such a person.

---

1   *al-Baqarah*, 2:3

Weeping and Crying

The milk of God's bounty and grace also requires tears. Hence, one ought to present tearful eyes before Him. Those who suggest that there is no use in crying and weeping before God Almighty are false and incorrect in their view. Such people do not believe in the Being of Allah Almighty, and in His attributes of power and control. If they developed true faith, they would never say such a thing. Whenever anyone has come in the presence of God, and has turned to Him with sincere repentance, Allah the Exalted has showered His grace on such a one. The man who has said the following verse is true indeed:

عاشق که شد که یار بحالش نظر نه کرد

اے خواجہ درد نیست و گرنہ طبیب ہست

What sort of a lover is he whose state does not
draw in the attention of the beloved;

Honourable sir! The pain simply does not exist,
for the physician is at hand.

God Almighty has always desired that you come to Him with a pure heart. The only condition is for you to make yourselves accord with Him and bring about within yourselves that true transformation which makes a person worthy of being presented before God Almighty. God Almighty possesses the most remarkable and wondrous of powers, and He possesses boundless grace and blessings. But develop the eye of love so that you can see them and receive them. If a person possesses true love, God Almighty listens to prayers in abundance and bestows His support. However, the condition is that one must love and show sincerity towards God Almighty.

The Love of God and His Grace

Love is a thing that burns a person's base life and transforms them into a new and purified individual. Then, the person in question sees that which previously they could not see, and hears that which previously they could not hear. Hence, where God Almighty has prepared a spiritual feast of divine bounty and grace for man, He has also blessed man with the capacities that are needed to benefit from it. If God Almighty had granted man the relevant capacities but not the means, or if God had provided the means but no capacities to man, even this would have been a failing. But no, this is not the case. Allah the Exalted has granted abilities to man, as well as the means. Similarly, on the one hand, God Almighty provides man with bread, and on the other hand, He has given man eyes, a tongue and teeth, and He has put a man's stomach, liver and intestines to work, and the proper functioning of all these things depends on food. If man consumed nothing, how would the heart be fuelled with blood and how would the body produce chyle?

In the same manner, first and foremost, God Almighty has showered His grace upon us and sent the Holy Prophet, peace and blessings of Allah be upon him, with a complete religion like Islam, and made him the Seal of the Prophets, and bestowed upon us a perfect book like the Holy Quran, which is the Seal of the Books. Now, until the Resurrection, neither shall any other book be sent, nor shall any other Prophet bring a new law.

Then, if we do not employ our faculties of reflection and contemplation, and if we do not advance towards God Almighty, how indolent, slothful and ungrateful would we be?

The Purpose of Human Life

Reflect on the elaborate manner in which Allah the Exalted has outlined the path of God's bounty in the very first chapter of the Holy Quran. In this first chapter, which is also known as the Seal of the Book and the Mother of the Book, we have been told clearly of the purpose of man's life and the path by which it can be attained. The words اِيَّاكَ نَعْبُدُ *(Thee alone do we worship)* express the fundamental demand and desire of man's inherent nature, and this cannot be fulfilled without اِيَّاكَ نَسْتَعِيْنُ *(Thee alone do we implore for help)*. However, by giving precedence to اِيَّاكَ نَعْبُدُ *(Thee alone do we worship)* over اِيَّاكَ نَسْتَعِيْنُ *(Thee alone do we implore for help)*, man has been taught that first, it is necessary for him to strive and toil to tread the paths of divine pleasure by means of his own strength, resolve and understanding, and by making full use of the faculties given to him by God Almighty; and after all this, then to pray to God Almighty so that He may complete these efforts and cause them to bear fruits. The purpose and objective of man's life is to tread upon and seek the 'straight path,' which has been mentioned in this chapter as follows:

اِهْدِنَاالصِّرَاطَ الْمُسْتَقِيْمَ صِرَاطَ الَّذِيْنَ اَنْعَمْتَ عَلَيْهِمْ [1]

This means, O Allah! Show us the straight path. The path of those upon whom You have bestowed Your favour. This is the supplication which is offered at all times, in every Prayer, within every *rak'at* of the Prayer. The number of times that this supplication is repeated demonstrates its importance.

The Prime Objective of the Ahmadiyya Community

Our community must remember that this is not a minor thing and the actual purpose is not to repeat these words like a parrot. In fact, this is an effective and faultless recipe that transforms an individual into the most excellent of people. One ought to keep this objective in mind as though it were an amulet.

The verse just mentioned is a supplication which seeks to beg for four classes of excellence. If man attains these four categories of excellence, he shall, as if, do justice to this prayer and in fact do justice to the purpose of his very own creation. Furthermore, in this way, man shall also fulfil his responsibility in making use of the abilities and faculties that have been given him.

A Commentary of 'Those Upon Whom God Has Bestowed His Blessings'

One should also not forget that certain parts of the Holy Quran are a commentary and explanation of other parts. In one instance, a matter will be alluded to in brief, but in another instance the very same matter is expounded in detail. In other words, the latter is a commentary of the former. Therefore, in the instance under discussion, here Allah the Exalted states:

صِرَاطَ الَّذِيْنَ اَنْعَمْتَ عَلَيْهِمْ [2]

The path of those upon whom Thou hast bestowed Thy blessings.

Now, this is an indication in brief. In another instance, however, the Holy Quran itself has expounded that 'those upon whom God has bestowed His blessings' are as follows:

---

[1]   *al-Fatihah*, 1:6-7
[2]   *al-Fatihah*, 1:7

مِنَ النَّبِيِّنَ وَالصِّدِّيقِيْنَ وَالشُّهَدَآءِ وَالصّٰلِحِيْنَ ¹

From among the Prophets, the Truthful, the Martyrs and the Righteous.

That is to say, those upon whom God has bestowed His blessings comprise four classes of people: the Prophets, the Truthful, the Martyrs and the Righteous. All four of these magnificent ranks are gathered in the Prophets, peace be upon them, because this is the highest rank among these four. It is obligatory upon each and every one of us to strive correctly to attain these excellences, in the manner that the Holy Prophet, peace and blessings of Allah be upon him, has shown us through his own actions.

Never Abandon the Way of the Holy Prophet[sa]

I would also like to tell you that there are many people who desire to attain these excellences by way of their own self-invented incantations and litanies. But let me tell you that if you adopt a method that was not practiced by the Holy Prophet, peace and blessings of Allah be upon him, then it is futile. Who could be more truly experienced in the path of those favoured by God than the Holy Prophet, peace and blessings of Allah be upon him? In fact, he was a man in whose person all the excellences of prophethood reached their final limit as well. The path adopted by the Holy Prophet[sa] is the most effective and nearest way to God. To abandon this path and invent another—irrespective of the joy that it may bring— in my opinion, leads to ruin. This is what God has disclosed to me. By truly following the Holy Prophet, peace and blessings of Allah be upon him, one finds God; but one who does not follow the Holy Prophet[sa]—even after an entire life of striving—shall not be able to attain the ultimate objective. As such, even Sa'di speaks of the necessity of subservience to the Holy Prophet, peace and blessings of Allah be upon him, in the following words:

زہد و ورع کوش و صدق و صفا

و لیکن میفزائے بر مصطفیٰ

Strive to forsake materialism, and to adopt piety, sincerity, and purity;
But do not step beyond (the practices taught by) Mustafa[sa].

So, do not abandon the path of the Holy Prophet, peace and blessings of Allah be

---
¹   *an-Nisa,* 4:70

upon him. I observe that people have invented a plethora of diverse incantations. They hang themselves upside down and undertake ascetic practices like yogis, but all of this is useless. It is not the custom of Prophets, peace be upon them, to hang upside down, or engage in meditative practices of 'negation and affirmation' (*nafi-o-asbat*), or perform the Sufi 'invocation of the saw' (*dhikr-e-arra*). This is why Allah the Exalted has referred to the Holy Prophet, peace and blessings of Allah be upon him, as a perfect exemplar:

لَكُمۡ فِىۡ رَسُوۡلِ اللهِ اُسۡوَةٌ حَسَنَةٌ ¹

Verily, you have in the Prophet of Allah an excellent model.

Follow in the footsteps of the Holy Prophet, peace and blessings of Allah be upon him, and do not try to deviate from his path even an inch.

The Purpose of the Establishment of the Ahmadiyya Community

In short, the real purpose of man is to aspire to the excellences of 'those upon whom Allah has bestowed his blessings,' and to which Allah the Exalted has alluded in the following:

صِرَاطَ الَّذِيۡنَ اَنۡعَمۡتَ عَلَيۡهِمۡ ²

The path of those on whom Thou hast bestowed Thy blessings.

Our community ought to pay special attention in this regard, for in establishing this community, the very desire of Allah the Exalted is to prepare a community like the one assembled by the Holy Prophet, peace and blessings of Allah be upon him, so that in the latter days, this community may serve as a testament to the truthfulness and greatness of the Holy Quran and the Holy Prophet, peace and blessings of Allah be upon him.

The Station of Prophethood

From among the excellences that are conferred upon those who receive the bounty of God, foremost is the excellence of prophethood, which sits at the loftiest of ranks. I regret that I am unable to find the words with which to expound the deeper reality of this excellence. It is a matter of principle that when something

---

¹   *al-Azhab*, 33:22
²   *al-Fatihah*, 1:7

grows in rank, words become all the more insufficient to describe it. And then, prophethood is a station that is the most supreme rank or level that any person can attain. How then can it be described? I can say, only briefly and inadequately, that when a human being abandons their base life, and separates themselves from this world just as a snake sloughs off its skin, the state of such a person becomes transformed. Such a one apparently walks about on the same earth, eats and drinks, and is subject to the law of nature, as are others, but despite all this, he is detached from this world; he continues to advance and progress until he finally reaches the point known as prophethood, where he converses with God Almighty. This converse begins when the person in question separates themselves from their own inner self and its relations, until ultimately forging a relationship with Allah the Exalted alone, after which it is with Him alone that the individual converses.

Converse with the Inner Self

The state of human beings is such that they can never remain idle or static, and the inner self cannot remain without engaging in some form of speech. If there is no one else with whom to converse, man will begin to speak with his own self or with Satan. On certain occasions, people will observe an individual to be completely silent, but actually they are not quiet—such people will be engaged in a string of conversation with their inner self, and at times this exchange will go on for an extended period of time. This exchange is lengthened due to its satanic and shameless nature. This continuous 'speech' as it were, is either in the form of transgression conceptualised in the mind, or in the form of indecent and inappropriate desires. It is impossible for one to free themselves of this until one abandons this base life. Also bear in mind that if an individual does not entertain this stream of desires and fancies for long, and if they arise in the heart as minor thoughts which quickly dissipate, then these will be forgiven. Sin is when an individual allows this chain of ideas to continue for an extended period of time and becomes firm upon them, and it is for this that they will be held accountable.[1]

When man repels these fancies which arise in the heart and does not allow them to continue for long, there is no doubt that they are worthy of being forgiven. However, when a person feels pleasure in their extended continuation and goes on increasing them, a person becomes accountable for these thoughts, because he

---

[1] *Al-Hakam*, vol. 9, no. 11, dated 31 March 1905, pp. 5-6

begins to cling to them firmly.

As I have mentioned earlier, bear well in mind that 'converse with the inner self' is of two kinds. At times it is satanic and spills over into the realm of imagined transgression and impiety, and spirals into an extended string of desires. So long as an individual is entangled in these two trains of thought, he cannot be free from satanic influence; he may suffer harm and it is possible that Satan may wound him. Let us take the example of a person who contrives a plan to kill someone because he feels that they are an obstruction in the way of his goal and purpose. Perhaps one may think that since a certain person has disrespected me, I will seek revenge by dishonouring him in return. A person who plots in this manner and remains drowned in such serpentine thoughts is diseased and suffers from a dangerous state. Such a one does not realise how they are harming their own soul, and damaging their own morals and spiritual powers. One should always refrain from such thoughts. Whenever a chain of immoral thoughts begin to arise, endeavour to repel them immediately. Seek forgiveness from God; seek God's help and support by reciting *la hawl*;[1] engage yourself in reciting the Book of God Almighty and realise that there is no benefit to be had in entertaining immoral thoughts; there is only harm and ruin. Even if an enemy of yours meets their death, so what? And if he remains alive, then what? To cause benefit or harm lies within the power and control of God Almighty. No human being can cause harm to another. Sa'di has written an anecdote in his *Gulistan* that someone brought the good news to Nusherwan that a certain enemy of his had been killed, and that his country and fortress had been taken over by Nusherwan's forces. Nusherwan gave a marvellous response:

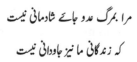

The death of my enemy brings me no joy;
for even our own life is not forever.

A person ought to reflect, what benefit and happiness can be reaped from such schemes and conspiracies? This train of thought is extremely dangerous and its cure is repentance, seeking forgiveness from God, reciting *la hawl*, and studying

---

1   This refers to the Arabic words *la hawla wa la quwwata illa billah* (There is no power and no strength except with Allah) recited as a prayer to seek God's protection and assistance. [Publisher]

the Book of God. When a person is idle and inactive, this immoral mindset prevails for a very long period of time.

The second form of converse with the inner self is to prolong the string of one's yearnings. This train of thought encourages inappropriate desires, and this gives rise to the ailments known as greed, jealousy and selfishness. Therefore, as soon as this way of thinking begins, put an end to it immediately. These two categories of converse with the inner self which I have mentioned ultimately destroy a person. However, a Prophet is pure from this form of discourse.

The Reality of the Station of Prophethood

What is prophethood? It is a God-given gift. If it were a station that could be earned, everyone would become a Prophet. The very nature of the Prophets is such that they do not fall prey to an inappropriate chain of discourse—they do not engage in this 'converse with the inner self' that I have just mentioned. Other people, however, take on a state where they become so engrossed in these exchanges that they lose sight of God altogether. Prophets, on the other hand, are free from this and they are so lost in God, and so absorbed in discourse and converse with Him, that their hearts and minds do not have the capacity or space to entertain such a series of thoughts. In fact, all that is left within them is the channel for discourse with God. As this is all that remains in them, God converses with them and they often speak to God. In solitude and in a state of inactivity, when a string of ill thoughts arise in an ordinary human being, if a Prophet is observed in a similar state of solitude and apparent inactivity, one may perhaps think out of misjudgment and a lack of knowledge that this individual is probably not engaged in converse with God. However, this is not the case. A Prophet converses with God at all times saying: 'O God! I love You and seek Your pleasure. Shower me with such grace that I may reach the point and station, which is the station of Your pleasure. Grant me the ability to perform such deeds which are pleasing in Your estimation. Open the eyes of the people so that they recognise You and fall at Your threshold.' These are the thoughts and yearnings of a Prophet, and he is so absorbed and lost in them that others cannot understand them. A Prophet constantly remains engaged in these thoughts with pleasure and then reaches a state where his heart melts; then his soul begins to flow forth and falls at the threshold of God with full force and vigour, and proclaims:

اَنْتَ رَبِّیْ اَنْتَ رَبِّیْ

You are my Lord! Indeed you are my Lord!

It is then that the grace and mercy of Allah Almighty surges forth, and God addresses him and responds to him with His converse. This is a most exquisite phenomenon which not all people can understand and the pleasure that is derived in this cannot be described in words. Hence, a Prophet knocks at the gate of divine providence *(rububiyyat)* again and again like one who thirsts for water, and it is here that he finds comfort and pleasure. Such a one lives in the world, but is not of the world. He does not desire anything of the world, but the world serves him, and God Almighty places the world before his feet.

This is the reality of prophethood in brief. At this stage, both of these forms of 'converse with the inner self' just mentioned are burnt to ashes and a third stream of converse begins—a form of converse that starts and ends with God alone. At this point, an individual draws in divine converse, which is free from the ambiguity and confused nature of 'converse with the inner self.' In fact, they are detached from this world completely like one enslaved by carnal pleasures who develops a relationship with a beautiful lover, and then constantly fantasises about them; the sensual pleasures of such an individual reach their apex in their lover, and they have no desire whatsoever to meet anyone else. In the same manner, a Prophet intensifies his relationship with God Almighty to such an extent that they are extremely averse to anyone else intruding in on their seclusion and privacy. They converse with their Beloved, and find pleasure and comfort in Him, and do not wish to part with this state of seclusion for even a moment. However, God Almighty brings them out into the world so that they may reform the people and serve as a mirror that reflects the image of God. It is in God Almighty that a Prophet seeks the natural pleasure and ecstasy that they experience. There is no other way in which I can describe this state. My heart is replete with this pleasure and the more I expound this subject, the more pleasure I feel. But where shall I find the words with which to express myself?

Why Do the Prophets Have Wives and Children?

Certain ignorant people raise the objection that when the Prophets, peace be upon them, are so annihilated in Allah, and when they turn away from the world and its pleasures, why then do they have wives and children? Such people fail to understand that on the one hand, where certain people become a slave of these things and lose themselves in these transient pleasures, on the other hand, the class of people known as Prophets are free from such things. Such relations serve their higher purpose. In addition to this, the Prophets, peace be upon them, come to bring about a reformation in every respect. Therefore, if they did not have wives and children, how could they bring about a complete reformation in this regard?

This is why I state: what example of the Messiah can the Christians present as far as his domestic interaction goes? Nothing at all. When he is ignorant of this path and inexperienced in dealing with these classes of people, what reformation can he bring about? This is the very excellence of the Holy Prophet, peace and blessings of Allah be upon him, for his example is complete in every respect. The world and its enjoyments have no influence over the Prophets, peace be upon them, and they could not care less about these ephemeral pleasures. In fact, their heart flows towards God Almighty as river water races down from a mountain in a waterfall. All the rubbish and debris that lies in its path is washed away.

In short, the Prophets, peace be upon them, are not slaves to such things; in fact, these things serve them. Moreover, due to the supreme moral excellences that they exhibit, these worldly things do not even slightly prove to be an obstruction in their remembrance of God, or in the enjoyment that they receive by reflecting over Him and being lost in Him. The Prophets are so absorbed and annihilated in God that they are beyond this world. When they become lost in God as such, they begin to hear the voice of God Almighty and begin to enjoy discourse with Him. It is a matter of principle that when something possesses a magnetic power, other things are attracted to it. This magnetism possesses such power that it burns to ash all the things of this world, and begins to pull in the grace and bounty of God Almighty. Ultimately, it is this very divine converse which then takes precedence and superiority over everything else. However, this requires proper struggle. This path is not opened in any other way, just as Allah the Exalted states:

$$وَالَّذِيْنَ جَاهَدُوْا فِيْنَا لَنَهْدِيَنَّهُمْ سُبُلَنَا ^{1}$$

And as for those who strive in Our path —
We will surely guide them in Our ways.

---

1   *al-Ankabut*, 29:70

Moreover, the words اِیَّاکَ نَعْبُدُ (*Thee alone do we worship*) also allude to this very fact. Undoubtedly, although اِیَّاکَ نَعْبُدُ (*Thee alone do we worship*) takes precedence over اِیَّاکَ نَسْتَعِیْنُ (*Thee alone do we implore for help*), if one contemplates, it becomes evident that the Graciousness (*rahmaniyyat*) of God Almighty takes even greater precedence. After all, there is a force that moves us to say اِیَّاکَ نَعْبُدُ (*Thee alone do we worship*) but where does this hidden force which moves us to make this declaration come from? Is it not God Almighty who has granted this power to us? Undoubtedly, this power is a gift from God Almighty, which He has bestowed upon us through His sheer Graciousness. It is through God's motivation and by the power endowed by Him that man proclaims اِیَّاکَ نَعْبُدُ (*Thee alone do we worship*) as well. Hence, if one reflects from this perspective, the worship of God is second in the greater scheme of things, but in another respect, it takes precedence. That is to say, in the context that God Almighty is the one who grants man the power to worship Him in the first place, اِیَّاکَ نَعْبُدُ (*Thee alone do we worship*) is second in rank, but in the first context, اِیَّاکَ نَعْبُدُ (*Thee alone do we worship*) takes precedence. The essence and deeper reality of the philosophy of prophethood can be understood in the same way.

The Necessary Aspects of Prophethood

Thousands and thousands of people may well claim to be the recipients of revelation from God, and in actuality, this is necessary to establish the truthfulness of prophethood and furnish evidence in favour of the fact that God speaks. However, there is another fundamental objective at the heart of prophethood which is specific to Prophets.

It is a general rule that all things come with their relevant essentials—they are never separated from their necessaries. For example, when food is presented, it is accompanied by its essentials: various pieces of crockery, water, and even toothpicks. In the same way, prophethood is also accompanied by its relevant essentials, and from among them, one is that 'converse with the inner self' comes to an end completely in the case of a Prophet. This is from among the essentials of the inherent nature of this institution known as prophethood, and the signs and hallmarks of this are the prophecies that are given to the Prophets by God Almighty.

Also bear in mind that Prophets have another name in heaven of which the common people are unaware, and when that heavenly name is put before the world, certain people stumble. For example, even in my case, God has named me the Messiah son of Mary. Some ignorant people raise the objection that your name is Ghulam Ahmad. They are unable to comprehend this secret; this is from among the secrets of prophethood.

In short, when both of these corrupt forms of discourse come to an end, the heart begins to speak, and continues to speak all the time. Even as it beats, the heart emits a voice. It is for this reason that the Prophets find pleasure in this discourse and remain engaged in conversing with their Beloved, even if thousands upon thousands of people around them are busy in other forms of conversation. This is the reason for their peace and tranquillity of heart and this is why no noise or clamour can disturb it. Normally, a lover desires to know all that they can know about the grace and beauty of their beloved, and desires to speak to them all the time. However, this does not happen, and these are base desires anyway. But a person who loves God Almighty and the class of people known as Prophets, who are lost in God's love, possess a fervour that is far greater than these false and transient loves. For God is He Who turns towards those who incline to Him. In fact, God pays greater attention to people than they show to Him. If a person advances towards God in small steps, Allah the Exalted runs towards them. Therefore, when a person develops a longing for God and becomes lost in His love, the fire of that love and passion for God burns away inner desires and carnal thoughts, after which their soul begins to speak. This pure speech that begins from within then becomes the speech of God Almighty. In other words, it could be said that man supplicates Allah the Exalted, and in turn, He responds. Hence, this is a hallmark of prophethood and has been alluded to in اَنْعَمْتَ عَلَيْهِمْ *(on whom Thou hast bestowed Thy blessings).* Therefore, one ought to seek to develop this particular distinction of prophethood within themselves when they offer the prayer:

اِهْدِنَا الصِّرَاطَ الْمُسْتَقِيْمَ صِرَاطَ الَّذِيْنَ اَنْعَمْتَ عَلَيْهِمْ [1]

Guide us in the right path — The path of those on
whom Thou hast bestowed Thy blessings.

The Station of the Truthful

The second form of excellence is that which characterises the Truthful *(Siddiqin)*. The Arabic word *siddiq* is in the superlative form, and refers to a person who is so

---

[1] *al-Fatihah,* 1:6-7

absorbed in the truth that nothing of his inner self remains. Such a one adheres to rectitude of the highest level, and is a sincere lover of the truth. It is at this point that one is referred to as a *Siddiq*. This is such a station that when a person reaches it, they gather within themselves all forms of truth and rectitude, and begin to draw them in. Just as a burning glass concentrates and draws in the rays of the sun, in the same way a *Siddiq* attracts towards themselves the excellences of truth *(sadaqat)*. As someone has said:

زر زر کشد در جہاں گنج گنج

In the world, gold attracts gold, and treasure attracts treasure.

When a thing grows and multiplies, it develops the power to draw towards itself other things of similar nature.

The Philosophy in Attaining to the Excellence of the Truthful

The philosophy in attaining to the excellence that is characteristic of the rank of the Truthful is that firstly, a person must realise their own weakness and helplessness. Then, in accordance with their individual strength and ability, they must proclaim اِیَّاکَ نَعْبُدُ *(Thee alone do we worship)* and adopt the truth, whilst abandoning falsehood. They must flee far from all forms of filth and impurity which are associated with falsehood. They must promise that they will never speak a lie, or give false testimony. They must promise that they will not allow the desires of the inner self to move them to utter any falsehood whatsoever, either as vain speech, neither in the cause of good, nor to repel evil—in no way and under no circumstances will they adopt falsehood. Now, when a person makes a promise that is as widely encompassing as this, they act upon the words اِیَّاکَ نَعْبُدُ *(Thee alone do we worship)* in a special way and such action is worship of the highest degree.

The words اِیَّاکَ نَعْبُدُ *(Thee alone do we worship)* are followed by اِیَّاکَ نَسْتَعِیْنُ *(Thee alone do we implore for help)*. Now, whether a person of the nature just described proclaims the latter by verbal profession or not, Allah the Exalted, nonetheless, who is the source of all grace and the fountainhead of all truth and rectitude, will definitely help and support such an individual, and open to them the sublime principles and verities of truth. It is an established fact that when a person involved in business follows ideal practices and principles, and holds fast to honesty and integrity, even if he starts with a penny, Allah the Exalted grants them hundreds and thousands of rupees in return for their penny.

The Insights of the Quran Are Opened to the Truthful

In the same way, generally, when a person loves virtue and rectitude, and makes truthfulness their way of life, that very same rectitude attracts the magnificent truthfulness that enables a person to behold God Almighty. That truth is embodied in the Holy Quran; that truth is the person of the Holy Prophet, peace and blessings of Allah be upon him. In the same manner, since those commissioned and sent by God Almighty are truth and rectitude embodied, such people reach this very 'truth' and their eyes are opened, whereafter they are blessed with a unique perception by which the insights of the Holy Quran are opened to them. I can never accept that a person who is averse to the truth and whose way of life is not characterised by rectitude should ever be able to comprehend the insights of the Holy Quran. For the heart of such a one has no affinity to such things. This is the fountain of truth and only a lover of truth can drink from it.

It should also be remembered that when insights of the Quran are referred to, this does not only mean that someone should present a subtle point of wisdom. For as the saying goes:

گاہ باشد کہ کود کے نادان

بغلط بر ہدف زند تیرے

At times, it so happens that even a foolish child,
manages to hit the arrow on target by coincidence.

In order to expound these very Quranic verities and insights, the heart develops an affinity, a magnetic force, and a relationship with truth and rectitude to such an extent that this increases and grows to the highest of degrees until such a person becomes an embodiment of the following verse:

مَايَنْطِقُ عَنِ الْهَوٰى[1]

He does not speak out of his own desire.

Their sights always fall upon the truth; they are granted a special ability and distinct power by which they are able to distinguish between truth and falsehood in an instant. Such a person's heart develops a power that is characterised by such a sharp sense that it can perceive the stench of falsehood from afar. This is the secret

---

[1] *an-Najm*, 53:4

that lies at the root of the following statement:

$$لَا يَمَسُّهُۥٓ إِلَّا الْمُطَهَّرُونَ^1$$

Which none shall touch except those who are purified.

One Cannot Become Pure Without Refraining from Lies

In reality, until a person abandons lies, he cannot become pure. Worthless materialists believe that they cannot survive without lies. However, this is an absurdity. If one cannot survive with truth, then lies definitely cannot sustain a person either. It is a pity that these wretched people do not give God the value He deserves. They do not know that it is without the grace of God Almighty that a person cannot survive. They consider the filth of falsehood to be their god and the resolver of their difficulties. This is precisely the reason that God Almighty has tied falsehood to the filth of idols and mentioned it in the Holy Quran. Know for certain that we cannot take a single step, rather, not even a single breath, without the grace of God. Our bodies are blessed with countless abilities, but what can we do with our own strength? Nothing at all.

The Meaning of Trust in God

Those people who trust in their own power and strength, and forsake God Almighty, do not meet with a good end. This does not mean that trust in God is to sit on one's hands and do nothing. To make use of means and to employ the faculties which God Almighty has granted us is also a manner in which we show gratitude to God. Those people who do not make use of their abilities and only verbally claim that they trust in God speak falsehood. Such people do not appreciate God. In fact, they test God and essentially suggest that the faculties and powers granted by Him are futile. In this manner, they are disrespectful and insolent towards God. They become distanced from the essence of اِيَّاكَ نَعْبُدُ *(Thee alone do we worship)* and do not act upon it, yet desire to see the results of اِيَّاكَ نَسْتَعِينُ *(Thee alone do we implore for help)* fulfilled in their favour. This is not right. Insofar as possible, and to the extent of one's ability, an individual ought to make recourse to means, but must not deem them to be his god and the resolver of his difficulties. On the contrary, man must first exhaust these avenues and then hand

---

1   *al-Waqi'ah*, 56:78-80

the matter over to Allah; he must offer prostrations of gratitude, thanking the very same God for having conferred upon him these faculties and strengths in the first place.[1]

The Rank of One Who Is Annihilated in Allah

A human being can do nothing without the grace and support of God Almighty. When man is pulled towards Allah the Exalted and becomes annihilated in Him, the actions which such a one performs are known as divine actions. The most sublime and supreme forms of light are manifested upon such a person. What can we say about human weakness—man cannot take even a single step without the grace and support of God Almighty. In fact, I believe that if God Almighty were not to lend His support, a man could not even do up his cloth after relieving himself from the call of nature. Physicians have written about a medical condition that causes death with a single sneeze. Always remember that human beings are weakness embodied and this is why God Almighty states:

[2]

Man has been created weak.

Nothing of man is his own. From head to toe, he does not even have as many limbs as he has illnesses. Now when man is prey to such a large collection of frailties, the only way that he can enjoy peace and security is to keep his affairs clean with God Almighty, and by becoming a true and loyal servant of His. For this, it is necessary that an individual adopts truth and sincerity. Even the workings of the physical system are based on truth as well. Those who abandon the truth and act unfaithfully consider falsehood to be the shield that will save them from the consequences of their crimes. However, such people are gravely mistaken.

Falsehood Darkens a Person's Heart

Momentarily and temporarily man may see some benefit, but in reality, the heart of man is darkened if he adopts a way of falsehood, and termites, as it were, begin to eat away at him from within. To cover one lie, a person must then conjure many more lies because the initial lie must be made to appear as if it were the

---

1   *Al-Hakam*, vol. 9, no. 13, dated 17 April 1905, p. 5
2   *an-Nisa*, 4:29

truth. It is in this way that one's moral and spiritual faculties begin to wither away from within, until finally one becomes so bold and impudent that he begins to forge lies against God Almighty as well, and will reject the Messengers of God and those divinely commissioned by Him, after which he is deemed 'the most unjust' or *azlam,* just as God Almighty states:

$$مَنْ اَظْلَمُ مِمَّنِ افْتَرٰى عَلَى اللّٰهِ كَذِبًا اَوْكَذَّبَ بِاٰيٰتِهٖ ^1$$

Meaning, who can be more unjust than the person who forges a lie and untruth against Allah the Exalted, or rejects His signs? Remember that falsehood is a most evil affliction and that it destroys a person. What could be a more grave consequence of falsehood than the fact that a person rejects the Messengers of God Almighty and becomes worthy of punishment from God by the rejection of His Signs? Therefore, adopt the truth.

An Incident of Hazrat Sheikh Abdul-Qadir Jilani[rh] Related to Truthfulness

There is an account narrated about Syed Abdul-Qadir Jilani, may Allah have mercy on him, that when he set out away from home for the purpose of his education, his noble mother sewed his share of eighty coins into the underarm of his shirt and advised him: 'Son, do not lie.' When Syed Abdul-Qadir[rh] departed, on the first day of his journey he passed through a jungle that was inhabited by a large band of thieves and robbers. A party of robbers confronted and apprehended him. The robbers asked: 'What have you in your possession?' Syed Abdul-Qadir[rh] thought to himself that he was being tested in the first stage of his journey; he reflected over his mother's advice and said: 'I have eighty coins which my noble mother has sewn into the underarm of my shirt.' The robbers were extremely surprised on hearing this and said: 'What is this dervish saying! We have never seen such a righteous man!' They took him and putting him before their chief, related the entire story. When the chief questioned him, Syed Abdul-Qadir Jilani[rh] gave the same response. Finally, when his shirt was torn at the place that he had described, it turned out that there were indeed eighty coins sewn into his shirt. All the robbers were astonished and the chief asked why Syed Abdul-Qadir[rh] had told them the truth. At this, Syed Abdul-Qadir Jilani[rh] mentioned the advice that his mother had given him before he departed. He said: 'I have set out as a student

---

1 *al-A'raf,* 7:38

of religion. If I had told a lie at the very first stage of my journey, what could I expect to attain? And so, I chose to stand by the truth.' When Syed Abdul-Qadir[rh] said these words, the chief burst into tears, fell at his feet and repented for his sins. It is said that this chief was the first follower of Syed Abdul-Qadir Jilani[rh].

In short, truth is a thing that delivers a person in even the most trying and difficult of times. Sa'di is true when he says:

کس ندیدم که گم شد از راه راست

Never have I seen go astray the one who treads the right path.

Therefore, the more a person adopts the truth and develops a love for the truth, the deeper a love and understanding they develop for the Word of God and also for His Prophets, because they are an example and source for all those who are truthful. This principle is also prevalent in the following instruction:

كُوْنُوْا مَعَ الصّٰدِقِيْنَ[1]

Be with the truthful.

The Truthful Are Graced with Insights of the Holy Quran

In short, the second excellence alluded to in اَنْعَمْتَ عَلَيْهِمْ is that of the Truthful. When a person attains to this excellence, the divine verities and insights of the Holy Quran are disclosed to them. However, this grace and bounty also comes through divine support. It is my belief that without the support and grace of God Almighty, one cannot so much as move their finger. It is, however, the responsibility of man to strive and make an effort insofar as possible, and he should seek this ability to do so from God as well. He should never lose hope in God, because a believer never loses hope. In this respect, God Almighty states Himself:

لَا يَايْئَسُ مِنْ رَّوْحِ اللّٰهِ اِلَّا الْقَوْمُ الْكٰفِرُوْنَ[2]

This means, only disbelievers despair of the mercy of Allah Almighty. Despair is a most wretched thing. In actuality, a person who loses hope in God Almighty is one who thinks ill of Him.

---

[1]   *at-Tawbah*, 9:119
[2]   *Yusuf*, 12:88

Ill-Thinking Cuts at the Root of Truth

Bear well in mind that all misery and evil stem from ill-thinking. This is why Allah the Exalted has strictly forbidden this and states:

For suspicion in some cases is a sin.

If the Muslim clergy had not thought ill of me, and if they had listened to my words with sincerity and steadfastness, and if they read our books and stayed with me to witness our circumstances, they would not have cast aspersions on me as they do. However, when they failed to give due regard to this instruction of God Almighty and did not act upon it, they thought ill of me and thought ill of my community as well; and thus, began to raise objections and allegations against me. Some even wrote, most insolently, that we are a group of atheists, and that we do not offer the Prayers and do not fast, and so on and so forth. Now, if they had refrained from this ill-thinking, they would not have to suffer the curse of falsehood and would be saved.

I truthfully declare that ill-thinking is a most evil affliction. It destroys a person's faith and throws them far away from sincerity and truth. It turns friends into enemies. In order to attain the excellence of the Truthful *(Siddiqin)*, it is necessary to strictly refrain from ill-thinking. If one begins to think unfavourably about a certain person, one ought to seek forgiveness from God profusely and make supplications before God Almighty, so that one may be saved from this sin and the evil consequences which follow through from ill-thinking. One must not deem this a light matter, for it is a terrible illness, which will cause a man to perish in the swiftest of ways.[2]

In short, ill-thinking destroys a man. This is to such an extent that when the hell-bound are cast into hell, Allah the Exalted will say that your sin was that you thought ill of Allah Almighty. There are certain people who believe that Allah the Exalted will forgive the wrongdoers but punish the righteous. This is also to think ill of God Almighty because it contradicts His attribute of justice and implies that virtue and its outcomes—as appointed by God in the Holy Quran—have been wasted, as though they were futile. Bear in mind, therefore, that the ultimate end of ill-thinking is hell, so do not consider this to be a minor illness. For ill-thinking

---

[1]   *al-Hujurat*, 49:13

[2]   *Al-Hakam*, vol. 9, no. 14, dated 24 April 1904, p. 2

results in despair, despair results in transgression, and transgression results in hell. It is a thing that cuts at the root of truth and sincerity *(sidq)*. Therefore, abstain from this vice and offer supplications to attain the excellences of one who is Truthful *(Siddiq)*.

The Unparalleled Truth of Hazrat Abu Bakr[ra]

The Holy Prophet, peace and blessings of Allah be upon him, bestowed the title of *Siddiq* (the Truthful) to Hazrat Abu Bakr[ra]. So Allah the Exalted knows best the countless excellences of Hazrat Abu Bakr[ra]. The Holy Prophet[sa] also said that the superiority of Hazrat Abu Bakr, may Allah be pleased with him, is owed to a quality that exists in his heart. In truth, the sincerity demonstrated by Abu Bakr, may Allah be pleased with him, is truly matchless. The fact of the matter is that in every era, anyone who desires to develop within themselves the excellences of a *Siddiq* and be one from among the Truthful must struggle, insofar as is possible, to inculcate within their being the nature and disposition of Abu Bakr[ra] and then pray for this purpose as much as possible. Until a person is covered by the shade of Abu Bakr's nature and does not take on the hue of his disposition, they cannot attain the excellences of the Truthful.

What is the Nature of Abu Bakr[ra]?

What is the nature of Abu Bakr[ra]? This is not the occasion for a detailed discussion and discourse on this subject, as much time would be required for such an exposition. To be brief, I shall narrate an incident. When the Holy Prophet, peace and blessings of Allah be upon him, made his claim to prophethood, Hazrat Abu Bakr Siddiq, may Allah be pleased with him, had travelled to Syria. On his return, he was still en route when he happened to meet someone. Hazrat Abu Bakr[ra] inquired of him as to the circumstances in Mecca and asked him if there was any current news. It is commonly observed that when a person returns from a journey, they will ask their fellow countrymen about the circumstances of their homeland. The individual responded: 'What is new is that your friend (Muhammad[sa]) has made a claim to prophethood.' As soon as Hazrat Abu Bakr[ra] heard this, he responded: 'If he has made such a claim, then he is truthful indeed.' This shows the degree to which Hazrat Abu Bakr[ra] thought well of the Holy Prophet[sa]. He felt no need to ask for a miracle. In actuality, only such a one who is uninformed of a claimant's circumstances, or who is unrelated to them, will ask to be shown a miracle for their heart's satisfaction. But as for the one who has no objection, what need has he for a miracle? In short, Hazrat Abu Bakr Siddiq[ra] affirmed his belief in the Holy Prophet[sa] even before he had returned home. When he arrived in Mecca, he presented himself before the Holy Prophet, peace and blessings of Allah be upon him, and inquired: 'Have you claimed to be a Prophet?' The Holy Prophet, peace and blessings of Allah be upon him, said: 'Yes, this is correct.' At this, Hazrat Abu Bakr Siddiq[ra] said: 'Bear witness that I am the first of those who have affirmed your truthfulness.' However, these were not mere words; in fact, Hazrat Abu Bakr[ra] demonstrated that his actions accorded with his words. This was to such an extent that he fulfilled his oath until his very last breath, and did not leave the Holy Prophet[sa] even after death.

Harmony in One's Word and Deed

In reality, there is a paramount need for man's words and deeds to be consistent with one another. If the two are not in harmony, then there is nothing. It is for this reason that Allah Almighty states in the Holy Quran:

$$اَتَاْمُرُوْنَ النَّاسَ بِالْبِرِّ وَتَنْسَوْنَ اَنْفُسَكُمْ^{1}$$

Meaning, you enjoin others to do good, yet you exempt yourselves of this command to act virtuously, and forget your own selves. Then, in another instance, Allah the Exalted states:

$$لِمَ تَقُوْلُوْنَ مَا لَا تَفْعَلُوْنَ^{2}$$

Why do you say what you do not do?

A believer must not act duplicitously. A believer is always far distanced from such cowardice and hypocrisy. Always keep your words and actions in order and exhibit harmony in both. Just as the companions manifested in their own lives, you too must follow in their footsteps and demonstrate examples of truth and loyalty.

Keep the Example of Hazrat Abu Bakr[ra] in View

Keep the example of Hazrat Abu Bakr Siddiq[ra] before you at all times. Think about the time of the Holy Prophet, peace and blessings of Allah be upon him,

---

1   *al-Baqarah*, 2:45
2   *as-Saff*, 61:3

when the Quraysh were bent on mischief on all fronts and the disbelievers hatched conspiracies to kill the Holy Prophet, peace and blessings of Allah be upon him. This era was a most trying time. All of you who are seated before me now ought to reflect that if today, a trial of this nature were to fall upon you, how many of you would stand by me? Or for example, what if the government began to investigate one by one the people who have sworn allegiance to me? How many of you would bravely say that they are among my followers? I am aware that some of you would lose the feeling in your hands and feet, and they would immediately begin to think about their properties and relatives, and how they would have to part with them. To stand by in times of difficulty is the sign of those who are true in faith. Hence, during the era in which the Holy Prophet, peace and blessings of Allah be upon him, was faced with grave trials and at a time when plans were being devised to kill him, the manner in which Hazrat Abu Bakr Siddiq^ra fulfilled his commitment of friendship is an example unparalleled in our world. Such strength and resilience is impossible without faith. Until a person practically instils faith within themselves, nothing can be achieved, for until such a time, a person's excuses will have no end. When the people are actually faced with a burning fire, there are few who prove firm. The disciples of the Messiah abandoned him and fled in his last hours when he was confronted with misfortune, and some even cursed him to his face.

This is a point where one ought to take a lesson. At one point, during the life of Hazrat Imam Husayn, may Allah be pleased with him, Muslim[1] offered the Prayer with a congregation of 70,000 people who had sworn allegiance to Hazrat Imam Husayn^ra. However, when a certain individual came and threatened them at the behest of Yazid, all of them fled.

Deeds Are the Ornaments of Faith

Such incidents are frightening. Weigh your faith, for deeds are the ornaments of faith. If one's practical condition is corrupt, then in reality he is devoid of faith as well. A believer is beautiful. If a beautiful person is adorned with even a simple and ordinary bangle, their beauty is enhanced manifold. In the same manner, deeds make a believing person appear more beautiful, but if a person performs evil deeds, then nothing remains. When one develops true faith within oneself, one begins to feel a pleasure in performing good deeds; one's eye of divine

---

[1] Muslim ibn Aqil who was sent to Kufa as an ambassador of Imam Husayn^ra. [Publisher]

understanding is opened; one offers the Prayer as it ought to be observed; one develops an aversion towards sin and detests vile gatherings; and one possesses a fervour and deep longing within one's heart for the greatness and glory of Allah Almighty and His Messenger to be manifested. That very same faith will give them the strength to be put on the cross like the Messiah[as]. For the sake of God, and indeed for the sake of God alone, such a one is willing to be thrown into a fire like Abraham[as]. When a person aligns his own will with the will of God, then Allah the Almighty who is [1]عَلِيمٌ بِذَاتِ الصُّدُوۡرِ (*He knows full well what is in your breasts*) becomes their Protector and Guardian. That God will take such a one down from the cross alive, and even pull him out of a fire, safe and sound. Only those who have full faith in God Almighty witness these miraculous wonders.

In short, the truth and sincerity of Abu Bakr Siddiq[ra] came to light as a fire was ablaze around him, at a time when the Holy Prophet, peace and blessings of Allah be upon him, was surrounded by his assailants. Although some of them were of the opinion that he should merely be banished from Mecca, most of them actually sought to put an end to his life. It was at that hour that Hazrat Abu Bakr Siddiq[ra] demonstrated his sincerity and loyalty, which will shine as an example until the end of time. In this trying hour, the very selection of the Holy Prophet, peace and blessings of Allah be upon him, is a powerful argument in favour of the excellence and supreme loyalty of Hazrat Abu Bakr Siddiq[ra]. For example, if the Viceroy of India were to choose someone for an important task, the opinion of the Viceroy would be better and more judicious than, say, a local watchman. It must be accepted, therefore, that the selection of the Viceroy is, in any case, better suited and more appropriate. For the government has appointed him as a deputy ruler, and has put its trust in his loyalty, farsightedness and experience. It is then that the government has handed over to him the reins of authority. It would, thus, be inappropriate to disregard the Viceroy's effective management and sound judgement, and take the choice of an ordinary watchman to be more correct.

The Secret in Selecting Hazrat Abu Bakr[ra] to Accompany the Holy Prophet[sa] on the Migration

This is also the case with the selection of the Holy Prophet, peace and blessings of Allah be upon him. At that time, the Holy Prophet[sa] had seventy or eighty companions, and even Hazrat Ali[ra] was with him, but from all of these companions,

---

[1]   *al-Mulk*, 67:14

the Holy Prophet^{sa} chose none other than Hazrat Abu Bakr^{ra}. What is the secret in this? The fact is that a Prophet sees through the eye of God Almighty, and his insight comes from God Almighty. Therefore, Allah the Exalted had informed the Holy Prophet, peace and blessings of Allah be upon him, by means of vision and revelation that the best and most appropriate person for this task was Hazrat Abu Bakr Siddiq^{ra}.[1]

Hazrat Abu Bakr, may Allah be pleased with him, accompanied the Holy Prophet^{sa} in this difficult hour. This was a time of perilous trial. When a similar time dawned upon the Messiah^{as}, his disciples abandoned him and fled, and one of them even stood before him and cursed him. But each and every one of the noble companions of the Holy Prophet^{sa} demonstrated complete loyalty. Therefore, Hazrat Abu Bakr Siddiq^{ra} stood by the Holy Prophet^{sa} and gave him full support, and when they reached a cave known as the Cave of Thaur, they both took refuge in the cave. The evil disbelievers who had conspired to harm the Holy Prophet^{sa} were led to this cave in their search. Hazrat Abu Bakr Siddiq^{ra} submitted to the Holy Prophet^{sa}: 'Now, these people are upon us, and if any one of them looks down even slightly, they will be able to see us, and we shall be apprehended.' At that time, the Holy Prophet^{sa} said:

لَا تَحْزَنْ اِنَّ اللّٰهَ مَعَنَا [2]

Meaning, do not fear in the least, for Allah the Exalted is with us. Reflect on these words. The Holy Prophet, peace and blessings of Allah be upon him, joins Hazrat Abu Bakr Siddiq^{ra} with himself and states:

اِنَّ اللّٰهَ مَعَنَا

Verily, Allah is with us.

The Arabic words *ma'ana* refer to both of them, i.e. 'with you and I.' Allah the Exalted placed the Holy Prophet, peace and blessings of Allah be upon him, on one side and Hazrat Abu Bakr Siddiq^{ra} on the other. At that time, both of them were in a state of trial. For it was at this point in time when the foundation of Islam was either going to be secured or brought to an end.

The enemy stood at the mouth of the cave and various opinions were being voiced. Some said that the cave ought to be searched because the footprints end-

---

[1]   *Al-Hakam*, vol. 9, no. 16, dated 10 May 1905, p. 2
[2]   *at-Taubah*, 9:40

ed at the cave, while others pointed out that it was impossible for a person to pass through here and enter the cave as a spider had woven a web at the mouth of the cave and a dove had laid its eggs. These discussions could be heard from within the cave and the Holy Prophet[sa] could also hear them clearly. In this state of affairs, the enemy had come to kill them both and had set out with immense vigour to complete their task, but just observe the remarkable courage of the Holy Prophet[sa], who says to his true friend:

$$لَا تَحْزَنْ اِنَّ اللّٰهَ مَعَنَا$$

Grieve not, for Allah is with us.

These words evidently demonstrate that the Holy Prophet[sa] said the aforementioned phrase with his tongue, because such words could only be expressed with a voice and not through sign language. The enemy stood outside consulting amongst themselves, and inside the cave, both servant and master are also engaged in discourse. The Holy Prophet[sa] had no concern that the enemy would hear his voice and this is proof of his remarkable faith and his insight into Allah the Exalted. It demonstrates that he had full trust in the promises of God Almighty. This one example alone is enough to show the bravery of the Holy Prophet, peace and blessings of Allah be upon him. In addition to the account just mentioned, there is another incident that bears testimony to the bravery of Abu Bakr Siddiq[ra] as well.

The Bravery of Hazrat Abu Bakr[ra] on the Demise of the Holy Prophet[sa]

When the Holy Prophet, peace and blessings of Allah be upon him, passed away, Hazrat Umar, may Allah be pleased with him, came forth, sword in hand, and said: 'I shall kill anyone who says that the Holy Prophet, peace and blessings of Allah be upon him, has died'. In these circumstances, Hazrat Abu Bakr Siddiq[ra] spoke with remarkable bravery and courage; he stood up and delivered an address. He recited the following verse of the Holy Quran:

$$مَا مُحَمَّدٌ اِلَّا رَسُوْلٌ قَدْ خَلَتْ مِنْ قَبْلِهِ الرُّسُلُ^1$$

Meaning, Muhammad, peace and blessings of Allah be upon him, is only a Messenger of Allah Almighty, and all the Prophets that have gone by before him, have all passed away. It was on this that emotion subsided. After this, the Arab nomads

---

1   *Aal-e-Imran*, 3:145

turned apostate. Hazrat Ayeshah, may Allah be pleased with her, describes these delicate times and says: 'When the Messenger, peace and blessings of Allah be upon him, passed away, there were a number of false claimants to prophethood who came forth. Some abandoned the Prayer and the circumstances changed completely. In this state of affairs and in this calamity, my father became the Caliph who succeeded the Holy Prophet, peace and blessings of Allah be upon him. My father was faced with such griefs that if they had descended upon the mountains, they would have crumbled.'

Now reflect, it is not the work of any ordinary man to stand firm with courage and resolve when overwhelmed with mountains of grief. This steadfastness requires a love for truth and sincerity *(sidq)* and it was this Truthful One *(Siddiq)* known as Abu Bakr[ra] who demonstrated this quality. It was impossible for any other person to confront these perils. All the companions were present at the time, but no one said that he was more deserving of the office of Caliphate. For they could see that a fire was ablaze around them. Who could have been willing to cast themselves into this fire? In these circumstances, Hazrat Umar, may Allah be pleased with him, extended his hand and swore his allegiance to Hazrat Abu Bakr[ra], after which everyone, one after the other, swore their allegiance as well. It was the sincerity *(sidq)* of Hazrat Abu Bakr[ra] that suppressed the uprising and put an end to the rebels. Musaylamah had an army of 100,000 and he taught a religious ideology that promoted freedom from divine law. When people would see his teachings of non-conformity, they would enter his religion in large numbers. However, God Almighty clearly demonstrated that He was with Hazrat Abu Bakr[ra] and eased all of his travails.

Incentives to Accept Christianity

To believe that the Messiah's blood serves as an atonement for our sins is also an easy route to take, because not only does it secure a person's livelihood, but also gives them an easy life of freedom from divine law. Where previously a person is expected to rise up for worship at the sound of *'Allahu Akbar'* (*Allah is the greatest*) when the call to Prayer is made, now all they have to do is have faith in the atonement through the blood of the Messiah[as] and then drink all night long, fall asleep and wake up whenever they so please, without any accountability whatsoever. In view of this, it is only natural that people would be inclined to Christianity. Now, the state of people is that they say:

لبہہ جہان مٹھا، اگلاکس نے ڈٹھا

Enjoy this life, who has ever seen the hereafter?

People feel that they might as well indulge in whatever they please here on earth, and they will see what happens in the hereafter. It is Christianity that can offer such people a free livelihood, coupled with an unrestrained life of comfort. Nothing is obligatory for them. If they so desire, they need not bathe for even ten years after consorting with their spouses. Hence, no one ought to be surprised on observing these people who have converted to Christianity. If these Muslims of atheistic bent, who have left Islam, had not become Christian, they were as good as apostates at heart anyway.

There are four types of people. Firstly, there are persistent disbelievers, who seek a life of unrestraint and non-conformity. Then, there are three kinds of believers: the one who suppresses his desires severely, the one who takes the middle course in goodness and the one who excels all others in acts of virtue. The first category of believers is of those who suppress their base desires, that is to say, their inner passions, to an extent, get the better of them. The second group of believers are those who follow a middle-course in virtue, and the third class of believers is of those who are goodness personified. What relation does a persisting disbeliever—whose only purpose and objective is to live an unbridled life and also gain wealth—have with Islam? Such people would obviously prefer Christianity where they can earn a wage without having a need for anything else. Even when they go to church, they do so in the thought that hundreds of attractive women go there in beautiful clothes, and so they will attend church to cast lustful glances as well. In short, people who seek an unrestricted life can have no relation with Islam.

Hazrat Abu Bakr[ra] Is a Second Adam for Islam

Even in that era, Musaylamah had gathered the people on teachings of freedom from divine law. It was in such a time that Hazrat Abu Bakr[ra] became the Caliph and so anyone can imagine the number of difficulties that would have arisen at such a juncture. If Hazrat Abu Bakr[ra] had not been strong-hearted and if his faith was not similar in nature to the faith of the Messenger, peace and blessings of Allah be upon him, he would have grown apprehensive and this could have spelled catastrophe. However, Hazrat Abu Bakr Siddiq[ra] was similar in hue to the Prophet[sa]. Moreover, the morals of the Holy Prophet[sa] had left an impress on his character, and his heart was replete with the light of certainty; this is why he exhibited an example of bravery and perseverance, which is unparalleled after the Holy Prophet, peace and blessings of Allah be upon him. Abu Bakr[ra] brought a death upon himself for the life of Islam.

This is an issue which does not require a lengthy discussion. Simply study the events of that era and then weigh the service that Abu Bakr, may Allah be pleased with him, rendered for Islam. I truthfully say that Abu Bakr[ra] was a second Adam for Islam. I am convinced that after the Holy Prophet, peace and blessings of Allah be upon him, if the person of Abu Bakr Siddiq[ra] had not existed, there would be no Islam. Abu Bakr Siddiq[ra] has done us an immense favour, for he established Islam again. Through the strength of his faith, he brought all of the rebels to account and established peace. God Almighty had stated and promised that he would bring peace at the hand of the true Caliph and this prophecy was fulfilled in the Caliphate of Hazrat Abu Bakr Siddiq[ra]. Heaven and earth bore witness to this practically as well. Hence, this is the definition of a Truthful One (*Siddiq*); such a person must possess within themselves a level of truth and sincerity (*sidq*) that is as great and excellent as what we have just described. Issues can easily be resolved through examples.

Joseph[as] and His Rank as a Truthful One

If one were to look into previous eras for an example, we have the truth and sincerity of Joseph[as]. Joseph[as] demonstrated such an outstanding level of truth and sincerity (*sidq*) that he was named the Truthful One (*Siddiq*). On the one hand, we have a beautiful, noble, young woman who makes brazen claims, and seeks to engage in fornication whilst in a state of complete privacy and seclusion, and on the other hand, one cannot help but praise this Truthful One, who would not transgress the limits set by God Almighty; and for this, he was ready to bear any calamity and grief that would befall him, to the extent that he even agreed to live the life of a prisoner. As such, Joseph[as] said:

$$رَبِّ السِّجْنُ اَحَبُّ اِلَیَّ مِمَّا یَدْعُوْنَنِیْ اِلَیْهِ$$ [1]

That is to say, he supplicated: 'O My Lord! I prefer prison over that to which this woman calls me.' This sheds light on the pure nature of Joseph, peace be upon

---

[1] *Yusuf,* 12:34

him, and on his indignation for the institution of Prophethood. He did not even mention the issue at hand. Why did he not mention by name the deed to which he was being called? In actuality, Joseph[as] was enamoured by the beauty and kindness of Allah the Exalted and was a passionate lover of the Divine. In his eyes, nothing else seemed attractive in front of his Beloved. He was strongly averse to transgressing the limits of Allah.

It is said that Joseph[as] remained in jail for a long period of time, a period that is said to have extended twelve long years. However, during this time, he never once uttered a word of complaint. He remained fully pleased with the decree of Allah Almighty. During that time, he did not even submit an appeal to the King so that his matter could be judged again or so that he could be released. In fact, it is narrated that this selfish woman only added to his spiral of pains, so that he would stumble. But this Truthful One did not let go of his truth and sincerity. God conferred upon him the title of the Truthful One. This is also a quality of one who has attained to the station of the Truthful in that no worldly calamity, no hardship and no disgrace moves such a one to transgress the limits set by Allah; the more that their afflictions and trials increase, their level of truth and sincerity grows all the more firm and pleasurable.

In summary, as I have mentioned, when a person declares اِيَّاكَ نَعْبُدُ (*Thee alone do we worship*) and moves forward with true sincerity and loyalty, God Almighty lets open a large stream of truth and sincerity, which falls upon a person's heart and fills it with truth and sincerity as well. The individual in question brings with them 'a paltry sum of money,' but Allah the Exalted grants them valuable goods of the highest quality in return. My purpose in stating this is to explain that a person ought to advance in this rank to such a degree that their truth and sincerity become an extraordinary sign in their favour. An ocean of divine insights and verities is opened to an individual of this nature to such an extent that they are granted a power against which it is beyond the strength of any ordinary person to contend.[1]

The Station of Martyrdom

The third station of excellence is that of the Martyrs (*Shuhada*). Generally, people believe that a Martyr (*Shaheed*) is simply a person who is killed by an arrow or a gun, or someone who meets a sudden, unexpected death. However, in the esti-

---

[1] *Al-Hakam*, vol. 3, no. 17, dated 17 May 1905, p. 2

mation of Allah the Exalted, the station of martyrdom *(shahadat)* is not limited to this alone. I must express with regret that the Pathans of the frontier region are also foolishly obsessed with attacking British officials and in turn, they only disgrace Islam with their madness. They believe that if they kill a non-believer or someone belonging to another religion, they will be deemed as fighting in the cause of Islam, and so if they are killed, they shall be martyrs. I am also disappointed in the wretched clergy who incite these mad Pathans. They do not tell them that if a person kills someone unjustly, they are not fighting in the cause of Islam, rather they are tyrants; if they are killed in such fighting, they are not martyrs, rather they die the illegitimate death of suicide, because Allah the Exalted states:

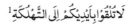

And cast not yourselves into ruin with your own hands.

Such people throw themselves into the hands of death themselves and thereby create disorder. I firmly believe that they are deserving of a severe punishment. In short, the common people have understood martyrdom in the limited sense that I have just mentioned, and confine the station of a Martyr to the aforementioned. However, in my view, the deeper reality of a Martyr, irrespective of whether or not their body is physically cut down or not, is something quite different. It is a state that relates to the heart. Bear in mind that one who sits at the rank of the Truthful enjoys nearness to the Prophet and is second in line after him; a Martyr bears resemblance in nature to the Truthful. Now a Prophet possesses all of these excellences; in other words, a Prophet is from among the Truthful, he is also from among the Martyrs and from among the Righteous as well. However, the station of the Truthful is distinct from that of a Martyr. There is no need to engage in a debate on whether the Truthful are also Martyrs or not. At both of these two ranks, the station of excellence that a person attains, which in every respect is deemed to be extraordinary and miraculous, is different in level and degree. Therefore, Allah the Exalted bestows upon a Martyr the strength which enables them to perform excellent deeds and morals in the most complete and purest sense, without any forced effort. No fear or expectation spurs these good deeds, rather, they become a part of their very nature and disposition. The nature of such a one need not strain themselves to do good. For example, if a beggar were to ap-

---

[1]   *al-Baqarah*, 2:196

proach someone, now whether the person has anything to give or not, they will feel compelled to give the beggar something—if not due to fear of God, then out of regard for what people will think. However, a Martyr is free from such strain and forced effort, and this power and strength of theirs continues to increase. As their power continues to grow stronger, the initial difficulty that is felt in doing good proportionally decreases, until they feel no burden whatsoever. For what would an elephant feel if an ant sat upon its head?

Does the Prayer Become Futile at Any Point?

In the *Futuhat*[1] a subtle point has been written whilst alluding to this station. It is written that when a person reaches a rank of perfection, the Prayer becomes useless for them. The foolish have understood this to imply that one becomes excused from offering the Prayer altogether, as certain free-minded dervishes claim. Such people are unaware of this station and fail to understand this subtle point of wisdom.

The fact of the matter is that in the initial stages of the spiritual quest, things like the Prayer and other good deeds feel as though they are a sort of burden, and the disposition is weighed down with feelings of indolence and inconvenience. However, when a person receives strength from God Almighty and reaches the rank of a Martyr *(Shaheed)*, they are granted such power and steadfastness that no difficulty is felt in performing these deeds. An individual becomes possessed and preoccupied in these deeds and fasting, the Prayer, Zakat, sympathy for humanity, kindness, and selflessness, in short, every good deed and sublime moral is performed with the power of faith. No misfortune, grief or pain can stop such a one from moving their steps towards God Almighty. A person will only be called a Martyr *(Shaheed)* when the power of their faith brings about through their person such actions that are performed with ease. Good deeds issue forth from a Martyr just as water falls from a height. A Martyr, as it were, sees God and witnesses His powers. When this rank reaches its point of perfection, it becomes a sign.

The Conduct of a Martyr in the Face of Trials and Tribulations

Some men have been observed to lose their composure in the face of trials and

---

[1]   *Al-Futuhat-ul-Makkiyyah* by Ibni 'Arabi [Publisher]

they begin to blame God. Their dispositions become dejected, because they do not enjoy the harmonious relations that ought to exist fully with God Almighty. An individual can only remain reconciled with God Almighty so long as they continue to obey Him. Also bear in mind that the relationship with God Almighty is like the relationships between friends. At times a friend will have their way, but at other times, they must accept the will of the other, and they must accept this happily, with an open heart, and not by compulsion. At a certain instance, God Almighty states:

$$ وَلَنَبْلُوَنَّكُمْ بِشَيْءٍ مِّنَ الْخَوْفِ وَالْجُوعِ^1 $$

In other words, We shall continue to test man, at times with fear or hunger, and at times with a loss of wealth, fruit and the like. Fruits can refer to a person's children as well; and is also applicable when someone prepares a crop with great effort, but then it is engulfed in a fire at once and is destroyed; or can allude to other cases when a person fails to gain the results of their labour and toil. In short, there are varying sorts of trials and diseases that afflict human beings, and these are a test from God Almighty. In these circumstances, those who are pleased in the will of Allah Almighty and who bow their heads in submission before His decree, declare with an open heart:

$$ إِنَّا لِلّٰهِ وَإِنَّا إِلَيْهِ رَاجِعُوْنَ^2 $$

Surely, to Allah we belong and to Him shall we return.

Such people do not complain or protest in any way, and it is about such people that Allah the Exalted states:

$$ أُولٰٓئِكَ عَلَيْهِمْ صَلَوٰتٌ مِّنْ رَّبِّهِمْ وَرَحْمَةٌ^3 $$

Meaning, it is these people who receive the special mercy of Allah Almighty. It is these very people to whom Allah the Exalted shows the way when faced with difficulties. Remember, Allah the Exalted is immensely generous, merciful and kind. When a person gives precedence to His pleasure and accepts His will, God does not leave them without granting them their recompense. This refers to occasions and instances when God Almighty desires for His will to be accepted. There are other instances as well about which God Almighty states:

---

1   *al-Baqarah*, 2:156
2   *al-Baqarah*, 2:157
3   *al-Baqarah*, 2:158 [Publisher]

اُدْعُوْنِیْٓ اَسْتَجِبْ لَكُمْ [1]

Pray unto Me; I will answer your prayer.

Here, God Almighty promises to accept whatever man desires. Therefore, a Martyr *(Shaheed)* is one who stands firmly at the point alluded to first; in other words, he is one who does the will of God with an open heart, and considers the pain that he sustains for the sake of his friend as though it were a reward.

The Station of the Righteous

The fourth station is that of the Righteous *(Salihin)* and this too at its highest level is a sign and a miracle. Perfect *salah* (i.e. being sound or pious) is when there are no traces of *fasad* (which in Arabic means to be corrupt or devoid of virtue). A sound body (that enjoys a state of *salah*) is pure from all kinds of corruption and infection. Only when a person is free from infection and full of elements that are conducive to health and well-being, can they be deemed a *salih* (in the physical sense). Further, until a person is good and sound, the elements that relate to them cannot be good and desirable either, to such an extent that even sweetness tastes bitter to an individual who is unwell. In the same manner, until a person becomes a *salih* and does not refrain from all forms of evil and is not purged of the corruption within, worship feels bitter. Such a one will attend the Prayer, but feels no pleasure and enjoyment; he pecks his head and finishes his Prayer with an ill-omened face and then leaves. However, pleasure is derived in worship when a person is cleansed of the impurity from within. It is then that one develops a desire, fervour and joy and it is from here that the point of man's reformation begins."[2]

After this address, the Promised Messiah[as] prayed and the gathering was brought to a close.

10 December 1899

Sunday 9 am—Qadian: Mufti Muhammad Sadiq Sahib[ra] had the English translation done of the announcement regarding the prophecy in which a sign had been sought within three years[3] and brought it from Lahore. Before going on his walk,

---

1   *al-Mu'min*, 40:61
2   *Al-Hakam*, vol. 9, no. 18, dated 24 May 1905, p. 8
3   This refers to an announcement of the Promised Messiah[as] dated 5 November 1899. Please refer to Supplement No. 5 to *Tiryaq-ul-Qulub*, Ruhani Khaza'in, vol. 15, pp. 507-512. [Publisher]

the Promised Messiah[as] said: "You have shown great resolve in accomplishing this task."

A Means for the Acquisition of Spiritual Reward

The Promised Messiah[as] said: "There is a wisdom of Allah the Exalted in my not studying English, for God desires to include you people in this spiritual reward. If I had been educated in English, every day I would have written a few pages in English as well, as I do in Urdu. But God desires that you and Maulvi Muhammad Ali Sahib, and others like you should also be given an opportunity to attain spiritual reward." At this, Mufti Muhammad Sadiq Sahib[ra] submitted: "This resolve and spiritual reward belongs to Maulvi Muhammad Ali Sahib."

The Promised Messiah[as] said: "In the era of Alamgir, the Shahi Mosque caught fire. The people made haste and ran to the noble King and submitted that the mosque had gone up in flames. Upon hearing this news, the King immediately fell into prostration and thanked God. The King's courtiers inquired in surprise: 'Your Noble Majesty! What time is this for thankfulness? The house of God has caught fire and the hearts of the Muslims are in immense pain.' The King responded: 'I have been thinking and yearning for quite some time that this grand and magnificent mosque that has been built, this building that is benefiting thousands of people, if only there was some way that I too could have a part in this good work. However, whenever I looked at this mosque, I would find it to be complete and flawless in every aspect, and so nothing would come to mind as to how I could partake of spiritual reward in this regard. So today, God Almighty has opened a way for me by which I too can attain spiritual reward. وَاللّٰهُ سَمِيۡعٌ عَلِيۡمٌ (*And Allah is All-Hearing, All-Knowing*).'"

Lekhram and His Associates

The Promised Messiah[as] said: "In attacking Islam and unjustly hurting the sentiments of the Muslims, there was almost a kind of trinity among the Aryas. More than anyone else, there was Lekhram, then Indraman, and then there was Alakhdhari."

The Promised Messiah[as] also said: "Dyanand was also one of them, but he did not have the same opportunity as the others, nor did he write books like the others. These three, and especially Lekhram, were guilty of gravely disrespecting, on numerous occasions, the Messenger of Allah, peace and blessings of Allah be upon him. It is the practice of Allah Almighty to seize an individual through the very avenue by which they chose to engage in transgression. Since Lekhram employed the dagger of the tongue against Islam and crossed all bounds, it was with the dagger that God Almighty punished him.

The Hidden Hand of God in the Matter of Lekhram

In the matter of Lekhram, the hidden hand of God can clearly be seen at work. The fact that the murderer had come to be made a Hindu; the fact that Lekhram trusted him to the extent that he took him home without hesitation; the fact that on the evening of the murder, all of Lekhram's other guests returned to their homes and he was left alone with the assailant; the fact that the murderer resolved to do the deed on exactly the second day of Eid; the fact that Lekhram stopped writing and stretched his arms, thus exposing his stomach; the fact that a clean strike was made with the knife; the fact that God silenced Lekhram such that despite being conscious and despite knowing that I had made a prophecy against him, his not expressing even for a moment that: 'I am suspicious of Mirza Sahib'; furthermore, the fact that to this day, the whereabouts of his murderer are unknown; all of these are the actions of God Almighty, which shed light on His awe-inspiring power and strength."

Then, the Promised Messiah[as] said: "Lekhram was a very rude man and no one like him was born after him. As the Hadith goes:

$$\text{اِذَا هَلَكَ كِسْرٰى فَلَا كِسْرٰى بَعْدَهُ}$$

When the Chosroes dies, there shall be no Chosroes after him like unto him.

Now Allah the Exalted will keep the land pure from such a person."

The Miracles of the Other Prophets

The Promised Messiah[as] said: "The signs that Moses[as] and the other Prophets showed to the world, like turning ropes into snakes with a staff, were all illusions—especially in view of the fact that these spectacles were shown in an era when showmen performed all sorts of sleight of hand and people would be left confounded as to how a certain thing had actually occurred. Conjurors from among the British can show such illusions and tricks that make it appear as if they can revive a dead man, or make broken things appear as if they are perfectly intact. For example, in the *Ain-i-Akbari* as well, Abul Fazal has narrated a tale that a magician ascended into the sky in front of a crowd of people and one after the other, parts of his body fell from the sky. His wife burned herself on the pyre as per the Hindu tradition known as *sati;* however, the magician returned from the sky and asked for his wife. When she could not be found, he suspected that a certain vizier had hid her because he had feelings for her. Then, the King granted the magician permission to search the vizier, after which he pulled his wife out from under the vizier's arm."

The Promised Messiah^{as} said: "In such circumstances, man is left with no choice but to have faith and deem the works of Prophets to be from God and consider the tricks of magicians to be deception and illusion. In this regard, the matter becomes a delicate one.

The Miracle of the Holy Quran

However, the miracle with which God Almighty has blessed the Holy Quran is its sublime moral teaching and values of social interaction, and its eloquence and articulacy, which are all things that no man can match in the least. So too is the case with its miracle that relates to news of the unseen and prophecy. In this era, no master magician claims to be able to do such things at all. In this manner, Allah the Almighty has granted my signs a clear distinction, so that no one is left with any room for excuse or objection. Thus, God Almighty has manifested His signs so openly and distinctly that there is no place for any doubt or suspicion to find its way in."

An individual submitted to the Promised Messiah^{as} that someone had raised the objection that Mirza Sahib was the one who had Lekhram murdered. To this the Promised Messiah^{as} said: "That is absurd and false. These people should at least stop to consider why the Messenger of Allah, peace and blessings of Allah be upon him, had Abu Rafi and Ka'b killed?"

The Promised Messiah^{as} said: "Our prophecies are ones which can be seen to possess divine power and this is a sign that demonstrates that they are from Allah the Exalted."

The Eloquence and Articulacy of the Holy Quran

The Promised Messiah[as] said: "The eloquence and articulacy of human beings is subject to vocabulary and possesses nothing more than rhymes. For example an Arab has written:

سَافَرْتُ اَلٰى رُوْمَ وَاَنَا علٰى جَمَلٍ مَّاتُوْم

This means, I set out for Rome, and set out I did on a camel whose bowels were closed. It is obvious that these words at the end have only been employed for the purpose of rhyme. It is a miracle of the Holy Quran, however, that all of its words have been strung like pearls and placed precisely where they belong in such a manner that not a single word can be moved from one place and put somewhere else, or replaced with another word more apt, and despite all this, it contains all the necessary elements of rhyme, eloquence and articulacy."

A certain individual praised a sufi who succeeded a line of religious divines and expressed his own view that the sufi apparently seemed to be a pious man, and if he was made to understand, it could be hoped that he would recognise the truth. The person submitted: "I have a relationship with him and if His Holiness would give me a letter addressed to him, I could take the letter to him and I trust that this will benefit him." To this, the Promised Messiah[as] responded: "Stay here for a few more days. I shall wait for God Almighty Himself to instill something in my heart firmly in this connection before I write you this letter." The Promised Messiah[as] went on to say: "Until such people receive an opportunity to stay in my company for a few days with steadfastness and good intentions, it is difficult that they should be moved. The heart must possess a passion for virtue and must be fearful out of a desire to attain the pleasure of God."

The Muslim Creed Fosters Bravery

The individual submitted: "These people are often hesitant because they feel that if others find out, they will take them to task." The Promised Messiah[as] said: "The reason for this is because such people do not fully believe in لَا اِلٰهَ اِلَّا اللهُ *(There is none worthy of worship except Allah)* and do not say these words in the true sense." The Promised Messiah[as] went on to say: "As long as a person's heart is fearful of a certain person or other, the impress of لَا اِلٰهَ اِلَّا اللهُ *(There is none worthy of worship except Allah)* cannot be firmly established on the heart."

The Promised Messiah[as] said: "When Muslims are encouraged and exhorted to proclaim the Muslim creed, it is for the very reason that without it, one can develop no courage at all. When a man says لَا اِلٰهَ اِلَّا اللّٰه *(There is none worthy of worship except Allah),* he deems the power and strength of all human beings and things, and of all rulers, officials, enemies and friends to be insignificant, and looks to Allah alone. Such a person deems all that is besides God to be worthless. And so, a person of this nature acts with bravery and courage, and nothing and no one is able to frighten them."

Insight

The Promised Messiah[as] said: "Insight is also a worthy quality. There is the example of the Jewish man who, upon seeing the Messenger of Allah, peace and blessings of Allah be upon him, instantly said: 'I see the signs of prophethood in this man.' Then, in the same manner, there were the Christians who chose not to come forth to contend with the Noble Messenger, peace and blessings of Allah be upon him, at the time of the prayer-duel, because their advisor had told them: 'I perceive such faces that if they tell the mountains to move, they shall move aside.'"

The Promised Messiah[as] said: "If a person has even a fraction of spirituality within them, they shall accept me."

A Desire to Write a Book of Teaching

The Promised Messiah[as] said: "It is my desire to write a book of teaching which Maulvi Muhammad Ali Sahib should then translate. This book will have three sections. The first section will be on our duties to Allah the Exalted, the second section will deal with the rights that we owe to our own souls, and the third section will provide an exposition on the rights that we owe to humanity at large."

A Miracle of the Saints

The Promised Messiah[as] said: "The era of prophethood could be described as نُوْرٌ عَلٰی نُوْر *(light upon light);* it was a shining sun. However, the miracles and wonders that are attributed to the saints after this era cannot be proven and one cannot clearly determine their historical authenticity. For example, the miracles of Sheikh Abdul-Qadir Jilani[rh] were penned some two hundred years after his demise. Furthermore, such saints were not met with circumstances where they contended against adversaries as have I, nor were they faced with the sort of trial by which I am confronted in this age."

A Matter Decreed

The Promised Messiah[as] said: "At present, there are many men from among our opponents about whom it is a matter decreed that they shall join our community. These people oppose us, but the angels look at them and laugh with the thought that: 'Ultimately, you are going to join these very people.' Such people constitute a hidden community of ours that will one day join us."[1]

On returning from his walk, the Promised Messiah[as] went inside and emerged when it was time for food. He spoke of the selfish nature of the Muslim clergy and also discussed, from various aspects, the despicable customs surrounding divorce and *halalah*. He joined with the congregation to offer his *Zuhr* and *Asr* Prayer, then after offering the evening Prayer, he remained among us until he became free from offering the *Isha* Prayer. After the evening Prayer, the Promised Messiah[as] heard a letter from a friend as well as readings from two other newspapers. Maulvi Abdul-Karim Sahib[ra] recited a poem by Mir Hamid Shah Sahib[ra], which pleased the Promised Messiah[as] greatly and he instructed that the poem be published in the newspaper. The poem was:

ڈنکا بجا جہاں میں مسیح کے نام کا

خادم ہے دین پاک رسول انام کا

The name of the Messiah gained fame far and wide;
he who is a servant of the Pure Religion of the Messenger of Mankind.

Luke

The following day, on his morning walk at 9 o'clock, there was a long discussion on what had been read out the previous day from a newspaper of Sialkot mentioning the Ointment of Jesus and a statement of Dr Luke. The Promised Messiah[as] instructed Mufti Muhammad Sadiq Sahib[ra] and Maulvi Allah Diya[ra] of Ludhiana to investigate further. During the course of discussion, the Promised Messiah[as] said: "In Arabic, *laqq* carries the meaning conveyed in the Urdu word

---

[1]   *Al-Badr,* dated 19 March 1905, p. 5

chutney[1]." On this Mufti Muhammad Sadiq Sahib[ra] said: "In English, *lick* is what we would say to express the Urdu verb *chaatnaa*." To this, the Promised Messiah[as] said: "Well, we have found a relation as far as *chutney* goes, I trust we will find a link to the extent of applying ointment and dressing wounds as well." Then, the Promised Messiah[as] went on to state: "English books and the history of the Christian Church ought to be studied further in this regard. This is a new point that has come to light." The Promised Messiah[as] also said: "This is not a difficult matter. If we desired, we could focus on Luke and gather all of the details in this way, but my disposition loathes the idea of turning my attention towards anyone other than Allah the Exalted. God Almighty tends to all of my affairs Himself.

Unveiling the State of the Dwellers of Graves

All of these stories about people who claim to be able to uncover the circumstances of the dead from their graves are nothing but lies, they are nonsensical and absurd; in fact, they are tantamount to associating partners with God. I have heard of a man who wanders these parts and makes tall claims about being able to gain an insight into the circumstances of the dead from their graves. If his knowledge is true, he ought to come to me and I shall take him to such graves of whose dwellers I am well aware. But as I have said, these are all nonsensical things and to pursue them is nothing but a waste of time. A fortunate man ought not to waste his time in such preoccupations. He ought to adopt the way taught by Allah, and follow the practice of Allah's Messenger[sa] and his companions."

Sufi Music and Songs

After this, regret was expressed at the condition of various sufi leaders, who were indulged in sufi music and singing *(surud)*, and other self-invented practices of this nature. In this context, the Promised Messiah[as] said: "Human beings possess a propensity to derive pleasure in things and this is what moves them to feel pleasure in sufi music and singing. The inner self of man is deceived into thinking that he is deriving pleasure from the subject matter being sung, but in actuality, their inner self is only concerned with the pleasure that it derives from the music itself, irrespective of whether Satan is being praised or God. When these people

---

[1] The word *chutney* is generally understood to refer to a sauce or condiment used to add flavour to food. In this instance, however, the Urdu word is used to refer to a finely ground, soft substance that can easily be swallowed. [Publisher]

become engrossed in this and lose themselves to it completely, be it the praise of Satan or the praise of God, both become one and the same." At this, the walk came to its conclusion. The Promised Messiah[as] returned later on when it was time for food, and after he had finished eating, he delivered the address that follows. I now present what I have remembered thereof.

The Greatest Form of Worship in This Era

Alluding to the trial and disorder that was prevalent in the present age, the Promised Messiah[as] said: "It is necessary for a Muslim, in this day and age, when Islam is overwhelmed by affliction, to play a part in dispelling this disorder. The greatest form of worship in these times is for each and every Muslim to partake in dispelling this disorder. At this time, everyone ought to strive sincerely through their speech, knowledge and every faculty with which they have been endowed, to remove from the world with sincere effort, all the evil and insolence that is currently prevalent.

What good is the comfort and pleasure that one receives in this world? If it is in this world that a person receives their reward then what has been attained? Prefer the reward of the hereafter, which has no limit. Each and every one of you ought to possess a passion for the Unity and Oneness of God, just as God Himself is passionate for His own Unity. Just reflect, where in the world will you find a person who has been wronged more so than our Prophet, peace and blessings of Allah be upon him? There is no filth, abuse or invective that has not been hurled at him. Is this a time when the Muslims should sit silently? At this time, if no one stands up to bear witness to the truth and to silence the ones who speak falsehood, and if one deems it acceptable for disbelievers to go on shamelessly casting aspersions against our Prophet and continue misguiding the people, then remember that such a Muslim shall undoubtedly be called to account severely. You ought to employ whatever knowledge and experience you have to serve in this cause and save the people from this misfortune. It is established in the Hadith that even if you do not strike the Antichrist, it will die anyway. There is a famous adage:

هر کمالے را زوالے

Every pinnacle sees a decline.

These afflictions began to arise in the thirteenth century, and now the time of their end is near. It is the responsibility of each and everyone of you to strive insofar as possible and show people the light.

A Yearning for the Manifestation of God's Greatness and Glory

In the sight of Allah the Exalted, a saint and a man of blessings is one who develops such passion. God desires for His glory to be manifested. In the Prayer, one repeats: سُبْحَانَ رَبِّيَ الْعَظِيْم (*Holy is my Lord the most Great*) and سُبْحَانَ رَبِّيَ الْأَعْلَى (*Holy is my Lord the most High*). This is also an expression of the desire that God's glory should shine forth and that His greatness be manifested in a manner that has no parallel. In the Prayer, when a person glorifies Allah and extols His Holiness, the same sentiment is expressed; and through these words, God encourages man to realise that he ought to demonstrate through his works and efforts—with a natural fervour—that nothing which goes against the greatness of God can dominate him. This is an exalted form of worship. Those people whose passion is aligned with the will of God are the ones who are known as divinely supported and it is they who receive blessings. Those who do not possess a fervour for the greatness, glory and holiness of God, the Prayers that they offer are disingenuous and their prostrations are futile. Until a person possesses a fervour for the sake of God, these prostrations are nothing more than futile incantations, by which they desire to attain paradise.

Bear in mind that anything physical in nature that is empty of spirit cannot prove beneficial. For example, just as the meat of sacrifices does not reach God, your bows and prostrations do not reach Him either, until they are performed with a true spirit. God desires the essence. God loves those who possess ardour for His honour and greatness. People of this nature tread a fine path on which others do not have the strength to follow them. Until the essence is present, a human being cannot progress. It is as though God has sworn to not grant a person any pleasure until they possess a zeal for His sake.

Every human being possesses desire, but a person cannot become a believer until they give precedence to the greatness of God over all of their desires. The Arabic word *wali* means a near one or a friend. Therefore, a person is referred to as a *wali* (or a saint) when they desire what their Friend, i.e. God, desires. Allah the Exalted states:

وَمَا خَلَقْتُ الْجِنَّ وَالْاِنْسَ اِلَّا لِيَعْبُدُوْنِ[1]

And I have not created the Jinn and the men but that they may worship Me.

An individual ought to possess a zeal for the sake of God and if they do, they shall outstrip their fellow man and become among those who enjoy the nearness of God. One must not be like a dead corpse—when something is put in from one side of the mouth, it comes out of the other. In the same manner, when someone is in a wretched state, nothing good can go inside. Remember that no worship or charity is accepted until one possesses a sincere fervour for the sake of Allah Almighty—a fervour that is free from traces of selfishness or personal motive. It ought to be such that even a person himself is unable to explain why they possess this fervour. There is a dire need for such people, but nothing is possible without the will of God.

The Present State of Affairs and the Need for a Reformer

Those who have been engaged in such service to religion ought to remember that they have done no favour upon God. There comes a time when every crop must be cut for harvesting. In the same manner, now the time has come for corruption to be dispelled. The worship of the Trinity has reached its highest limit and the Truthful One has been slandered and insulted to the greatest possible extent. The Messenger of Allah, peace and blessings of Allah be upon him, has not been valued even to the extent of a bee or a wasp. People fear wasps and are even apprehensive of ants, but no one has hesitated in speaking ill of the Messenger of Allah, peace and blessings of Allah be upon him. Such people fall true to the following statement of God Almighty:

كَذَّبُوْا بِاٰيٰتِنَا[2]

They rejected our signs.

They have lashed out against the Holy Prophet[sa] as much as they could and have openly spewed out vulgarities and invectives against him. Now the time has truly come for God to recompense them. In such an era, Allah the Exalted always raises a man. As God Almighty states:

---

1   *adh-Dhariyat*, 51:57
2   *Aal-e-Imran*, 3:12

وَلَنْ تَجِدَ لِسُنَّةِ اللهِ تَبْدِيلًا ¹

And thou wilt never find a change in the way of Allah.

God raises a man who possesses an immense passion for His greatness and glory. That man is supported by a hidden, divine succour. In actuality, everything is done by God Almighty Himself, but His raising a man for this purpose is in accordance with His custom. Now the time has come. In the Holy Quran, God advised the Christians to not exceed the limits in their religion, but they did not act upon this exhortation and having first been misguided themselves, they have now begun to misguide others as well. If one studies the 'scriptures of nature,' it becomes evident that when a thing exceeds the limits, preparations begin in the heavens. The fact that the time for preparation has now arrived is the very sign of the coming of that man. A chief sign of the appearance of a true Prophet, Messenger or Reformer is that he appears at the proper time and in an era of need; he appears in a time when people swear on oath that the time has now come for something to be done in heaven. But remember that God Almighty does everything Himself. If all the members of my community—myself included—were to retreat into seclusion, the task at hand would still be accomplished and the Antichrist will fall. As Allah the Exalted states:

تِلْكَ الْأَيَّامُ نُدَاوِلُهَا بَيْنَ النَّاسِ ²

These days We cause to alternate among men that they may be admonished.

The ascendancy of the Antichrist at this time proves that the time for its downfall has now come; its height demonstrates that now it shall see a low; its flourishing is a sign of its imminent destruction. Indeed! The cool breeze has now begun. The works of God follow their course gradually and softly.

Even if I had no argument in my support, the Muslims still ought to have wandered frantically in search of the Messiah and asked why he has not yet appeared. Indeed, he has come to break the cross. The Muslims should not have engaged him in disputes with themselves, for his purpose was to break the cross; this is what the present time calls for and this is why he was named the 'Promised Messiah'. If the Muslim clergy had the well-being of mankind in view, they surely would not have acted in this manner. They would have realised that nothing is to be accomplished by issuing edicts against me. When God says that a certain thing

---

¹   *al-Ahzab*, 33:63
²   *Aal-e-Imran*, 3:141

should be, who has the power to say that it should not be? In a way, my opponents are actually my servants and helpers, because they convey my message to the east and to the west. I have just heard that the *pir* from Golra is about to write a book against me, and so I am pleased that those of his followers who were unaware of me shall now come to know about me and they will have a reason to see my books as well."[1]

---

[1] *Badr,* vol. 7, no. 11, dated 19 March 1908, pp. 3-6

An Address Delivered by the Promised Messiah^{as} on 28 December 1899 at the Annual Convention

A Speech or Sermon Must Be For the Sake of God Alone

The Promised Messiah^{as} states: "Would all the gentlemen listen attentively. I wish and desire for my community, and even for my own person and soul, that we must not be pleased with empty words and expressions that are to be found in lectures. Our entire aim and focus must not culminate merely on the spell-binding nature of a certain individual's speech and the power of their words. This does not please me. What pleases me—and not by any pretence or affectation, but rather as a natural and inherent demand of my soul—is that everything be done for the sake of Allah, and to serve God. If the pleasure of Allah and obedience to His commands had not been my objective, Allah the Exalted knows well that I have always preferred to remain in seclusion and I feel such pleasure in solitude that is beyond me to explain—delivering speeches and sermons is quite another matter. But what am I to do? My sympathy for mankind draws and pulls me out into the public, and then, I am also bound by the command of Allah Almighty, who has appointed me to convey His message.

The reason that I have mentioned that we must not be pleased with hollow words and expressions is because even in all things that are good, Satan has a part. Hence, when a person stands up to exhort the people, there is no doubt that enjoining goodness and forbidding evil is a most excellent deed; but the one who stands in this place ought to be fearful, for in this deed, Satan seeks to have his share. A part of this relates to the one who delivers the address, and a part relates to the audience. The reality of this is that when speakers stand up to deliver their addresses, it is observed that their purpose and heartfelt desire is nothing more than to deliver a speech that pleases the audience. They aim to use such words and expressions so that sounds of praise and acclaim can be heard from all directions. I find that this is the only purpose of such speakers, just as the main effort of entertainers, actors, *qawwali* performers and singers is to receive praise from their audience.

Hence, when a person has a large audience before them, which comprises people of all dispositions and levels, the eye with which one perceives God is shut, except in the case of whom God wills. Otherwise, the objective of most people is simply to garner praise and acclaim, and to be applauded and given cheers of appreciation. In short, this is Satan's part as it relates to a preacher or speaker.

The share of Satan, as it relates to the audience that listens to an address, is for them to appreciate and praise a speaker for their eloquence, articulate speech, mastery of the language, powerful expression, and for their apt use of poetic verses and stories and jokes that spur laughter, only so that they may be deemed as ones who have an understanding of poetry and prose. In other words, their purpose is far distanced from God, while the speaker has his own motives. The speaker speaks, but not for the sake of God; the audience listens, but does not give these words a place in their hearts because they do not listen for the sake of God. Why does this happen? Only so that they can feel pleasure. Remember! Human beings experience two forms of pleasure: a pleasure of the soul and a pleasure of the baser self.

Spiritual pleasure is a fine and profound secret. If someone were to learn about it or if a person was to experience this pleasure and delight even once in their life, this would be enough to intoxicate them and they would lose their senses. Carnal pleasures are always short-lived and temporary. Carnal pleasures refer to the pleasure, for example, with which a harlot dances in the streets, and from whom people also derive a pleasure. For example, when a Muslim cleric sings as he admonishes an audience, this pleases the people who sit before him. In the same manner, people are pleased when they hear a harlot sing. This clearly demonstrates that a person's baser self attains the same pleasure from the address of a preacher, as it does from the singing of a prostitute. Despite knowing full well that the woman before them is a prostitute, whose morals and way of life are extremely despicable, if a person feels a pleasure in her words and songs, and is not averse, or does not perceive a foul smell, then know for certain that this is a carnal pleasure. Otherwise, the soul would never be pleased with such a disgusting and foetid thing. In the example I have just mentioned, the pitiful preacher does not know that he is bereft of purity, just as these members of the audience, who wrong their souls, do not realise that they experience nothing but a baser pleasure that has nothing to do with God.

Hence, I seek refuge with God Almighty and pray that may He keep our speeches and speakers, and those who listen to them, free from this foul and impure spirit, and may He fill them with a nature that is wholly devoted to God. Whatever we say, may we say for the sake of God and to attain His pleasure; and whatever we hear, may we hear as the words of God and so that we may act upon them; may the share that we partake from a gathering in which an exhortation is made, not be limited to us merely saying that today a most wonderful speech was delivered.

Righteousness and Godly Preachers

This was a significant reason for the decadence and downfall of the Muslims. Countless conferences are held, and a plethora of bodies and councils exist, where renowned and prolific speakers and lecturers read out their papers and deliver addresses and poets mourn the state of our religion in their poetry. But why does none of this have any effect? Instead of moving forward, with every passing day, our people only fall further and further into decline. The fact of the matter is that those who participate in these gatherings do not come with sincerity. The aim of the lecturers who speak in these gatherings, as I have just mentioned, whether they are maulvis, leading modern-day intellectuals, or sufis, is nothing but to hear voices of praise and acclaim. When they deliver speeches, their audience is their god. It is their satisfaction and approval that they seek, not the pleasure of God. However, this will never be the intention and purpose of the righteous and the divine. Their aim and purpose is God, and true sympathy and sincere compassion for mankind, which is also a great means by which to acquire the pleasure of Allah Almighty. They desire to show the world what they have witnessed themselves. Their true longing is to manifest the glory of Allah Almighty and for this reason whatever they say, they say without fear of reproach. In their view, the listeners who sit before them are like dead insects, from whom they neither seek reward nor praise. It is for this reason that on certain occasions, the people become agitated on hearing their words and will even stand up and leave in the middle of their speech; often they will curse at them; they do not suffice at hurling verbal abuse alone, but rather, inflict various forms of pain and agony upon them as well.

From this we clearly come to know of those who seek and yearn for carnal pleasure and what is actually implied by 'carnal pleasure.' There are people who will stay up all night to watch a prostitute perform and dance, and they have no problem in falling true to the saying:

زر دادن و دردِ سر خریدن

To give gold and purchase a headache.

However, these same people find it difficult and burdensome to hear even a few words from the holy mouth of a divine preacher, who speaks out of immense sincerity, sincere fervour and true sympathy. However, this community of divine preachers is never worried in saying these things, nor do they tire. Why? Because they have God in view, who manifests Himself upon them with His boundless powers and extraordinary might, and Who sends down tranquillity and perseverance upon them. How then could they be bothered by dead materialists?

The Effect of Godly Preachers on the Soul

One ought to bear in mind that human birth is characterised by two aspects. The soul makes up one part of it, while the baser self, which is expansive and widespread, constitutes the other part. Now you can all easily understand that anything that is larger will carry a greater effect. The fervour of the soul in man, however, may be likened to a foreigner who has come to reside in a place far from home among strangers. Therefore, the soul which is in a state unknown is given very little attention. A sign of the influence of the soul is that when a godly preacher and divine reformer speaks, he considers his listeners to be non-existent and conveys his words in the likeness of a messenger. In this state, the soul melts until it uncontrollably descends in the likeness of a waterfall that flows from a high river bank to lower ground, after which the soul flows towards God Almighty, and in this flow it experiences a pleasure and joy which I cannot express in words. Hence, in his expositions and speeches, he looks at the countenance of Allah. He does not care about what his listeners will say when they hear his words. He receives pleasure from another source, and is filled with inner delight over the fact that he is conveying the command and message of His Master and Ruler. The difficulties and pains that he experiences in conveying this message is also a source of pleasure in itself and a means of comfort for him.

The Immense Sympathy and Compassion of the Noble Prophet[sa]

Since such people are overwhelmed by feelings of sympathy for mankind, they remain engaged in thoughts day and night, and are absorbed in grief for the people so that they will come to the path of God in some way or other, and so that they will drink just one sip from this fountain. This sympathy and this fervour was present in our chief and master, the Noble Prophet, peace and blessings of Allah be upon him, to an immense degree—no one else could ever possess a greater share. As such, the state of the sympathy and compassion with which the Holy Prophet[sa] was possessed has been illustrated by Allah the Exalted Himself in the following words:

$$ لَعَلَّكَ بَاخِعٌ نَّفْسَكَ اَلَّا يَكُوْنُوْا مُؤْمِنِيْنَ ^1 $$

Meaning, will you grieve yourself to death because they do not believe? Whether you are able to grasp the deeper reality of this verse or not, the fact is that it circulates in my heart, just as blood flows throughout the body.

بدل دردیکہ دارم از برائے طالبانِ حق

نے گردبیان آں درد از تقریر کو تاہم

The pain that I feel in my heart for those who seek the truth;
is pain which I cannot express in one small speech.

I understand full well the sort of heart-wrenching pain by which godly preachers are consumed for the reformation of mankind.

The Capacity to Be Influenced

It should also be borne in mind that listeners are influenced according to their capacity in a manner that is commensurate with the nature and power of the teacher himself—so long as their capacity has potential. Those people who have a greater affinity with God Almighty and have a fear for Him will be influenced more than others. The proof of this is that the soul makes haste and races uncontrollably towards God Almighty so that it may be purified. If one has a stronger connection with the soul that incites one to commit evil and is ruled by it, the disposition feels an anxiety, strain and aversion to listening to the words of a divine reformer. Such people do not feel comfortable sitting with them and listening to their words, and even feel disturbed. When an individual feels such restlessness and discontent in listening to the words of a divine preacher, it is crucial for them to begin worrying about their soul, for such a soul has reached the edge of the pit of destruction.

---

1   *Al-Shu'ara*, 26:4

The Cure for Spiritual Maladies

What could be more destructive in this world than feeling an aversion or distaste in listening to God's teachings? What is the cure to such feelings? The cure is to seek forgiveness from Allah and to turn towards God, and pray for one's sins to be forgiven, and then to continue in this without fail. If this remedy is employed, I can say with surety that their displeasure will turn into a pleasure and their distaste will turn into a liking. Then, the same soul that would flee from God's presence and was averse to listening to God's teachings, will race towards Him in the likeness of a rolling ball.

Three States of the Human Soul

There are three states of the soul: the self that incites to evil, the reproving self and the soul at rest. One state of the soul at rest is known as the soul that is pure. The soul that is pure is the one found to exist in children. It is the soul that has not been defiled by the winds of this world, and which moves forward on a smooth and level plain, without any highs or lows. The self that incites to evil is the self that has been adulterated by worldly elements. The reproving self is the self that develops a sense of understanding, reflects over its lapses, and strives and prays to save itself from vices, and is cognisant of its own weaknesses. The soul at rest is one which, by the grace of Allah, finds the strength and power to abstain from all forms of evil, and feels safe from all sorts of calamities and afflictions, and in turn, feels tranquillity and comfort at heart, with no traces of apprehension or restlessness.

The Jurisdiction of the Brain, Heart and Tongue

This may be elaborated with an example. Allah the Exalted has put in place three ruling forces within human beings. The first of them is the brain, the second is the heart, and thirdly, the tongue. The brain is supported by the intellect and makes use of argumentation. The task of the brain is to remain forever engaged in formulating and constructing ideas, and to reflect upon new arguments and proofs. The service entrusted to the brain is to compile data and then go on generating results.

The heart is the king of man's entire being. The heart does not operate with the use of argumentation because it holds a connection with the King of all kings, and therefore receives knowledge either by way of manifest revelation, or by means of hidden revelation. It could also be said that the brain is a vizier and since the task of a vizier is to devise plans, therefore, the brain remains engaged in formulating proposals, reflecting on the necessary means, weighing arguments and producing results. In this, the heart has no part. For God Almighty has vested the heart with the faculty of sense. For example, an ant will find its way at once to a location where there is something sweet, although it is moved by no argument which proves that there is something sweet to be found in that location. On the contrary, God Almighty has granted the ant an instinct, which guides it to the relevant location. Likewise, the heart is similar to an ant, because like an ant, it too possesses the same faculty of sense which guides it. The heart does not require argumentation and proofs, nor does it have a need to analyse facts in order to extract results. Notwithstanding that fact, the brain does, nonetheless, provide the heart with these means and resources anyway.

The Heart in Arabic

The word *qalb*, which is used for 'heart' in Arabic, has two meanings. Firstly, there is the apparent and physical meaning, and then there is the spiritual meaning. The apparent meaning of *qalb* is one of 'turning about'. Since it is the heart that causes the circulation of blood in our bodies, it is referred to as *qalb* in Arabic. In the spiritual sense, this word implies that any progress an individual hopes to attain in terms of spirituality can only be attained through the power of the heart. Just as the circulation of blood, which is absolutely critical in sustaining human life, is powered by the heart or *qalb*, in the same manner, all forms of spiritual advancement are dependent on the power of the heart.

The Nature of the Heart and Brain

There are certain ignorant philosophers in this day and age, who attribute all positive advancement to the brain. However, such people do not realise that the brain only possesses the ability to weigh arguments and evidence. Although it is the brain that possesses the faculty of reflection and retention, the heart possesses a quality which moves it to the position of a chief. The mind follows a forced, mechanical process, while the heart is free of this and functions in an unforced, natural way. It is for this reason that the heart holds an affinity with the Lord of the Throne, and is able to determine the truth merely through its faculty of sense, without any evidence or proof. This is why it is narrated in a Hadith:

$$ اِسْتَفْتِ الْقَلْبَ $$

Meaning, seek a verdict from your heart. One has not been instructed to seek a verdict from one's brain. It is the heart with which the line of divinity is linked. No one ought to view this as improbable. This concept is deep and difficult indeed, but those who are experienced in purifying the soul know that all good values inherently exist within the heart. If the heart had not possessed these powers, the very being of man itself would be without purpose. Sufis who remain engaged in mystic practices and those who undertake spiritual exercises know well that the heart can be seen to visibly emit columns of light, which flow towards the sky in the form of a straight line. This is a clearly visible and categorically established phenomenon. I cannot explain this with any specific examples, but indeed, those who have had to engage in exercises in spirituality, or who have sought to traverse the stages of the spiritual quest, have found this spectacle and experience to be true.

It is as though a thin line exists between the heart and the throne of God, and the heart experiences a pleasure in whatever command it receives from the Lord's throne. The heart is not in need of external evidence or proofs; in fact, it receives revelation from God and is enlightened by God from within, whereafter it gives a verdict. It is a fact, however, that until a heart becomes a heart in the true sense, it may be aptly described by the following verse:

$$ لَوۡ كُنَّا نَسۡمَعُ اَوۡ نَعۡقِلُ مَا كُنَّا فِیۡۤ اَصۡحٰبِ السَّعِیۡرِ ۚ [1] $$

If we had but listened or possessed sense, we should not
have been among the inmates of the blazing Fire.

To further explain, man experiences a time when both the heart and mind do not possess any faculties or powers at all. Then a time comes when the brain begins to grow and develop. Then a stage arrives when the faculties and powers of the heart are developed, after which the heart becomes enlightened, ignited and il-luminated. When the heart arrives at this point, a human being reaches the stage of spiritual maturity, and the brain becomes subservient to the heart, and the faculties of the mind no longer control the qualities and faculties of the heart.

---

[1] *al-Mulk*, 67:11

It should also be remembered that these various states of the mind are not specific to believers alone. Hindus and people from among the scheduled classes all make use of the brain. Moreover, those who are engaged in worldly affairs and business, all make use of their brains. The mental faculties of such people have grown and developed fully, and it is through these faculties that they come up with new and innovative ideas to further their business. Look at Europe and the New World, and you will see how its people make use of their mental faculties, and the pace at which they invent new technologies. The work of the heart begins when a person becomes devoted to God. At such a time, all the inner faculties and authorities of man cease to exist and the rule of the heart gains a power and strength. It is then that a human being may be deemed complete. It is this very state in which a human being becomes an embodiment of the verse:

نَفَخْتُ فِيهِ مِنْ رُّوْحِيْ[1]

I have breathed into him of My Spirit.

It is in this very state that even the angels prostrate before such a person. At this time, the individual in question becomes a new person altogether, and their soul becomes fully absorbed in pleasure and joy. It must also be remembered that this pleasure cannot be likened to the pleasure that an impulsive evil-doer feels in fornication, or to the enjoyment that an admirer of good voices experiences on hearing a melodious person sing—not in the least; one must not be deceived. The soul experiences pleasure[2] when a human being melts and begins to flow towards God in the likeness of water, due to fear and awe of Him. At this stage, the person in question becomes the 'Word of God' and the following verse begins to show its effects in them:

اِنَّمَآ اَمْرُهٗٓ اِذَآ اَرَادَ شَيْئًا اَنْ يَّقُوْلَ لَهٗ كُنْ فَيَكُوْنُ[3]

*Verily His command, when He intends a thing, is
only that He says to it, 'Be!,' and it is.*

The Deeper Reality of the Word of Allah and the Soul

People have gravely misunderstood the term 'Word of Allah' which is used for

---

1 *al-Hijr,* 15:30
2 *Al-Hakam,* vol. 5, no. 9, dated 10 March 1901, pp. 1-4
3 *Yasin,* 36:83

the Messiah[as]. They have understood this as being a means of some distinction for the Messiah[as], but this is not the case at all. Every human being becomes a 'Word of Allah' when they emerge from the darkness, impurity and gloom of the baser self.

Bear in mind that every human being is a Word of Allah because they possess a soul, which has been referred to as the command of the Lord *(amri-rabi)* in the Holy Quran. However, on account of his foolishness and ignorance, as man does not give due importance to the soul, he essentially chains it in fetters and shackles, blinding its vision and blackening its pure state with perilous darkness and evil, marring the soul to such an extent that it becomes so dim that it can hardly be perceived. But when man repents and turns towards Allah the Exalted, and removes the cloak of his impure life of darkness, the heart begins to shine, and the journey to the original source—which is God—begins, until finally, when a person reaches the highest state of righteousness, all of their dirt and filth is removed and what remains of man is Allah's Word. This is a subtle point of knowledge and wisdom. All people do not have the ability to attain to the depth of this matter.

The Excellence of Man

The excellence of man is for him to develop true cognisance of the Divine and true insight, i.e. the insight one receives through faith—an insight that is accompanied by the light of Allah and guides man on every path. Without this, a person cannot be safe from the possibility of deception, and by habit or custom, such a person will oftentimes, even happily, consume a deadly poison. The sufi leaders and inheritors of shrines throughout the Punjab and all across India consider the height of their divine understanding and excellence to be limited merely to the songs of *qawwali* reciters, raising slogans of هُوَ حَقّ, and hanging upside down. Moreover, the ignorant masses, who worship these sufi leaders witness these things, and look to these people to find the satisfaction and comfort of their soul. Observe closely, for if these people do not actively deceive others, in the least, they are themselves deceived. These acrobatics have nothing to do with the true relationship between man's servitude *(ubudiyyat)* and God's divinity *(uluhiyyat);* for if this true bond exists, it emits a light and brilliance, producing a pleasure the like of which cannot be compared with any other joy.

I say with the purest of intentions, and God knows my intentions well, that if such exercises were a means of worshipping God, attaining divine understanding and a means for the soul to attain to excellence, then we ought to consider acrobatic performers to have attained to the pinnacle of divine understanding. The British have progressed even more remarkably in such tricks and acrobatics; but despite their advancements in this field, the level of their understanding of God is that they are non-believers or atheists altogether, and those who do believe in God, deify a weak, helpless human being who was born from the womb of a woman, Mary. These people have left aside belief in One God and believe in three, one of whom they believe was accursed and stayed in hell for three days.

O you who are wise, reflect! O you who possess a pure nature, contemplate! If hanging upside down, or musical instruments like the tabla and sarangi were the means by which divine insight and human excellence was attained, why have the British—who are experts in the art, and who produce new and innovative instruments of sound and music—stumbled, either rejecting God completely or subscribing to the concept of trinity, even though they are deemed to possess developed minds in the field of invention and innovation? Moreover, do reflect and contemplate that if this is the means by which understanding of God is attained, then those who perform at theatres, in fact all singers and dancers, must be godly and excellent individuals of the highest degree! Alas! These people have no idea as to what constitutes true understanding of the Divine. They are unaware of what constitutes human excellence and are unable to see the share of Satan in these things.

Emotion, Weeping and Lamentation

Such people deem that the satisfaction and comfort of the soul lies in shedding a few tears and letting out a few cries. Often, when reading a novel, a person will reach a painful turn in the plot, and even though they know that this is a made-up tale of fiction, they are unable to control their emotions, and at times they will burst into tears. This demonstrates that mere weeping and crying also, in itself, has no value. I have heard that during the reign of the Chughtai Kings, there were people who would wager on the fact that they would certainly make their audience cry or laugh. Now we have a clear example in countless sorts of novels. On reading certain novels, a person will be unable to contain their laughter, while certain others uncontrollably move a person's heart to feel pain, even though the readers know that these are made-up stories and tales of fiction.

This evidently demonstrates that man is susceptible to deception, and this happens when a person is unable to distinguish between the cravings of the baser-self and spiritual objectives. There is a very large number from among the people of this world who are bereft of the true signs of spirituality. Although their speech has nothing to do with divine insights and verities, yet they are able to make the people weep. The people do not weep because these speakers are blessed with knowledge of divine insights and verities, or because they are coloured in the hue of servitude to God, and fearful and in awe of the greatness and glory of God's divinity when they speak. In fact, at the depth of this phenomenon is what I have just mentioned in the context of novels and stories. These people themselves are enthralled by their baser desires, and mere weeping in this manner has no benefit.

Even One Tear Forbids Hell

Of course, if a heart is overwhelmed by the greatness, omnipotence and fear of Allah the Exalted, causing it to melt with emotion, and if this moves a person to shed even one tear for the sake of God, this one tear surely makes hell forbidden for such a person. Hence, one must not be deceived by the fact that they weep often. Empty crying serves no purpose and will only strain the eyes until a person falls victim to various ailments of the eye.

I advise you that when a person is moved by the fear of Allah and weeps in His presence, hell is forbidden on such a person. However, such emotion and weeping is not possible until a person believes in God and His Messenger[sa] in the true sense, and until they learn about His True Book—and not only learn about it, but rather, believe in it.

When a physician gives a laxative medicine to someone who is ill, this clears their bowels through light, repeated diarrhoea, but this is not enough to cure the illness. It is only through diarrhoea caused by a liver flush that the body is cleared of all its toxins and impurities, and all the filth and harmful matter, which had weakened and agitated the patient, is cleansed. It is then that a person is restored to health. In the same manner, emotion and tears at the threshold of God purge an individual of their inner impurities and foul matter, and makes them pure and clean, but only when it comes from the innermost depths, as though one's liver would burst, as it were. Even one tear shed by a servant of God, at a time of sincere repentance, has greater worth and value than an ocean of tears shed by one who is a slave of carnal passions and desires, and who is engulfed in ostentation and darkness. The former weeps for God, while the latter does so for the people or for their own self.

Sincerity and honesty is what holds value in the estimation of God Almighty—never let this fade from your hearts. Affectation and pretence can be of no use before God.

The Means to Attain an Understanding of Allah Almighty

Now one may inquire as to the manner in which one can reach this state and ask what means the Holy Quran has set forth in this regard. The response is that God Almighty has put forth two principles in this connection. Firstly, there is prayer. Indeed, it is true:

Man has been created weak.

Man is a weak creature. He can do nothing without the grace and mercy of Allah the Exalted. His very existence, and the means for his nourishment and sustenance are based entirely on the grace of Allah Almighty. Foolish is the one who prides himself on his own intellect or wisdom, or on his wealth and property, for all the aforementioned are a gift from Allah the Exalted. Where did man bring these from? Now, for prayer to be effective it is necessary for man to fully accept and be cognisant of his own weakness and infirmity. The more an individual reflects over their own weakness, the more they will find themselves in need of the support of Allah Almighty, and this will produce a fervour within them to supplicate. When a person is grappling with a calamity, or feels grief or difficulty, they will cry out and call for help so that someone will come to their aid. In the same manner, if a person reflects over their own weaknesses and lapses, and feels in need of the support of Allah Almighty at every moment, then their soul falls and wails at the threshold of divinity with immense vigour, grief and restlessness, and cries out: 'O Lord! O Lord!' If you contemplate, you shall see that in the very first chapter of the Holy Quran, Allah the Exalted has taught us to supplicate:

اِهْدِنَا الصِّرَاطَ الْمُسْتَقِيْمَ صِرَاطَ الَّذِيْنَ اَنْعَمْتَ عَلَيْهِمْ غَيْرِ الْمَغْضُوْبِ عَلَيْهِمْ وَ لَا الضَّآلِّيْنَ[2]

Guide us in the right path — the path of those on whom Thou hast bestowed Thy blessings, those who have not incurred

---

[1] *an-Nisa*, 4:29
[2] *al-Fatihah*, 1:6-7

Thy displeasure, and those who have not gone astray.

A prayer can only be complete if it encompasses every possible benefit and advantage, and if it saves one from every possible harm or loss. Hence, this prayer seeks all of the best possible advantages and makes a submission to be saved from even the greatest of things which could inflict harm and destroy a person.

The Four Classes of Those Upon Whom God Has Bestowed His Blessings

I have explained repeatedly that those upon whom God has bestowed His blessings are divided into four classes of people: firstly, the Prophets; secondly, the Truthful; thirdly, the Martyrs; fourthly, the Righteous. Hence, in this supplication, the excellences of these four classes of people have been sought.

The Prophets

The magnificent excellence of the Prophets is that they receive news from God. As such, the Holy Quran states:

$$\text{لَا يُظْهِرُ عَلَى غَيْبِهِ أَحَدًا إِلَّا مَنِ ارْتَضَى مِنْ رَّسُوْلٍ}^{1}$$

He reveals not His secrets to any one, except to him
whom He chooses, namely a Messenger of His.

Meaning, God Almighty does not disclose His hidden secrets to just anyone; of course, He does reveal them to whomsoever He pleases from among those who are blessed with the excellences of Prophethood. Allah the Exalted informs these people in advance of events that will occur in the future, and this is a grand and supremely magnificent sign in favour of those who are commissioned and sent by God. No miracle is greater than this. Prophecy is a truly extraordinary miracle. All the past scriptures —and the Holy Quran as well—prove that there is no greater sign than prophecy.

The Perpetual and Everlasting Miracles of the Holy Prophet[sa]

Foolish and spiteful opponents have never thought about this aforementioned knowledge; instead, they have levelled allegations upon the miracles manifested by our Noble Prophet, peace and blessings of Allah be upon him. However, these

---
[1]   *al-Jinn*, 72:27-28

critics who shut their eyes and level allegations fail to realise that even if all the miracles of all the Prophets of the world were compared to the miracles of the Holy Prophet[sa], I can honestly say that the miracles of the Messenger of God, peace and blessings of Allah be upon him, would prove to be greater. Irrespective of the fact that the Holy Quran is replete with prophecies of the Messenger of Allah, peace and blessings of Allah be upon him, which extend not only to the Day of Resurrection, but even speak of events after that time, the strongest evidence in support of his prophecies is that in every era there is someone present to provide living proof of his prophecies. As such, in this era, Allah the Exalted has raised me as a sign, and has bestowed upon me the magnificent sign of prophecies, so that I may show those who are ignorant of divine verities and deprived of divine insight, the perpetual and everlasting nature of the miracles of our Messenger, peace and blessings of Allah be upon him, as clearly as the light of day.

Prophet Muhammad[sa] Is the Only Living Messenger Until the End of Time

Is there anyone from among the remaining Jews belonging to the Children of Israel, or anyone from among the Christians, who calls upon the Messiah saying: 'O Lord! O Lord!' who can contend with me in these signs? I loudly proclaim that there is no one. Not even one. This is a proof of the power of our Prophet, peace and blessings of Allah be upon him, to show miracles that display divine power. For it is an accepted principle that miracles manifested at the hands of a follower are deemed to be miracles of the Prophet who is their Master. Therefore, the extraordinary signs that have been given to me, and the magnificent sign of prophecies that has been bestowed upon me, are actually fresh and living miracles of the Messenger of Allah, peace and blessings of Allah be upon him. No follower of any other Prophet has been blessed with the honour of being able to claim that even today, they can show miracles due to the spiritual influence of the Prophet who is their chief. This honour is reserved for Islam alone and this very fact establishes that only Muhammad, the Messenger of Allah, peace and blessings of Allah be upon him, can be deemed to be the living Messenger who shall remain until the end of time. Moreover, it is through the blessings of his pious followers and his own spiritual influence that in every era, a man of God shows the countenance of God to the people.

The Greatest Excellence of a Prophet Is Their Disclosing the Unseen

In short, the actual point was that in the aforementioned prayer, a supplication has been made so that one may partake of the excellences of the Prophets. For the chief class from among those upon whom God has bestowed His blessings is that of the Prophets, peace be upon them all. Further, the greatest excellence of this group is that matters of the unseen—also referred to as prophecies—are revealed to them. It ought to be remembered that in this prayer, the supplicant does not actually pray to be given prophecies, but rather only seeks to attain that station at which he then makes prophecies. The station at which one makes prophecies requires the highest levels of nearness to God. For this is the station where a person becomes an embodiment of the following verse:

مَا يَنْطِقُ عَنِ الْهَوٰى[1]

He does not speak out of his own desire.

This level is attained when a person reaches the station that is illustrated in the following verse:

دَنَا فَتَدَلّٰى[2]

He drew nearer to God; then he came down to mankind.

Until a person discards the mantle of their human nature and cloaks themselves under the mantle of divinity, so as to become a reflection of the divine, how can they be conferred the rank just mentioned? This is the rank at which certain sufis, ignorant of the stages in the spiritual quest, arrived but stumbled, and then considered themselves to be God. This misunderstanding of theirs has resulted in the spread of a grave error, which has ruined many. The issue that I speak of is the concept of Unity of Being *(wahdat-e-wujud)*. The people are unaware of the deeper reality of this concept.

My purpose is only to tell you that until a person reaches the rank described in مَا يَنْطِقُ عَنِ الْهَوٰى[3] (*He does not speak out of his own desire*), they cannot be granted the power of prophecy, and this rank is attained when a person attains nearness of the Divine. In order to attain the nearness of Allah, one must act upon the following:

---

[1]   *an-Najm*, 53:4
[2]   *an-Najm*, 53:9
[3]   *an-Najm*, 53:4

تَخَلَّقُوْا بِاَخْلَاقِ اللهِ

Develop within yourselves the attributes of Allah.

Until one keeps the attributes of Allah Almighty in the forefront of their heart and honours them, and shows a reflection of them in one's own state and morals, how can one be admitted in the presence of God? For example, one of the attributes of God is *Quddus* or 'the Holy.' How then, can an impure, filthy individual, who indulges in the impurity of all sorts of sin and transgression, be admitted into the presence of Allah Almighty and develop a relationship with Him?[1]

To summarise, in this prayer, a supplication is made initially to attain the excellent ranks of the class upon which Allah has bestowed His blessings. Hence, until an individual abandons their inner thoughts and desires and hears the voice of God: اَنَا الْمَوْجُوْدُ *(I am present)*, they should continue to pray. This is the rank of absolute perfection.

The Truthful

The second station is of one who has attained to the rank of the Truthful, i.e. a *Siddiq*. The quality of perfect truth and sincerity cannot be absorbed until one draws it in with sincere repentance. The Holy Quran is a compendium of all truths and is in fact an embodiment of perfect truth itself. Until man becomes truthful himself, how can he become cognisant of the excellence of truth and its ranks?

When one reaches the stage of the Truthful, one develops an insight and love for the Holy Quran, and learns of its divine verities and points of wisdom. For falsehood attracts falsehood and therefore, a liar can never be enlightened with the divine insights and verities of the Quran. It is for this reason that the Holy Quran states:

لَا يَمَسُّهٗٓ اِلَّا الْمُطَهَّرُوْنَ[2]

None shall touch it except those who are purified.

The Martyrs

The third station is of one who has attained to the rank of the Martyrs, i.e. a

---

[1]   *Al-Hakam*, vol. 5, no. 10, dated 17 March 1901, pp. 1-4
[2]   *al-Waqi'ah*, 56:80

Shaheed. The common people have generally understood this word to merely refer to a person who dies in battle, or drowns in a river, or dies in an epidemic, etc. However, I declare that to suffice on this alone and to limit the word to this alone, is far from the greatness of a believer. A *Shaheed* is one who gains the strength from God Almighty to remain steadfast and composed, and who cannot be weakened in the face of tribulations and calamities. He is one who remains firm with courage when confronted by misfortunes and difficulties, to such an extent that even if he is required to lay down his life purely for the sake of God Almighty, then he is granted an extraordinary resolve. He is one who will lay down his head without any feelings of sorrow and grief, and desires that he be granted life again and again so that he may sacrifice it in the way of Allah again and again. He is one whose soul is so permeated by pleasure and comfort that every sword that strikes his body and every crushing blow grants him a new life, a new joy and a new freshness. This is what it means to be a Martyr or a *Shaheed.*

Further, this word is also derived from the word *shahd* (which means honey). Those who engage in strenuous worship, and endure bitterness and enmity, and are prepared to bear such things, are granted a sweet and pleasant taste, just as one gains from honey. Moreover, just as honey is described as: [1] فِيهِ شِفَآءٌ لِّلنَّاسِ *(therein is cure for men),* these individuals, too, are a cure. Those who spend time in their company are cured from many an ailment.

Moreover, a *Shaheed,* which in Arabic means 'a witness', also refers to the rank at which a human being, as it were, beholds God before them whenever they perform any action, or in the least, firmly believes that God sees them. This concept is also referred to as *ihsan.*

The Righteous

The fourth station is of one who has attained to the rank of the Righteous, i.e. a *Salih.* These people are ones who have been cleansed of their foul elements, and their hearts have become clean. It is an obvious fact that until the foul elements in the body are dispelled and so long as one's disposition is unwell, even the taste in one's tongue is spoiled and seems bitter. However, when a state of *salahiyyat* prevails in the body, i.e. when it is healthy and well, it is then that the proper taste of everything is experienced, and the disposition is in a state of pleasure, comfort, energy and alertness. Likewise, when a person is drowned in the impurity of sin,

---
[1]   *an-Nahl,* 16:70

and the nature of the soul is disturbed, the spiritual faculties begin to fall weak, to the extent that one is unable to experience the pleasure of worship. In this state, the disposition is agitated and apprehensive. However, when the foul elements, which were produced by a life of sin, begin to be expelled from the body by means of sincere repentance, this agitation and apprehension of the soul starts to subside, until finally one attains a comfort and satisfaction. Prior to this state, one felt a pleasure in submitting to sin and experienced a delight in committing that act, as a result of carnal desire. But now, the same person feels a pain and grief in turning to evil. The soul begins to tremble even at the thought of this previous life of darkness, and then a pleasure, enjoyment, fervour and passion for worship is aroused. The spiritual faculties of that individual, which were once dying due to a life adulterated with sin, begin to develop and grow again, and moral powers manifest themselves.

Man has been commanded to attain these four ranks on earth, and prayer is the most potent means to attain this end. We have been given an opportunity five times daily to implore that we are granted these ranks.

Etiquettes of the Acceptance of Prayer

There is another point to note in this context. Allah the Exalted states:

$$اُدْعُوْنِیْ اَسْتَجِبْ لَكُمْ ^1$$

Pray unto Me; I will answer your prayer.

Furthermore, He also states:

$$اُجِیْبُ دَعْوَةَ الدَّاعِ اِذَا دَعَانِ ^2$$

I answer the prayer of the supplicant when he prays to Me.

Moreover, a reflection on the Holy Quran will reveal that Allah the Exalted does in fact listen to prayers and He is very near. However, if an individual supplicates without proper consideration of the attributes and names of God Almighty, prayer has no effect whatsoever. It is due to the fact that people are unaware of this secret, or rather, have never endeavoured to learn about this secret, that the world is being ruined. I have heard many people say that they prayed profusely, but there was no outcome. In turn, these people become atheists. The fact of the

---

1   *al-Mu'min*, 40:61
2   *al-Baqarah*, 2:187

matter is that there are rules and laws in every realm. Similarly, there are laws and regulations that have been put in place for prayer. Those who claim that their prayer was not accepted do so because they do not give due consideration to the rules and requirements that are necessary for the acceptance of prayer.

Allah the Exalted has put before us a matchless and precious treasure that we can find and attain. For it cannot be accepted that on the one hand we believe in Allah Almighty to be Powerful, but then suggest that whatever He has put before us and shown us is nothing but a mere mirage and an illusion. Even such a thought can ruin a person. Not at all. In fact, each and every individual can have this treasure. Allah Almighty has no shortage. He has the power to give everyone these treasures, yet there would be no decrease in them.

In short, Allah the Exalted is even prepared to bestow upon us the excellences of prophethood. However, we must endeavour to seek them. The assertion, therefore, that a certain individual's prayer was not accepted is an evil suggestion and a deception of Satan. The fact is that such a prayer is wholly devoid of the etiquettes and means that are necessary for the acceptance of prayer, and so the gates of heaven are not opened to such supplications. Hear the words of the Holy Quran:

$$اِنَّمَا یَتَقَبَّلُ اللّٰهُ مِنَ الْمُتَّقِیْنَ ^{1}$$

Meaning, Allah the Exalted accepts the prayers of those who are righteous. The prayers of those who are not righteous are without the garb of acceptance. The providence and graciousness of Allah Almighty work to support such people, nonetheless.

The Wisdom in Certain Prayers of the Righteous Not Being Accepted

The bounty of the acceptance of prayer is bestowed upon those who are righteous. Now I shall inform you as to who are the righteous. However, before this, I deem it necessary to remove another misconception as well. There are certain individuals who are righteous, yet even some of their prayers are not accepted as per their will. Why is this so? It ought to be remembered that none of the prayers of such people are actually wasted. However, since human beings are not knowers of the unseen, they cannot know the effects that the acceptance of a certain prayer will have on them. Therefore, Allah the Exalted—out of boundless affection and kindness—accepts the supplication of His servant in a manner that is

---

1 *al-Ma'idah*, 5:28

beneficial and favourable for them. For example, if an innocent child fearlessly desired to take hold of a snake, considering it to be a soft and beautiful thing, or asked its mother to hand over a burning piece of coal, considering it to be bright and attractive, is it possible that the mother—no matter how utterly foolish she may be—would ever approve of her child taking hold of a snake, or would willingly put a bright, burning piece of coal in her child's hand? Of course not. For she knows that these are a threat to her child's life. Hence, how can Allah the Exalted, Who is the Knower of the unseen, and in fact the Knower of all things, and Who is more gracious and kind than even a mother, and Who is the very Being who instilled this love into the hearts of mothers, bear to accept immediately the prayer of a dear servant of His who has, out of his human weakness, error and ignorance, asked for something that is harmful for him? Not at all. God rejects such requests and grants His servant something better in return. The supplicant is able to understand with certainty that a certain something in their life is the effect and result of a previous prayer, and then the servant learns of his own error as well. Therefore, it is absolutely incorrect to say that even certain prayers of the righteous are not accepted; nay, their every prayer is accepted. Of course, if on account of their weakness and ignorance, they happen to pray for something that will not bring positive results in their favour, Allah the Exalted grants them a better alternative for what they had originally requested, as a return for their prayer.

Who Are the Righteous?

After this, I now return to my actual objective and proceed to tell you about the definition of a righteous person. In actuality, there are magnificent promises for the righteous. What could be more than the fact that Allah the Exalted is a friend of the righteous? Those who claim to enjoy the nearness of Allah, without being righteous, are liars; in fact, such people lead a life of sin and transgression. They commit an immensely grave injustice when they claim for themselves the rank of sainthood and nearness to God, because Allah the Exalted has stipulated that one must be righteous in order to attain these ranks.

Divine Succour

Another condition that Allah the Exalted has stipulated in this context, or rather—one could say—a sign of the righteous as stated by God, is as follows:

اِنَّ اللہَ مَعَ الَّذِیۡنَ اتَّقَوۡا[1]

Meaning, God is with those, i.e. bestows divine succour, to those who are righteous. The greatest proof of the fact that God stands by a certain person is the succour and support that He bestows upon them. Since people are no longer righteous, the door to saintliness has been closed to them, and as they are no longer righteous, the gate of God's company and support has also been shut on them. Always remember that the succour of God is never granted to the impure, nor to those who are transgressors, for divine succour depends on righteousness. The help of God is reserved for the righteous.

Affluence

Then, there is another aspect as well. Human beings suffer from various difficulties and hardships, and have various needs. Again, it is righteousness that is the fundamental means by which one can see their difficulties resolved and their needs fulfilled. Righteousness alone is the path of deliverance from financial hardship and other difficulties as well. Allah the Exalted states:

وَمَنۡ یَّتَّقِ اللہَ یَجۡعَلۡ لَّہٗ مَخۡرَجًا وَّیَرۡزُقۡہُ مِنۡ حَیۡثُ لَا یَحۡتَسِبُ[2]

Meaning, in every difficulty, he who fears Allah—He will make for him a way out, and provide for him the means of deliverance from the unseen; and grant him provision from where he expects not.

Now reflect and observe, what more does a human being want in this life? The greatest desire a person has in this world is to find peace and happiness, and for this purpose, Allah the Exalted has made only one path available—the path known as righteousness. This could be described in other words as the path of the Holy Quran, which is synonymous with the straight path *(sirat-e-mustaqim)*.

The Wealth and Riches of the Disbelievers

No one should be misled by the fact that disbelievers possess wealth, riches and property as well, and live in pleasure, engrossed in their luxury and enjoyment. I tell you truthfully that these people appear happy only in the eyes of the world, rather, only in the eyes of despicable materialists and those taken by outward ap-

---

[1]　*an-Nahl*, 16:129
[2]　*at-Talaq*, 65:3-4

pearances. In actuality, these people are burning from within and are drowned in grief. You look at the faces of these people, but I see their hearts. They are engulfed in a blazing fire, and entangled in chains and iron-collars, just as Allah the Exalted states:

$$اِنَّآ اَعۡتَدۡنَا لِلۡكٰفِرِيۡنَ سَلٰسِلَا۟ وَاَغۡلٰلًا وَّسَعِيۡرًا١$$

Verily, We have prepared for the disbelievers chains
and iron-collars and a blazing Fire.

It is impossible for them to adopt virtue. The weight of these collars hold them down in such a way that they are shackled like animals and beasts, and therefore cannot advance towards God. Their eye is forever set upon the world and they themselves incline towards it. Then, they constantly experience a pain and burning sensation from within. If they experience a loss in their wealth, or if—contrary to their wishes—they fail to succeed in a certain endeavour, they grieve and burn from within. This is to the extent that they will even go mad and lose their senses, or wander helplessly to and from court. It is true that an irreligious man is in a blazing fire, because he cannot find peace and comfort, which is the definite result of pleasure and satisfaction. An alcoholic, for example, will drink a glass of alcohol and then ask for another, and continue asking for more and more, and all the while, is consumed by a burning longing. In the same way, a worldly person is engulfed in a blazing fire; for his fire of greed can never be extinguished for even a moment. True happiness, in actuality, is reserved for a God-fearing person, in relation to whom, Allah the Exalted states that there are two paradises.

True Happiness

A God-fearing person can find more happiness in a hut, than a worldly person, who is a slave to greed and avarice, can ever find even in a magnificent castle. The more a worldly person acquires the material wealth of this world, the more they are confronted with afflictions. Hence, remember that true comfort and pleasure is not partaken of by worldly people. Do not be mislead to believe that abundant wealth, expensive and elegant clothing, and fine foods can bring happiness. Absolutely not. True happiness depends on righteousness alone.

---

[1] *ad-Dahr*, 76:5

Controlling One's Tongue

When all of these points make it evident that no comfort and happiness can be attained without true righteousness, one must know that righteousness has various aspects, like the divided sections made by the strands of a spider's web. Righteousness relates to all of a person's limbs, their beliefs, their tongue, morals, etc. The most sensitive of these affairs relates to the tongue. Often, a person will abandon the fear of God and make a statement; then they will feel pleased at heart for saying such and such thing, though it was immoral.

At this, I am reminded of a story. A worldly man invited a holy man. When the holy man arrived for food, the host, who was an arrogant man of a worldly bent, said to his servant: 'Bring such and such tray, which I brought back from my first Hajj.' Then he said: 'Bring the second tray as well, which I brought from my second Hajj.' Then he proceeded to say: 'Bring the one from the third Hajj as well.' The holy man said: 'You are deserving of immense pity. In these three sentences, you have ruined your three pilgrimages. Your only purpose in making these statements was to show that you have gone to pilgrimage three times.' Therefore, God has taught that a person ought to control his tongue, and abstain from making useless, absurd, inappropriate, needless comments.

Observe how Allah the Almighty has given us the teaching of اِيَّاكَ نَعْبُدُ (*Thee alone do we worship*). Now, since there was a possibility of man depending on his own faculties and distancing himself from God, immediately after these words, God also teaches us to supplicate: اِيَّاكَ نَسْتَعِيْنُ (*Thee alone do we beseech for help*), and tells us that a person must not surmise that whatever worship he performs, he does so of his own power or strength. Not at all. On the contrary, without the help of Allah Almighty and until God—the Holy One—confers this ability and strength Himself, man can achieve nothing. Moreover, God does not teach us to say: اِيَّاكَ اَعْبُدُ (*Thee alone do I worship*) and اِيَّاكَ اَسْتَعِيْنُ (*Thee alone do I beseech for help*), because this carries an unpleasant air of giving preference to one's own ego, while this is contrary to righteousness. A person who is righteous always keeps the whole of humanity in consideration. The tongue alone is sufficient to distance a man from righteousness. It is with the tongue that one expresses conceit and it is with the tongue that one begins to develop Pharaoh-like tendencies. It is by this very tongue that an individual turns his hidden deeds of virtue into ostentation. The tongue is quick to cause harm. It is narrated in a Hadith: 'I guarantee paradise to one who safeguards from evil the organ beneath the naval and the tongue.' Eating that which is forbidden is not as detrimental as speaking falsehood. Let no one be misled to believe that there is no harm in eating that which is unlawful. Anyone who thinks this way is gravely mistaken. My purpose is to highlight that it is one thing for a person to consume the flesh of swine themselves under compelling circumstances, but if they were to issue an edict with their tongue, permitting the consumption of swine, such a one would be guilty of an action that moves them away from Islam to a far greater extent. For such a one declares permissible a thing which has been forbidden by Allah the Exalted. Therefore, this demonstrates that the harm caused by the tongue is dangerous. Therefore, a righteous person must keep control over their tongue. A God-fearing person does not say anything that is contrary to righteousness. So rule over your tongues, let not your tongues rule over you, such that you should speak nonsense without consideration.

Before you say anything, reflect over the consequences that your words will bring. Reflect as to whether Allah the Exalted permits you to say such a thing, and until you contemplate over this, do not speak. It is better to not speak at all than to say something that causes evil and disorder. However, notwithstanding that fact, it is also against the greatness of a believer to refrain from expressing a matter of truth. When such an occasion arises, let not the reproach of any critic or any fear stand in the way of your tongue. When our Noble Messenger, peace and blessings of Allah be upon him, announced his claim to prophethood, his relatives and even strangers became his enemy, but he did not care about any of these people for even a heartbeat. When Abu Talib, the uncle of the Holy Prophet^{sa}, could bear to hear no more complaints and raised the matter with the Holy Prophet^{sa}, the Prophet of Islam clearly stated: 'I cannot refrain from expressing the truth. You are free to stand by me if you wish, or leave me.'

Therefore, one must hold back the tongue from saying anything that is contrary to the pleasure of God Almighty. Yet, it is necessary to use the tongue to express the truth. The greatness of the believers is described as follows:

$$يَأْمُرُوْنَ بِالْمَعْرُوْفِ وَيَنْهَوْنَ عَنِ الْمُنْكَرِ^{1}$$

They enjoin what is good and forbid evil.

Before one enjoins goodness and forbids evil to others, it is incumbent for an in-

---

[1] *Aal-e-Imran*, 3:115

dividual to prove through their own practical state that they possess the strength within themselves to act accordingly. The reason being that before an individual can exert an influence on others, they must first make their own state influential. So remember, never hold back your tongue from enjoining goodness and forbidding evil. It is necessary, however, to be considerate of time and place, and one's manner of speech must be kind and gentle. Similarly, it is a grave sin to engage the tongue in speech that is contrary to righteousness.[1]

The Ultimate Cause of the Holy Quran is Righteousness☒Then, one may observe that righteousness is such a highly significant and necessary quality that Allah the Exalted has deemed it to be the ultimate cause behind the revelation of the Holy Quran. As such, at the start of the second chapter, Allah the Exalted states:

$$الٓمّٓ ذٰلِكَ الْكِتٰبُ لَا رَيْبَ فِيْهِ هُدًى لِّلْمُتَّقِيْنَ^2$$

Alif Lam Mim (I am Allah the All-Knowing). This is a perfect
Book; there is no doubt in it; it is a guidance for the righteous.

My belief is that this sequence of the Holy Quran is extraordinary to say the least. In these verses, Allah the Exalted has alluded to the four causes: the efficient cause, the material cause, the formal cause and the ultimate cause. All things are characterised by these four causes. The Holy Quran manifests these causes in a most perfect manner. Firstly, Allah the Exalted states:

Alif Lam Mim—I am Allah, the All-Knowing.

This indicates that Allah the Exalted who is the All-Knowing, has revealed this Word upon Muhammad, the Messenger of Allah, peace and blessings of Allah be upon him, i.e. God is the Agent in this context. Then, there are the words:

This is a perfect Book.

This describes the matter in this case, or one could say, alludes to the material cause of the Holy Quran. Moving onwards, there are the words:

---

1   *Al-Hakam*, vol. 5, no. 11, dated 24 March 1901, pp. 1-4
2   *al-Baqarah*, 2:2-3

لَا رَيْبَ فِيْهِ[1]

There is no doubt in it.

These words allude to the formal cause of the Holy Quran and indicate that all things are susceptible to doubt, suspicion and corrupt thoughts, but the Holy Quran is a book that is free from all forms of doubt. The words لَا رَيْبَ *(no doubt)* indicate that the Holy Quran is free from all doubts. Now when Allah the Exalted has described the greatness of this Book with the words: لَا رَيْبَ فِيْهِ, naturally, the soul of any good-natured and blessed individual would be thrilled and would desire to act upon the instructions of the Holy Quran. I must say with regret that the manifestly clear and radiant grandeur of the Holy Quran is not presented before the world. For the Holy Quran possesses such qualities and excellences, such beauty within itself, and such attraction and allure that hearts are drawn to it helplessly. For example, if someone were to praise a beautiful garden, if they were to speak of its fragrant trees, its refreshing and revitalising plants and pathways, and its streams and rivers flowing with pure water, anyone would desire to visit and walk through that garden, and enjoy its beauty. Moreover, if it was said that some of the flowing streams in the garden cure chronic and deadly ailments, people would flock there with even more fervour and desire. In the same manner, if the qualities and excellences of the Holy Quran are described in the exceedingly beautiful manner that behoves it, and in effective words, the soul races towards it with extreme ardour.

Righteousness Is a Necessary Condition for the Discovery of Quranic Knowledge

In reality, the means by which the soul is satisfied, satiated and the manner in which the need of the soul is truly fulfilled, are contained within the Holy Quran. This is why Allah the Exalted has stated:

هُدًى لِّلْمُتَّقِيْنَ[2]

It is a guidance for the righteous.

At another instance, God Almighty states:

---

1   *al-Baqarah*, 2:2-3
2   *al-Baqarah*, 2:3

لَا يَمَسُّهُ إِلَّا الْمُطَهَّرُونَ [1]

None shall touch it except those who are purified.

The word *'mutahharun'* refers to the very same *'muttaqin'* referred to in the verse: هُدًى لِّلْمُتَّقِينَ [2] *(it is a guidance for the righteous).* And this makes it clearly evident that righteousness is necessary for the discovery of knowledge contained within the Quran. There is a stark difference between secular knowledge and the knowledge of the Quran. Righteousness is not a prerequisite for the acquisition of worldly and traditional knowledge. It is not incumbent that one who learns Arabic morphology, grammatical syntax, natural science, philosophy, astronomy, or medicine must regularly observe the Prayer or fasting, and be forever mindful of the commandments and prohibitions of God, and keep their every action or statement in line with the injunctions of Allah the Exalted. In fact, it is often observed and generally the case that experts and students in secular knowledge have an atheistic bent of mind, and are indulged in every form of sin and transgression.

In this day and age, we have a clear example before us in the people of Europe and America. Despite these people attaining outstanding and considerable progress in the field of worldly knowledge, and despite the new inventions they produce every other day, their spiritual and moral state is shameful to say the least. The stories that are published about what goes on in London's parks and hotels in Paris, I cannot even mention. However, righteousness is the first condition for the acquisition of heavenly knowledge and insight into the secrets of the Quran. This requires sincere repentance. Until a person adheres to the injunctions of Allah Almighty with complete humility and modesty, and meekly turns towards Him, trembling in awe of His glory and might, the gate of Quranic knowledge cannot be opened. Moreover, such a person cannot derive from the Holy Quran those means by which the inherent properties and faculties of the soul are nurtured, and the acquisition of which grants the soul pleasure and comfort.

The Holy Quran is the Book of Allah Almighty and the knowledge contained within it is in the hand of God, and righteousness serves as a staircase leading to this knowledge. How then can the faithless, evil and corrupt, and those who are slaves of earthly desire be fortunate enough to receive this knowledge? For this reason, a Muslim, who is a Muslim by name, could well be the greatest scholar of Arabic morphology, syntax, etymology, literary critique, and other such sci-

---

[1]   *al-Waqi'ah,* 56:80
[2]   *al-Baqarah,* 2:3

ences, and in the eyes of the world, could well be the greatest expert in all fields of knowledge, but if such an individual does not purify their soul, the knowledge of the Holy Quran is not granted to them. I observe in this day and age that the world's attention is greatly inclined towards the acquisition of worldly knowledge, and the enlightenment of the West has astonished the world with its new inventions and creations. The path that Muslims have thought to follow in order to secure their own prosperity and success, unfortunately, is by making the people of the West their leaders and priding themselves on following Europe. This is the state of modern Muslim thinkers. Then, there are those Muslims who are old-fashioned in their thoughts and who consider themselves to be the guardians of the Faith. The summary and sum-total of their lifelong achievements is that they are entangled in intricacies and disputes that relate to Arabic morphology and syntax; and they are at daggers drawn over the correct pronunciation of the Arabic word *daleen*. They pay no attention whatsoever to the Holy Quran, and how could they, when they pay no attention to the purification of their souls?

There is one class among the Muslims nonetheless that does claim to undertake the purification of the soul. This group is composed of sufis and the successors of saints, however, these people have abandoned the Holy Quran and have invented their own practices. Some of them perform forty-day retreats in seclusion; others raise slogans of الله إلا (*there is none but Allah*), while some of them are indulged in meditative practices of 'negation and affirmation' *(nafi-o-asbat)*, concentration, breath control, etc. In short, these people have invented practices that are not taught by the Messenger of Allah, peace and blessings of Allah be upon him, and do not align with the teaching of the Holy Quran—practices which have never been favoured by the institution of prophethood.

In short, it ought to be remembered that until an individual brings about a pure transformation and purifies the soul, one cannot gain an understanding of the insights and excellences of the Holy Quran. The points of wisdom and divine verities comprised in the Holy Quran are ones which quench the thirst of the soul. Alas! If only the world knew of that which brings pleasure to the soul, and then came to realise that what they require is comprised within the Holy Quran, and the Holy Quran alone.

Who Are the Saints?

Hearken! The greater a transformation one brings about in oneself, the more one is admitted into the class known as 'saints.' The divine verities of the Holy Quran are not unveiled until one enters the class of the saints. People have erred in understanding what the word 'saints' actually implies; they have understood it in a strange manner of their own. The fact of the matter is that saints are those people who inculcate within themselves a pure transformation and then, due to this transformation, their hearts are cleansed of the darkness and rust that covers it in the form of sin. Satan's rule over them is eradicated and the throne of Allah Almighty then reigns over their hearts. Then, such people are strengthened by the Holy Spirit and receive the bounty of God Almighty.

I give you glad-tidings and proclaim that whosoever among you transforms themselves from within is from among the saints. If a human being takes even one step towards God, the grace of Allah the Exalted races towards them and supports them. It is true and I also inform you that an individual cannot attain the knowledge comprised within the Quran through cunning. Intellectual ability and mental progress on their own cannot attract the knowledge of the Quran. The actual means is righteousness. God is the teacher of a righteous person. This is why the Prophets are often uneducated in secular fields of study. This is why our Prophet, peace and blessings of Allah be upon him, was sent as an unlettered man. Despite the fact that he was not educated in any school nor taught by any teacher, he still presented insights and verities that have stunned and astonished experts in the worldly sciences. A holy and perfect book like the Holy Quran was made to flow from his lips, which silenced the whole of Arabia through its literary eloquence and articulacy. What was the underlying quality in the Holy Prophet, peace and blessings of Allah be upon him, such that he outstripped all others in knowledge? It was righteousness. What could be greater proof of the pure life of the Messenger of Allah, peace and blessings of Allah be upon him, than the fact that he brought a book like the Holy Quran, which has astounded the world with the knowledge that it contains. The fact that the Holy Prophet[sa] was unlettered is an example and an argument to show that righteousness is required for the acquisition of Quranic and heavenly knowledge, rather than worldly guile.

The Purpose of the Recitation of the Holy Quran

Therefore, the actual purpose and objective of the Holy Quran is to teach the world righteousness, so that it receives guidance. In the following verse, Allah the Exalted has alluded to three stages of righteousness:

اَلَّذِيْنَ يُؤْمِنُوْنَ بِالْغَيْبِ وَيُقِيْمُوْنَ الصَّلٰوةَ وَمِمَّا رَزَقْنٰهُمْ يُنْفِقُوْنَ [1]

Who believe in the unseen and observe Prayer, and
spend out of what We have provided for them.

People recite the Holy Quran, but they do so like a parrot without thinking, just like a Pundit who goes on blindly reciting the scripture. Neither does the reciter understand what they are reciting, nor are the listeners aware of what is being said. In the same manner, all that is left of the recitation of the Holy Quran is for people to recite a few parts, without knowing what they have read. At most, people will recite the Holy Quran in tune, paying special attention to the pronunciation of the letters *qaf* and *ayn*. No doubt, it is commendable to recite the Holy Quran in a melodious voice, but the actual purpose behind the recitation of the Holy Quran is to learn about its divine verities and insights, and so that human beings can bring about a transformation within themselves as a result.

The Order in the Holy Quran and the Sequence in the Verse About the Death of Jesus[as]

Bear in mind that there is a strange, wondrous and veracious philosophy present within the Holy Quran. There is an order in the Holy Quran, which is not given its due value. Until the order and sequence of the Quran is kept in view and reflected upon, the objectives in the recitation of the Holy Quran cannot be fulfilled. If these people, who quarrel and argue over the pronunciation of the letter *qaf, ayn* or *duad* and who declare one another sinners and disbelievers, gave due regard to the order present in the Holy Quran, why would they war with me over the interpretation of the verse: اِنِّىْ مُتَوَفِّيْكَ وَرَافِعُكَ اِلَىَّ [2] (*I will cause thee to die a natural death and will exalt thee to Myself*), when they know that the Holy Quran states the relevant accounts in this context in an appropriate sequence, according to the manner in which they transpired? Allah the Exalted states: 'O Jesus, I shall cause you to die.' One ought to think, why has the Holy Quran stated:

يٰعِيْسٰى اِنِّىْ مُتَوَفِّيْكَ وَرَافِعُكَ اِلَىَّ [3]

O Jesus, I will cause thee to die a natural death and will exalt thee to Myself.

After all, what was the need for stating these words? If these people were to

---

[1] *al-Baqarah*, 2:4
[2] *Aal-e-Imran*, 3:56
[3] *Aal-e-Imran*, 3:56

ask the Jews, they could have found their answer. The actual fact, which I have mentioned countless times, is that the Jews declared that the Messiah[as] was accursed, God forbid. The proof that the Jews gave to support their view was that the Messiah[as] was killed on the cross. The Holy Quran, however, has refuted this allegation and has in fact charged the Jews with wrongdoing. Allah the Exalted never disgraces His holy servants and His promise is true when He states:

$$لَنْ يَّجْعَلَ اللهُ لِلْكٰفِرِيْنَ عَلَى الْمُؤْمِنِيْنَ سَبِيْلًا ^1$$

Allah will not grant the disbelievers a way to prevail against the believers.

When the Messiah[as] was put on the cross, he apprehended that the Jews of the time would take his life on the cross and thus charge him with an accursed death. In this hour of death, Allah the Exalted gave glad tidings to the Messiah[as] saying: 'I will cause you to die a natural death, and will exalt you, and will clear you of the charges against you.' Each and every word of this statement is full of truth. It is a pity, however, that these people do not reflect, and seek to distort the meaning of the Holy Quran by altering its order.

Did Allah Almighty not have the power to say:

$$يَا عِيْسٰى اِنِّىْ رَافِعُكَ اِلَى السَّمَآءِ$$

O Jesus, I shall lift you into the sky.

What difficulty then was God faced with so that He was compelled to say:

$$يٰعِيْسٰى اِنِّىْ مُتَوَفِّيْكَ ^2$$

O Jesus, I will cause thee to die a natural death.

Therefore, the sequence that has been followed in this verse is in accordance with the events as they unfolded. Foolish is the one who states that sequence is not set out by use of the conjunction 'and.'

If there is anyone so dull as to think otherwise, then in the least they ought to look over the events in this relation, and think about whether a person is cleared of charges before or after they are exalted. This 'clearing of charges' referred to in the verse under discussion alludes to the fact that after Jesus[as], a Messenger would appear as the Arbiter and give a verdict on this issue of contention, and he would vindicate Jesus[as] of all the allegations that are levelled against him by the Jews.

Even our opponents accept the sequence of the three fragments that form the following statement of the Holy Quran:

رَافِعُكَ اِلَيَّ وَمُطَهِّرُكَ مِنَ الَّذِيْنَ كَفَرُوْا وَجَاعِلُ الَّذِيْنَ اتَّبَعُوْكَ فَوْقَ الَّذِيْنَ كَفَرُوْا[1]

I shall exalt thee to Myself, and will clear thee from the charges of those who disbelieve, and will place those who follow thee above those who disbelieve.

They agree that this statement is a well-ordered sentence and all that Allah the Exalted promised herein has been fulfilled. Those who believe in the physical ascension of Jesus[as] cannot say anything in their support. It astonishes me that when such people accept the sequence of the three fragments in this statement, why do they make a futile attempt to interpret the word *tawaffi* (which means to die) in the sense of 'taking up the body'? Do tell me that by adopting the nature of the Jews, where will they place this word? If they place the word *tawaffi* after *rafa* (which means to be raised), this would clearly contradict the events as they actually transpired. There is no break between the word *rafa* (to be exalted) and the word *tat-heer* (the clearing of charges)— both words appear together. As a matter of fact, it is the clearing of charges which takes place after exaltation. The Holy Prophet, peace and blessings of Allah be upon him, absolved Jesus, peace be upon him, of the charges levelled against him by the Jews who believed that he was not a true Prophet and was accursed. He also absolved him from the calumny of the Christians who believed that Jesus[as] was the son of God and God himself, and who was raised into the heaven and suffered a curse for their sake. Jesus[as] being exalted, and then as a result, being cleared of the charges against him, are like two fingers, which cannot be separated. Then, Allah the Exalted states:

جَاعِلُ الَّذِيْنَ اتَّبَعُوْكَ

I shall place those who follow you (above those who disbelieve).

Now, if one reflects over these words, they do not permit for any other word to be placed after *mutah-hiruka* (I shall clear you of the charges). Then, where else can one place the word *tawaffi* if not where it sits already? Allah the Exalted has stated the events in the sequence that they transpired. How can one flip and re-arrange them in any other way? I ask why, after all, do you harbour such animosity towards the words of God Almighty to the extent that you wish to alter their order?

---

[1] *Aal-e-Imran*, 3:56

The Harm in Believing that Jesus[as] Is Still Alive

Does it please you more than anything else that the divinity of the Messiah[as] be established? After all, why do you not let this lifeless god of the Christians die? It is surprising to note that on the one hand, you claim that the Messiah is a mere mortal and a Prophet, while on the other hand, you desire to hold fast to such doctrines that deify him. This is like the example of two people: one says that such and such person has died, while the other says, no, he is not dead; but he does not have a pulse, his body is cold and he has stopped breathing.

O wise ones! Do reflect. What doubt can there be in the fact that someone who has no signs of life in them is dead? You say that the Messiah is not God, yet you believe that he is alive even to this day, and is untouched by the effects of time, and has remained unchanged and unaltered. You say that the Messiah[as] is not the Creator, yet you believe that he created a number of birds that flew in to join those created by God. You say that the Messiah[as] is not the knower of the unseen, yet you believe that he is aware of what the people eat and drink, and what they gather in their homes. It is shameful that you call yourselves Muslims and despite believing in a God who possesses every perfect attribute, you ascribe His attributes to a humble human being. Do you have no fear of God? It is these very beliefs that have given confidence to the Christians, with which they have misguided a large group from among the Muslims.

When will you realise? When your entire house is looted? You do not harbour enmity towards me, you only wrong your own souls. What have I said that is unusual? Have I asked you for anything? Why then do you hold animosity towards me? Is it because I say that there is only One Being Who is the Possesser of perfect attributes, Who is worthy of worship, and that you should not ascribe His attributes to any human being? Is it because I say that there is only one perfect man who has walked the face of the earth, whose name is Muhammad, the Messenger of Allah, peace and blessings of Allah be upon him? Is it because I say that you should not attribute ranks to the Messiah that are higher than those of Allah's Messenger, peace and blessings of Allah be upon him, because Jesus[as] does not possess the attributes that you ascribe to him? In God's name! Reflect! Remember that one day you must die and stand before God.

Three Stages of Righteousness

In short, my point was that it is necessary to consider the sequence that is present in the Holy Quran, and that the verse which I recited earlier has also kept sequence and order in view. The verse is as follows:

$$يُؤْمِنُوْنَ بِالْغَيْبِ وَيُقِيْمُوْنَ الصَّلٰوةَ وَمِمَّا رَزَقْنٰهُمْ يُنْفِقُوْنَ^1$$

They believe in the unseen and observe Prayer, and
spend out of what We have provided for them.

Bear in mind that righteousness is of three categories. The first category of righteousness is doctrinal in nature and is applicable when a person possesses belief. The second category is practical in nature as stated in: يُقِيْمُوْنَ الصَّلٰوةَ *(He establishes the Prayer).* Those Prayers of a person that are plagued by suspicions and evil suggestions do not stand erect, as it were. Allah the Exalted does not say *yaqra'una* (to recite or read), he uses the word *yuqimuna* (which means to erect or establish) and this implies that the Prayer must be observed in the manner that does it justice.

Hear me when I say that all things have an ultimate purpose. If this remains unfulfilled, the thing itself becomes useless. For example, an ox that is bought to plough the land will be deemed to fulfil its purpose when it does its task. However, if the aim and objective of the ox is limited to eating and drinking, it does not fulfil its ultimate purpose and ought to be slaughtered.

The Establishment of Prayer

In the same vein, the ultimate end or pinnacle alluded to in يُقِيْمُوْنَ الصَّلٰوةَ *(They establish the Prayer)* are the essential aspects or outcomes of Prayer. This refers to the state when a person begins to develop a relationship with Allah the Exalted and experiences visions and true dreams; they become detached from people and begin to develop a bond with God, to the extent that they ultimately meet God as a result of their complete devotion to Him alone.

The Arabic word *sala* means 'to burn'. Just as mincemeat is roasted on a fire, in the same way, a burning sensation must be felt in the Prayer. Until the heart burns, there can be no pleasure and delight in Prayer. As a matter of fact, this state is precisely what characterises Prayer in the true sense. One of the fundamental

---

[1] *al-Baqarah*, 2:4

aspects of Prayer is for it to be offered with all its conditions. Until Prayer is observed in this manner, it is no Prayer at all, and neither can that state be achieved which inclines a person to Prayer, as alluded to in the word *salat* (Prayer).

Remember that it is necessary in the Prayer for both physical state and verbal expression to unite. On certain occasions, expression is visual. At times, an illustration is shown which enables an observer to understand the message that is intended. Similarly, the Prayer depicts an illustration of God's will. In Prayer, just as the tongue recites certain words, so too the physical movements of one's body and limbs display a certain image.

When a person stands to praise and glorify God, this posture is known as *qiyam* or 'the standing position.' Now, everyone knows that the standing position is the physical state best suited for praise and glorification. After all, when eulogies are recited before kings, they are done so whilst standing. And so, in the Prayer, the apparent posture prescribed is the standing position, while the tongue is instructed to praise and glorify God in this state. The purpose in this is so that man stands before Allah the Exalted in the spiritual sense as well. Praise is expressed by standing firm on one point. A person who truthfully and sincerely praises someone, stands firm on one view. Therefore, an individual who says: اَلْحَمْدُ لِلهِ (*All praise belongs to Allah*) can only sincerely proclaim these words when they develop a firm belief in the fact that Allah Almighty is the Possessor of all forms of praise in totality. When a person accepts this fact with complete open-heartedness, this is known as *qiyam* or 'standing' in the spiritual sense, because the heart begins to 'stand' firm in this belief, as though it were upright, so to speak. Therefore, in the Prayer, a person stands demonstrating an apparent state, so that they may be blessed with the ability to 'stand' in the spiritual sense.

After this, a person says: سُبْحَانَ رَبِّيَ الْعَظِيْم (*Holy is my Lord the most Great*) in the bowing position. It is a matter of principle that when someone accepts the greatness of another, they bow in their presence. A person must bow in the face of greatness. Hence, with the tongue a person states: سُبْحَانَ رَبِّيَ الْعَظِيْم (*Holy is my Lord the most Great*) and through their outwardly state, they demonstrate this by bowing. This statement is expressed visually through the bowing position.

The third statement is: سُبْحَانَ رَبِّيَ الْأَعْلٰى (*Holy is my Lord the most High*). The word *a'la* (the most high) is in the grammatical form that expresses the superlative degree. This naturally calls for prostration. Therefore, along with these words, the image that one shows in practice is that of prostration. Hence, a person immediately assumes this form along with this verbal declaration.

These three verbal expressions correspond with three physical states or positions. This is an illustration or image that one displays before God Almighty. An individual performs all of these physical postures; the tongue which is a part of the body also makes expressions and participates in these movements.

There is a third thing as well, which if absent from the Prayer, leaves it incomplete. What is it? It is the heart. For the Prayer, it is necessary that the heart 'stands' as it were. Allah the Exalted must see that one's heart not only praises Him in the true sense and remains in a standing position, but that the soul also stands and praises God; not only the body alone, but that the soul also stands before God. When the heart proclaims: سُبْحَانَ رَبِّیَ الْعَظِیْم (*Holy is my Lord the most Great*) God must see that it not only proclaims His greatness, but also bows before Him, and He must also see that the soul has bowed with the heart as well. Then, in the third place, God must see that the heart has fallen in prostration and that the soul has also fallen at the divine threshold in view of the lofty grandeur of God. In short, until one is able to develop such a condition, one must not rest, for this is the true meaning of: یُقِیْمُوْنَ الصَّلٰوۃ (*They establish the Prayer*).

If the question arises as to how such a condition may be fostered, the simple answer is that one must remain persistent in observing the Prayer, and must not fret in the face of evil inspirations and doubts. In the beginning, a war ensues against doubts and suspicions, but the cure is that one must keep at it with an untiring perseverance and patience, and continue to offer supplications before God Almighty. Ultimately, the condition that I have just referred to is developed. This is a part of the practical aspect of righteousness.

The Spending of Provision

Another part of the practical aspect of righteousness is as follows:

$$مِمَّا رَزَقْنٰهُمْ یُنْفِقُوْنَ^1$$

That is to say, they spend out of what they have been given. Generally, people understand provision (*rizq*) to refer to food. This is incorrect. All that is given to one's faculties is also provision—whether it is knowledge, skill, insight and verities, etc. or apparent things like affluence and wealth.

Provision refers to authority as well, and sublime morals are also encompassed

---

[1] *al-Baqarah*, 2:4

by the term. In this verse, Allah the Exalted states that the righteous spend out of whatever they have been given by God. In other words, they give bread from their own bread, knowledge from their own knowledge, and morals from their own morals. Sharing knowledge is obvious, of course.

Avarice

Remember that a miser is not only one who does not share a portion of his wealth with those in need. In fact, even such a one who hesitates in teaching others from the knowledge that Allah the Exalted has bestowed upon them is a miser. To hide one's own knowledge and skill in view of the fact that if others learn, then our own worth will diminish, or our own profits will decrease, is equivalent to associating partners with Allah. For in such a case, the individual in question considers their knowledge and skill to be their provider and God. Similarly, a person who does not act with morality is also a miser. The giving of morals means to treat the rest of humanity with the exemplary morals that Allah the Exalted has granted an individual out of His sheer grace. As a result, the people will witness the individual's morals and strive to develop them within themselves as well.

The Definition of Morality

Morality does not only mean to speak gently or use soft words. Not at all. In fact, courage, generosity, forgiveness, all the abilities granted to man, are in actuality moral abilities. Their appropriate use is what makes them moral qualities. Even anger, when expressed at the appropriate occasion, possesses a spirit of morality. This is a view that is different from the teaching of the Gospel, which is one-sided and instructs a person to turn the other cheek when struck on the first. This is not morality, nor can such a teaching be based on the principles of wisdom. For if this were true, every army in the Christian world would have to be demobilised, and all of their weapons of war would have to be destroyed; the Christian world would have to live a life of servitude, because if someone were to ask them for their shirt, they would be obliged to give them their cloak as well. The teaching states that if someone forces a Christian to walk one mile, they ought to walk with them for two. In such circumstances, the Christians would be faced with momentous difficulties. If they were to act upon this teaching, they would not only be deprived of the necessities of life, but would have all their comfort stripped from them. For if someone were to demand their possessions, they would be left with nothing, and if a Christian sought to find work, they would be forced into labour without wages.

In short, this teaching is greatly emphasised, and the Christian clergy can be seen to preach it in the public, vigorously praising this teaching, but when a practical example is sought after, nothing can be found. It is as though all this is limited to words alone, and nothing is to be acted upon. This is why none of this can be referred to as morality. Morality means to employ all the faculties that Allah the Exalted has granted man in their appropriate place and time. For example, human beings have been granted wisdom. Now if someone who was unacquainted in a certain area needed counsel from someone who was experienced in the subject at hand, morality would demand that the latter offer their full assistance and sincere advice to the person in need through their own sound wisdom. People view these things lightly and say that they have nothing to lose; let the other person suffer. This is a satanic action. It is inhumane for an individual to see someone else being ruined and not be prepared to help them. No, in fact, one ought to listen to the other person with full attention and regard, and give them the necessary assistance that they need, according to one's own wisdom and understanding.

Someone may raise the allegation that here: مِمَّا رَزَقْنٰهُمْ (*They spend out of what We have provided for them*) has been stated, and the words *mimma* or 'a part out of what' express an air of avarice, and what ought to have been instructed is the following:

ہر چہ داری خرچ کن در راہِ اُو

Spend in his way, whatever you possess.

The fact of the matter is that this verse does not encourage avarice. The Holy Quran is the word of the All-Wise God. The meaning of wisdom is:

شے را بر محل داشتن

To place a thing at its appropriate place.

Hence, the words مِمَّا رَزَقْنٰهُمْ indicate that an individual ought to spend in a manner that is appropriate in view of time and place. In other words, where spending less is better suited, one ought to spend less, and where greater spending is needed, one spends to a greater degree.

Forgiveness

Now, forgiveness, for example, is a moral strength. In this context, one must see whether a certain person is deserving of forgiveness or not. There are two categories of offenders. The first kind is of those who happen to commit a deed that does rouse anger, but they are worthy of being forgiven. There are others, however, who if forgiven and turned a blind eye to, become further emboldened and cause further harm. Take the example of a servant who is immensely virtuous and obedient. Let us say this servant was bringing a cup of tea. The servant happens to stumble and the cup falls on the ground and breaks. As a result, the tea falls on his master as well. Now in this case, if the master stood up to strike the servant, and acted harshly and furiously towards him, this would be foolish. This is a time that calls for forgiveness because the servant has not been guilty of intentional mischief, and forgiveness will only make the servant more repentant and he will exercise greater caution in the future. However, if a wretched servant were to break things on a daily basis and damage things in this manner, mercy on such a person would demand that they are punished. Therefore, this is the wisdom in the following words:

$$\text{مِمَّا رَزَقْنٰهُمْ يُنْفِقُوْنَ}^{1}$$

And they spend out of what We have provided for them.

Every believer is responsible for judging their own soul and ought to determine the nature of various situations and circumstances, so that they can spend appropriately.

The Impractical Teaching of the Gospel

I have just stated that the teaching of the Holy Quran possesses a wise order within itself. In contrast to this, look at the teaching of the Gospel, which instructs a person to turn the other cheek when struck on the first, among other such things. This teaching is so objectionable that one cannot hide this fact, and its application in society is impossible. So much so that even the most gentle and holiest of priests cannot act upon this teaching. If someone were to seek a practical example of this teaching and slap a Christian priest on the face, instead of turning the other cheek, the priest would run to the police and hand over his offender to the

---

1   *al-Baqarah*, 2:4

authorities.

This clearly establishes that the Gospel is redundant, while the Holy Quran is being acted upon. A poor and needy old woman who has a piece of barley bread can share a portion of that piece and act upon the teaching of: مِمَّا رَزَقْنٰهُمْ *(they spend out of what We have provided for them)*. However, even the holiest of priests cannot act upon the teaching of turning the other cheek as taught by the Gospel.

بہ بیں تفاوتِ راہ از کجاست تا بہ کجا

Observe the distance that exists between these paths.

The Gospel is so deficient in this regard that what to talk of others, even the Messiah himself could not fully act upon its teachings. He demonstrated practically that the teaching which he gave himself, was nothing more than words. Otherwise, he ought to have handed himself over to his enemies even before he was arrested; what need was there to offer supplications and express such restlessness? If he had handed himself over, this would not only have proven that he practiced what he preached, but would also have demonstrated that he did actually come for no other purpose than to atone for the sins of man. For if the purpose of his life was none other than to commit suicide in order to give salvation to the world, and if—as the Christians say—there was no other way for God to grant salvation, Jesus[as] ought to have done what he was sent for; why did he bother to preach and teach? Why did he not say as soon as he came: 'Take me and hang me, so that the people may be delivered.'[1]

The Teaching of the Quran Perfects Human Faculties

In short, the teaching of the Holy Quran proves that Allah the Exalted is All-Wise and all things to the very last shred are in His knowledge; and He has given a teaching that perfects human faculties. You will find no better teaching than this, which instructs the proper and appropriate exercise of forgiveness and retribution. Anyone who presents a teaching that is contrary to this, as it were, seeks to overturn the law of God. Certain dispositions naturally require forgiveness, while others are worthy of being chastised. Any court of law can operate in accordance with the teaching of the Holy Quran. However, if the Gospel was used as a standard, everything would shut down immediately, and you would see the

---

[1] *Al-Hakam*, vol. 5, no. 13, dated 10 April 1901, pp. 1-4

results of following such a teaching. A human being simply cannot act upon the Gospel teaching. Hence, these are two examples of righteousness in the doctrinal and practical sense.

Belief in the Word of God

In addition to this, however, there is a third category of righteousness and it is described in the following verse:

$$يُؤْمِنُوْنَ بِمَآ اُنْزِلَ اِلَيْكَ^1$$

They believe in that which has been revealed to thee.

Human beings depend on the power of testimony. One must not follow a path that goes against authentic testimony. A path that is at odds with the testimonies of the truthful is a dangerous one. The path of righteousness is that which is vouched for by powerful testimony that is living and present in every age. For example, you ask someone directions and they tell you that a certain path leads in such and such direction. However, ten other people say otherwise and explain that this route leads in some other direction. Now, righteousness would demand that one accepts the word of these good-natured people.

Remember that only the testimony of the virtuous is acceptable and proper. The testimony of those who are immoral can never be accepted. This is the third category of righteousness that is alluded to in the following verse:

$$يُؤْمِنُوْنَ بِمَآ اُنْزِلَ اِلَيْكَ^2$$

They believe in that which has been revealed to thee.

By forsaking this principle as well, many people are ruined. Those people who have opposed me have done so for the very reason that they have abandoned this third category of righteousness.

The Death of Jesus[as]

The Word of God Almighty supports me with thirty verses. On one occasion, it supports me in the following words:

---

1. *al-Baqarah*, 2:5
2. *al-Baqarah*, 2:5

يَعِيْسَىٰٓ اِنِّىْ مُتَوَفِّيْكَ[1]

O Jesus, I will cause thee to die a natural death.

At another place, it speaks in my favour by stating:

فَلَمَّا تَوَفَّيْتَنِىْ[2]

But since Thou didst cause me to die.

Still, in another instance, it states:

مَا مُحَمَّدٌ اِلَّا رَسُوْلٌ قَدْ خَلَتْ مِنْ قَبْلِهِ الرُّسُلُ[3]

*And Muhammad is only a Messenger. Verily, all
Messengers have passed away before him.*

Hence, on various occasions, in different ways, the Word of God loudly proclaims that the path which I follow is the one that is true by the grace of God Almighty. It is on this path that the Messenger of Allah, peace and blessings of Allah be upon him, saw the Messiah[as] with John[as] on the night of the *Mi'raj*. And it is conclusively established that the Holy Prophet[sa] did not speak of any difference between the two, as would indicate that one was living and the other was dead. On a certain occasion, the Holy Prophet, peace and blessings of Allah be upon him, bore testimony to the death of Jesus[as] by speaking of his age. In another instance, he explained to us that Jesus[as] has died by describing the differing appearance of the Promised Messiah who was to come and the Messiah of the Israelites. These testimonies are from the Hadith and the Quran.

In addition to the above, the unanimous testimony of all the companions at the demise of the Holy Prophet, peace and blessings of Allah be upon him, was that all the Prophets had died. Hazrat Umar, may Allah be pleased with him, said that the Messenger of Allah, peace and blessings of Allah be upon him, had not yet died, and stood with an unsheathed sword. But then Hazrat Abu Bakr Siddiq, may Allah be pleased with him, stood to deliver an address and recited the following verse:

---

[1] *Aal-e-Imran*, 3:56
[2] *al-Ma'idah*, 5:118
[3] *Aal-e-Imran*, 3:145

مَامُحَمَّدٌاِلَّا رَسُوْلٌ قَدْ خَلَتْ مِنْ قَبْلِهِ الرُّسُلُ[1]

And Muhammad is only a Messenger. Verily, all
Messengers have passed away before him.

Now on this occasion—a doomsday so to speak—the Noble Prophet, peace and blessings of Allah be upon him, had passed away from this world and all the companions were present. The army of Usamah[ra] had not yet departed. Hazrat Abu Bakr[ra] loudly proclaimed in response to Hazrat Umar[ra] that Muhammad, peace and blessings of Allah be upon him, had died, and the argument that he presented in favour of this was:

مَامُحَمَّدٌاِلَّا رَسُوْلٌ

Muhammad is but a Messenger.

Now, if the companions even faintly believed or held that Jesus, peace be upon him, was alive, they would surely have spoken up, but all of them remained silent. As a matter of fact, the companions began to recite this verse in public and say: 'It is as though this verse was revealed today.'

The companions did not take to silence out of awe of Hazrat Abu Bakr, may Allah be pleased with him; they did not hold back from responding out of hypocrisy, God forbid. Not at all. The reality was as Hazrat Abu Bakr[ra] had stated and this is why all the companions bowed their heads. This was the consensus of the companions. After all, Hazrat Umar[ra] also suggested a similar thing when he said that the Messenger of Allah, peace and blessings of Allah be upon him, would return again. Now, if the argumentation of Hazrat Abu Bakr[ra] had not been perfectly sound—and it could only be as such if it bore no exceptions, for if Jesus[as] had ascended into the heaven alive and was to return, this would be a jest rather than an argument—in the least, Hazrat Umar[ra] would have refuted him.

Hazrat Abu Bakr[ra] and His Insight into the Holy Quran

Therefore, since there were no exceptions in the verse alluded to earlier and this was the true state of affairs, all of the companions unanimously accepted this point. The following verse of the Holy Quran was revealed upon the Messenger of Allah, peace and blessings of Allah be upon him:

---

[1]   *Aal-e-Imran*, 3:145

اَلۡیَوۡمَ اَکۡمَلۡتُ لَکُمۡ دِیۡنَکُمۡ وَاَتۡمَمۡتُ عَلَیۡکُمۡ نِعۡمَتِیۡ[1]

This day have I perfected your religion for you
and completed My favour upon you.

When he read out this verse, Hazrat Abu Bakr[ra] began to weep. Such was his insight into the Holy Quran. Someone asked: 'Why does this old man weep?' Hazrat Abu Bakr[ra] said: 'I can sense from this verse that the demise of the Prophet of God, peace and blessings of Allah be upon him, is imminent.' The Prophets of God are like officials. When a surveyor of land boundaries finishes their work at a certain place, they move on. In the same way, when the Prophets complete the task for which they are sent into the world, they take their leave. Therefore, when the announcement اَکۡمَلۡتُ لَکُمۡ دِیۡنَکُمۡ (*I have perfected your religion for you*) was heard, Hazrat Abu Bakr Siddiq, may Allah be pleased with him, understood that this is the final call. This evidently demonstrates that the insight of Hazrat Abu Bakr[ra] was immensely deep.

It is also narrated in a Hadith: 'Close all the gates that lead to the moque, but the window of Abu Bakr shall remain open.' The hidden message in this is that since the mosque is where divine secrets are manifested, the entrance that opens towards Abu Bakr Siddiq[ra] will not be closed. The Prophets make use of metaphors and symbols. An individual who, like a dull Muslim cleric, says that everything must be literal, is gravely mistaken. For example, Abraham, on whom be peace, telling his son to 'change the threshold of his gate' or the Holy Prophet, peace and blessings of Allah be upon him, seeing gold bangles etc. are all things that were not taken literally; they were metaphors and allegories, and encompassed a deeper reality.

In short, the point is that from all the companions, Hazrat Abu Bakr[ra] was blessed with the deepest understanding of the Quran. Now when Abu Bakr, may Allah be pleased with him, derived this argument from the verse mentioned earlier, it is my belief that even if his interpretation was apparently at odds with what we observe, righteousness and honesty would demand that we agree with Abu Bakr[ra]. But in this case, there is not a single word in the Holy Quran that opposes the interpretation of Hazrat Abu Bakr[ra].

Now the Muslim clergy ought to be asked: was Abu Bakr[ra] a wise man or not? Is this Abu Bakr[ra] not the same person who was given the title *Siddiq* (the Truth-

---

[1] *al-Ma'idah*, 5:4

ful). Is this not the same person who became the first Caliph of the Messenger of Allah, peace and blessings of Allah be upon him? Is he not the same man who rendered the magnificent service to Islam of stopping in its tracks the dangerous epidemic of apostasy? Alright, put everything else to one side. Just tell me this: what need was there for Abu Bakr[ra] to take a stand at the pulpit in the first place? Then, do tell me, keeping righteousness in consideration, when Hazrat Abu Bakr[ra] recited the verse: [1] مَا مُحَمَّدٌ اِلَّا رَسُوْلٌ قَدْ خَلَتْ مِنْ قَبْلِهِ الرُّسُلُ *(And Muhammad is only a Messenger. Verily, all Messengers have passed away before him)*, did he do so to present a perfectly sound argument or would he present such a flawed argument that even a child could say that anyone who believes that Jesus[as] was among the dead turns into a disbeliever?

Alas! In harbouring hostility and enmity towards me, my opponents have not only forsaken the Quran; in fact, their animosity towards me has taken them to the extent that they have practically, for all intents and purposes, issued a verdict of disbelief against the entire community of the companions and have looked down upon the argument derived by Hazrat Abu Bakr[ra] in this context.

The Consensus of the Companions on the Death of Jesus[as]

The whole of the Holy Quran is on our side. Thirty verses particularly testify to the death of the Messiah, on whom be peace. The night of the *Mi'raj,* the speech by Abu Bakr Siddiq[ra] and the consensus of the companions all testify to this fact. Those people who oppose us and say that I have gone against the consensus *(ijma)* are liars. The consensus is not in their favour at all. Firstly, 'consensus' can only be limited to the companions, and as I have just mentioned, the consensus of the companions of the Messenger of Allah, peace and blessings of Allah be upon him, was on the death of the Messiah[as]. Imam Ahmad ibn Hanbal[rh] states that any claim of a consensus after the companions is false, but notwithstanding this fact, there are many others who are against our opponents and support my point of view. The Mutazilites do not believe that the Messiah[as] was lifted into the heaven alive. The Sufis believe that the coming of the Messiah will be in the form of a spiritual manifestation *(buruz).* Then, it is narrated:

وَقَالَ مَالِكٌ مَاتَ

That is to say, Imam Malik[rh] believes in the death of Jesus[as]. Furthermore, Ibni

---

[1] *Aal-e-Imran, 3:145*

Hazm also holds the same belief. Therefore, the Malikis, Ibni Hazm's followers and the Mutazilites stand with us on this issue. However, even stepping down a degree, if I were to accept that no one supports me in this view, I would say that the era following the first three centuries of Islam was given the name *fayj-e-a'waj*, i.e. a crooked group, by the Messenger of Allah, peace and blessings of Allah be upon him. In respect of these people, the Holy Prophet[sa] says:

$$لَيْسُوْا مِنِّىْ وَلَسْتُ مِنْهُمْ$$

They are not from among me, nor am I from among them.

What do these people have left in their hands?[1] Therefore, it is we who are the heirs of the companions, and it is established that we are the inheritors of the deeper essence of the Quran and Hadith. Now, what remains is that the word *nazil* or 'one who will descend' has been used for the Messiah. However, let it be known that the word *nuzul* has a very wide connotation; a traveller is referred to as a *nazeel* as well.

The Concept of Spiritual Manifestation

In addition to this, the actual fact of the matter that ought to be remembered is that in light of the knowledge that the Messenger of Allah, peace and blessings of Allah be upon him, was granted of the latter days, he foretold of the appearance of two spiritual manifestations. The saints believe that there are only two kinds of being, and I believe the same. This is what we derive from the Holy Quran as well. The esteemed Sufis believe that the nature, disposition and morals of people who have passed away reappear in the persons of other human beings. In the terminology of the Sufis, it is said that such and such person is an appearance of Adam or an appearance of Noah, and some of them use the term *buruz* (which means the spiritual manifestation of a person). They believe that there is a spiritual manifestation for all eras, just as Seth, on whom be peace, was the spiritual manifestation of Abel *(Habil)*—the first of all spiritual manifestations. *Habal* means 'to mourn'. God conferred this spiritual manifestation upon Seth. Then this system continued until the spiritual person of Abraham, on whom be peace, was manifested in the Holy Prophet, peace and blessings of Allah be upon him. This is the wisdom in the following words:

---

[1]   *Al-Hakam*, vol. 5, no. 14, dated 17 April 1901, pp. 1-2

عَلَىٰ مِلَّةِ اِبْرَاهِيمَ حَنِيْفًا

Upon the way of Abraham, who was ever inclined to God.

This is the underlying secret here—Abraham[as] reappeared in the home of Abdullah after some two or two and a half thousand years. In short, the concept of *buruz* or spiritual manifestation is an accepted concept in the context of advents.

Two Trials of the Latter Days

Now, the Holy Prophet, peace and blessings of Allah be upon him, had foretold in relation to the latter days that two trials would exist in this era. One would be internal and the other external. The internal disorder would be that the Muslims would not be following true guidance, and would be weighed down by Satanic influences. They would transgress the limits of Allah due to their being indulged in gambling, fornication, alcohol and diverse forms of sin and vice, and they will have no concern for the prohibitions set by God Almighty. They will abandon the Prayer and fasting, and the commandments of God will be seen with contempt; the people will mock and ridicule the injunctions of the Quran.

The external disorder would be that the sacred personage of the Holy Prophet, peace and blessings of Allah be upon him, would be slandered and attempts would be made to dishonour and destroy Islam through hurtful attacks of every kind. All sorts of schemes and strategies would be employed to prove the divinity of the Messiah and to move people to believe in this curse of the cross.

In short, when the Holy Prophet, peace and blessings of Allah be upon him, was informed of these two forms of disorder—internal and external—he was also given the glad-tiding that a man from his community would be raised. That man would expose the reality of this external disorder and of the religion of the cross; he would break the cross, and it is in this connection that he would be the Messiah son of Mary. Moreover, he would dispel internal dissension and misguidance, and would set people on the true path of guidance, and it is in this connection that he would be referred to as the Mahdi. It is this glad-tiding to which the following verse alludes:

وَّاٰخَرِيْنَ مِنْهُمْ [1]

And among others from among them.

---

[1]   *al-Jumu'ah*, 62:4

Both of these disorders will be prevalent in that era, and their foundation will rest on two evil things. One group will be referred to as *ad-Dajjal* (the Antichrist) and the other *Yajooj* (Gog).

The Antichrist

The Antichrist is referred to as *ad-Dajjal*. In Arabic, *dajlun* refers to a thing that is artificial from inside but seemingly pure on the exterior. Copper that is gilded with gold from the outside is an example. This form of deception has existed in the world since the beginning of time. No era has been free from such fraud and deceit. What do we observe of goldsmiths? Just as there is deception in worldly matters, so too there is deception in spiritual affairs as well. It is deception that is alluded to in the following verse:

$$ يُحَرِّفُوْنَ الْكَلِمَ عَنْ مَّوَاضِعِهٖ ^1 $$

They pervert words from their proper places.

The Holy Quran states:

$$ يٰعِيْسٰٓى اِنِّىْ مُتَوَفِّيْكَ ^2 $$

O Jesus, I will cause thee to die a natural death.

Those who misrepresent this verse are also guilty of deception. However, the deception of the latter days was destined to be grave in nature. As though an ocean of deception would surge forth. The definite article *'al'* in *ad-Dajjal* conveys a meaning of absolute totality. Hence, *ad-Dajjal* (i.e. the Antichrist) was destined to be a manifestation of diverse forms of deception. In other words, previously there were individual forms of fraud, schemes, misguidance and disbelief. In a certain time the wicked said one thing, while others said something else. Various allegations were levelled against Islam individually, but they were to a limit. However, Allah the Exalted knew that a time was approaching when an ocean of allegations would flow forth. Just as smaller rivulets and tributaries join to make an ocean, in the same manner, all these smaller forms of deceit would join to make one great surge of deception.

Therefore, just observe in this era how deception is so greatly prevalent. Criticism and allegations are raised against Islam on all fronts. The Christians have

---

1   *an-Nisa*, 4:47

2   *Aal-e-Imran*, 3:56

crossed all bounds. I have gathered the allegations that the Christians have lev-elled against the Messenger of Allah, peace and blessings of Allah be upon him, and they have reached three thousand in number. Moreover, the books, periodi-cals and announcements that these people publish every other day in the form of objections against the Messenger of Allah, peace and blessings of Allah be upon him, have reached sixty million. In other words, they can hand one book to each and every Muslim in India. Therefore, the greatest disorder in this era is this trial of the Christians, and is a manifestation of *ad-Dajjal* (i.e. the Antichrist).

Gog and Magog

In the same manner, Gog is referred to as *Yajooj* in Arabic. The word *Yajooj* is derived from *ajeej*. This alludes to the fact that this party will have a very close relationship with work that relates to fire; they will be experts in wielding fire, as though fire will be in their control. Others will fail to contend with them in the use of fire. This fact is evidently clear. One can observe the connection that this nation has with fire. There are countless machines in operation and day after day; these people are advancing in the use of fire. These are two manifestations. Both of these individual characters have come together in one; and *Ma'jooj* (Magog) is implied here as well. It is an incontestable fact that:

$$اَلنَّاسُ عَلٰى دِيْنِ مُلُوْكِهِمْ$$

The people follow the way of their kings.

Human beings are heavily influenced by their kings. Kings are far greater in status; indeed, even insignificant village heads command influence. In the time of the Sikh reign, many people began to keep a *kesh* (long hair) and wear a *kachera* (traditional shorts). There was a man who lived in a nearby village whose name was Khuda Bakhsh. He changed his name to Khuda Singh.

In the village of Dalla there were two brothers named Gulab Shah and Mahtab Shah. They would only recite the Garanth. It is a known fact that the views of kings along with their religion, including their manner of dress etc. and all other values, whether moral or religious, bear a significant influence on the citizens. This is in the same way that the male influences the female. This is why Allah the Exalted states:

اَلرِّجَالُ قَوَّامُوۡنَ عَلَى النِّسَآءِ[1]

Men are guardians over women.

In the same way, the influence that kings have on their subjects is unavoidable. In the Sikh reign, they would wear turbans and this custom has continued even today within various states. When people would meet one another, everyone would say: 'This person is a Sikh'.

Similarly, even in this period of rule, the Empire has had an influence on its subjects. Observe the people's manner of dress alone. Everyone feels a sense of pride in wearing British-styled clothing—a coat and trousers. There are some who even wear British-styled hats. The government does not encourage this in any way, nor are official orders given that people must wear this clothing, and yet there is an ever-increasing interest that naturally grows within the people.

Despite the large number of people who do not see this change of dressing style in a positive light and who strive in their own way to stop this growing trend, nothing can be done—this is an ocean that just continues to flow forth and cannot be stopped. Along with western education, the dressing style of the English is also on the rise. This is to such an extent that even when people visit the barber, they prefer the style and fashion that is prevalent among the British. Why is this the case? Only because:

اَلنَّاسُ عَلٰى دِيۡنِ مُلُوۡكِهِمۡ

The people follow the way of their kings.

Do not think that dressing style is the only change that is on the rise. Nay, this manner in itself is a dangerous shift that will encourage many other trends as well.

After English clothing is adopted, the character of English gatherings will also flourish, and this is happening even now. Christianity has not forbidden alcohol, and segregation of men and women is deemed unnecessary; gambling is also not prohibited, and then there is no distinction between foods that are permissible or impermissible. Hence, the inevitable consequence of this freedom is that people have begun to overstep the bounds within which true religion seeks to keep human beings. Alcohol is intrinsic to English-style gatherings. A gathering without alcohol is looked upon with contempt, as it were. Hence, how can those who are fond of British style and fashion ever accept to remain within the limits of reli-

---

[1] *an-Nisa*, 4:35

gion? How will such people develop an inclination towards those who call them to religion?

I am correct when I say that people have not contemplated as to why Christianity continues to plant itself into the people without anyone noticing. I have reflected on this matter deeply. I have found that everything at this time pushes people towards Christianity—especially when the Christian clergy have left no stone unturned in spreading their faith. They have employed every means for the propagation of their religion, irrespective of whether it is lawful or not. It is due to the effects of British fashion that now alcohol is consumed openly. There is nothing to restrain one from committing fornication; in fact, factors that encourage and support this act continue to multiply. Though gambling is forbidden under the law, ways have been devised which for all intents and purposes bring it within the bounds of the law. Then, Christian women walk about unveiled and generally mix with unrelated men. This has caused such dangerous outcomes that many men enjoy walking in public with their wives unveiled. They raise objections against the Muslims and assert that men and women have equal rights, so women should not be made to take the veil, arguing that this is cruel.

The Islamic Veil

To raise allegations against the Islamic concept of the veil is foolish on the part of these people. Allah the Exalted has not given any such instructions in relation to the veil that are objectionable. The Quran instructs Muslim men and women to lower their gaze. When both men and women do not cast glances at one another, both will remain protected. The Quran is not like the Gospel, which commands a person to not look with lust. It is regretful that the writer of the Gospel was unable to realise that a 'lustful glance' means nothing. It is the glance itself which arouses lustful thoughts in a person. The outcome of this teaching is not hidden to those who read the newspapers; they are probably aware of the utterly shameful displays that are reported to take place in London's parks and Parisian hotels.

The Islamic veil does not at all mean that women be imprisoned as though they were locked in jail. The purport of the Holy Quran is that women cover themselves and refrain from gazing at men that are beyond the permissible bounds. Women are not barred from leaving the house to tend to their societal needs. They are welcome to go out and about, but must control their gaze.

Islam has made no distinction between men and women in acts of virtue, nor have they been prohibited from being like men in goodness. Where does Islam state that women should be bound in chains? Islam cuts at the root of lust. Just look at what is happening in Europe. We are told that people fornicate like they were dogs and alcohol is so widespread that if liquor stores were put in a line they would extend for three miles. What teaching has lead to this result? Is this on account of the veil or due to removing the veil?

It is unjust to misrepresent Islam and raise objections blindly. Islam has come to teach the world righteousness. I was mentioning that the people follow the way of their kings and I have demonstrated this through various examples. Now you can observe that the terrible state of affairs that exists in this country cannot be seen in any other land, not even in Mecca or Medina. The freedom and non-conformity to religious law that is prevalent here has no parallel in any other country. Since such stimulating factors have not arisen in those places, the views of people in other countries have not deteriorated as much either.

Two Manifestations of Evil—The Antichrist and Gog and Magog

Now I return to my actual subject. I have stated that there are two manifestations: firstly, the Antichrist *(ad-Dajjal)* and secondly, Gog and Magog *(Yajooj Majooj)*. The Antichrist, therefore, is manifested by what we observe as a constant phenomenon spanning from Adam, peace be upon him, to the present time. All the various forms of evil and mischief that have emerged in various eras have now come together in this age and a wondrous spectacle of God's power has been displayed. As humans reach their end, God Almighty has shown manifestations of evil and goodness.

The manifestation of evil is what I have described as the Antichrist. The Antichrist is the sum total of all evil schemes and mischief. In these, the latter days, a group of people have been given such wisdom in worldly matters that previously, all that was hidden has now come to light. This group has shown two forms of deception. In one respect, it has attacked the very institution of prophethood, and in another aspect, it has attacked God. The attack on prophethood is characterised by their distorting the commandments of God. Then, they have progressed to the highest levels in their mental abilities and have attacked God by taking His divinity into their own hands. For example, they have shown great interest in curing chronic diseases; with instruments they are able to take a person's sperm and impregnate a womb; they are even inventing machines that will cause rainfall, and so on and so forth. All of these things demonstrate that these people seek to take the work of God into their own hands. This group of people seek to become God, while another group deifies a human being. What is the underlying purpose in developments that are taking place in Europe? It is nothing other than to exploit the free nature and greed that has arisen in society so that the secrets of divine providence may be uncovered and people can free themselves from God. Hence, these people engage in experiments to give life, revive the dead and induce rainfall. But this is not all, they are in fact striving to take control over everything that happens on earth.

Although I accept that making appropriate provisions is not forbidden, it should also be remembered that sin is always caused by taking an extreme—either in excess or insufficiency. For example, if you were to place your hand on someone, this would not be a sin, but if you punched them, this would be a sin and an excessive extreme. An extreme on the side of insufficiency would be if, for example, someone needed a glass of water, but they were given a mere drop.

In this era, therefore, the Antichrist is a mixture of various elements. On the one side, an attack is being waged against God and in another respect, against the institution of prophethood; one group deifies a human being, while another party seeks to become God themselves. Is this not true? Look at various books and read the newspapers, and you will come to know how great a disorder has erupted and how this hypocrisy is inflicting cruelty upon the world.

In relation to the disorder of Gog and Magog, I have already mentioned that its effects influence the heart, and this disorder is dominant at present. It is becoming more and more difficult to turn to God, and show honesty and integrity, and to refrain from alcohol, fornication, lustful glances and gambling. There are very few—perhaps one out of a thousand—who stay away from such evils.

Two Manifestations of Goodness

Now, it is obvious that when there were destined to be two manifestations of evil, in the same way, it was necessary for there to be two manifestations of goodness that would stand against this evil. Therefore, by God's will there were two manifestations of goodness. In actuality, this too is one entity that is referred to by two names, just as one person can hold the position of a magistrate and a clerk at the same time. These two manifestations of goodness relate to two aspects: internal issues and external issues. The Mahdi has a relation with internal issues and the

Messiah son of Mary is associated with external issues.

The Messiah Son of Mary

What is the task of the Messiah in the 'external sense', on account of which he has been given this name? The task of the Messiah son of Mary would be to repel evil, and the task of the Mahdi would be to restore virtue. As such, reflect on the fact that it has been narrated that the tasks of the Messiah are that يَقْتُلُ الْخِنْزِيرَ *(he would kill the swine)* and يَكْسُرُ الصَّلِيبَ *(he would break the cross)*. This is the repelling of evil. However, I do not believe that the Messiah would set out with swords and spears for this purpose.

Those scholars who assert that the Messiah would wage war are mistaken; in fact, they are wrong completely. What sort of reformation is this that as soon as the Messiah appears, he should take up the sword and enter the field of battle for war? This cannot happen. The truth and reality is what has been disclosed to me, and which accords with the Hadith, and it is that the Messiah will wage no bloody wars, nor is his task to pick up the sword and fight. In fact, the Messiah will come for the purpose of reformation. Of course, I do believe that he will come to repel evil, but he shall do so with proofs and arguments.

The Mahdi

The task of the Mahdi is to restore virtue. That is to say, although innovations in the faith, sin and vice would have become rampant, he would replace this with guidance. The word *Isa* (Jesus) is derived from *aws*, which alludes to the repelling of evil. The secret in both these manifestations is that the spiritual manifestation known as the Mahdi is superlative, because his task is to propagate virtue, which is a more superior quality than the mere repelling of evil. For example, a person who removes a thorn from someone's path does a great deed no doubt, but an individual who gives that someone a ride to their house and feeds them as well, does an even greater deed than the first. Therefore, the Mahdi is superior in rank. This is why he is the vicegerent of Allah. This is the secret in Jesus son of Mary swearing the oath of allegiance at the hand of the Mahdi, who is the vicegerent of Allah. Moreover, the manifestation known as the Mahdi is also superior because he is actually a spiritual manifestation of the Messenger of Allah, peace and blessings of Allah be upon him, who was the Seal of the Prophets, and the most

Perfect of all the Prophets; this is why the spiritual manifestation of the Holy Prophet[sa] was bound to be superior.

These were the two spiritual manifestations that were destined to appear. How unjust are these scholars who have accepted that one of these manifestations—that is the Mahdi—would be a reflection of the Messenger of Allah, peace and blessings of Allah be upon him, in his morals and would come in his name, but suggest that Jesus son of Mary would physically descend from the heaven. It is truly astonishing that the minds of people have degenerated to such an extent that they make contradictory statements, yet fail to realise this fact. On the one hand, they believe in a spiritual manifestation of the Messenger of Allah, peace and blessings of Allah be upon him, and hold that his representative would be the vicegerent of Allah. Yet it is strange indeed for them to assert that he who is lower in rank would return himself, physically. These people believe that the Mahdi, who would come to spread virtue and was greater in rank, would appear in the form of a spiritual manifestation, but claim that the Messiah son of Mary would return himself in bodily form to swear allegiance to this Mahdi.

یہ بیں تفاوت راہ از کجاست تا بہ کجا

Observe the distance that exists between these paths.

The Meaning of 'Leaders from Among the Quraish'

When such people are asked why they believe that a Prophet would descend to take the oath of allegiance at the hand of the Mahdi, they respond by saying: 'What can be done? It is narrated in the Hadith: اَلْاَئِمَّةُ مِنْ قُرَيْشٍ (*The leaders are from among the Quraish*).' I say in response that if the meaning of this Hadith is as these people suggest, then all the people of the Ottoman empire ought to have rebelled.

If this Hadith was not in the form of a prophecy—as is my view—why do the same Muslims then refer to the Ottoman sultan as the Caliph of the Muslims? The fact of the matter is that the Prophet of God, peace and blessings of Allah be upon him, was shown in the form of a vision that Caliphs would be from among the Quraish, either in the apparent sense or in the metaphoric sense as manifestations. Earlier, I alluded to the manifestation of the Antichrist. In the same manner, the Mughal kings etc. are also manifestations of the Quraish. For they bore the responsibility that was given to them, and for as long as God willed, they continued to rule. Until an individual understands this concept of *buruz*, i.e. manifestations in the metaphoric sense, the reality of this prophecy cannot be understood and ultimately one will have to reject this prophecy.

When the actual Quraish lost their ability and another people become more worthy, God gave the responsibility of leadership to them. This is precisely the reason that people have followed the Ottoman empire and have accepted its rule with sincere love, not out of pretext or hypocrisy; and their hearts have given the verdict that the Ottomans are the custodians of the two holy cities of Mecca and Medina. There have always been examples of such metaphoric concepts, and there shall be in the future as well. This is the meaning of ٱلْأَئِمَّةُ مِنْ قُرَيْشٍ *(The leaders are from among the Quraish).*

Therefore, both these appellations belong to one man. One title referred to his rank as a restorer of virtue and the other alluded to his duty of repelling evil. Since the cultivation of goodness is greater than simply repelling evil, this is the reason that the Mahdi has been given a great status and was conferred the title 'Vicegerent of Allah'. Therefore, just as there were two manifestations of evil, there were in contrast to them the two manifestations of virtue just mentioned.

Now, I would like to state one more point in this regard and then I shall bring my discussions to a close. The name *Isa* (Jesus) possesses the meaning of repelling evil. The name Ahmad[sa] or Muhammad[sa] alludes in one sense or the other to the giving of goodness. The meaning of Muhammad is 'one who is praised abundantly' (and Ahmad means 'one who praises abundantly'). When a person is beneficent, those who are in receipt of the person's favour will naturally praise them. The giving of praise is intrinsically tied to the receipt of favour. The Holy Prophet[sa] was named Muhammad because he showered favour upon mankind at large. Ahmad is the 'one who praises' and Muhammad is the 'receiver of praise'; the word Isa (Jesus) means 'one who is saved' and this connotes the repelling of evil. This is why God has reminded us of the incident mentioned in the following verse:

$$اِذْ قَالَ رَبُّكَ لِلْمَلٰٓئِكَةِ اِنِّى جَاعِلٌ فِى الْاَرْضِ خَلِيْفَةً ۭ[1]$$

And when thy Lord said to the angels: 'I am about to place a vicegerent in the earth.'

---

[1] *al-Baqarah,* 2:31

There is a prophecy in the incident mentioned in this verse. Now, I do not wish to prolong the discussion any further. I conclude by stating that the titles 'Mahdi' and 'Messiah' are two designations for the same individual, and they shed light on the two capacities of one man—namely his duty to repel evil and propagate goodness. It is a shame that while the scholars accept in the spiritual sense the manifestation that will come to propagate goodness, they reject the manifestation of the one whose task it was to repel evil."[1]

Emphasis on Returning to the Centre Repeatedly

In December of 1899 very few people came to attend the Annual Convention (in Qadian). His Holiness, the Promised Messiah, on whom be peace, expressed deep regret and said: "At present, people are ignorant of our objectives and are unaware of what I would like to see them become. The objective that I seek and the purpose for which God Almighty has raised me cannot be fulfilled until people come here again and again, and do not tire in the least from travelling here."

Then, the Promised Messiah[as] said: "Anyone who believes that it is burdensome for them to come here, or who thinks that their staying here will burden me, should fear, for they are guilty of associating partners with Allah. I believe that even if the entire world was to become my household, it is God Almighty who would see to my affairs. I am not burdened in the least. The presence of my friends gives me immense pleasure. Such an idea is an evil thought that must be thrown away from the heart. I have heard people say: 'Why should we sit here and burden his Holiness? We are useless; why sit here and break bread for nothing?' Such people must remember that these are satanic thoughts which Satan plants in their hearts so that they may be turned away from here."

One day, Hakeem Fazl Din Sahib[ra] submitted: "Your holiness, what do I do sitting here idle? If you instruct, I shall return to Bhera. There, at least I can teach the Holy Quran. Here, I feel a sense of extreme embarrassment, because I am of no use to you, and perhaps I may be guilty of sin, sitting here idle." The Promised Messiah[as] said: "Your sitting here is a Jihad and your 'uselessness' is a great task."

In short, the Promised Messiah[as] expressed his displeasure at those who did not attend with words full of immense anguish and regret. He said: "These people who make excuses are of the same ilk as those who made excuses before his Holiness, the Chief of the World, peace and blessings of Allah be upon him saying:

---

[1]   *Al-Hakam*, vol. 5, no. 15, dated 24 April 1901, pp. 1-5

اِنَّ بُيُوْتَنَا عَوْرَةٌ¹ (*Our houses are exposed and defenceless*). God Almighty, however, refuted these people in the following words: ²اِنْ يُّرِيْدُوْنَ اِلَّا فِرَارًا (*They only seek to flee away*)."

The Promised Messiah[as] said: "Who has told our friends that life is long? No one knows when death will come crashing down on them. It is appropriate, therefore, to consider the time that one is given to be a blessing."

The Promised Messiah[as] said: "These days will not come again and all of this will be nothing more than stories."

Control Over the Inner Self

The Promised Messiah[as] said: "I possess such control over myself and God Almighty has made my soul so true a Muslim that if someone were to sit before me and went on uttering—for an entire year—the most filthy and obscene profanities that one could imagine, ultimately, they would be embarrassed themselves and would have no choice but to concede that they were unable to weaken my patience."

The Promised Messiah[as] was never frightened by the pains inflicted upon him by others or by their mischief. In this respect, he said: "No event takes place on earth before it is first determined in heaven. Nothing can transpire without the will of God Almighty, and God never disgraces or ruins His servant."

The State of the Promised Messiah[as] in a Time of Trial

In Jalandhar, the Promised Messiah[as] said: "At a time of trial, it is the weak-hearted from among my community for whom I worry. My state of affairs is that even if I were to hear a clear voice saying: 'You are forsaken and not a single one of your desires will be fulfilled,' I swear by God's Being that there would be no decrease in my passion and love for God or in my service to the Faith, because I have already seen God."

Then, the Promised Messiah[as] recited the following verse:

³هَلْ تَعْلَمُ لَهُ سَمِيًّا

Dost thou know any equal of His?

---

1. *al-Ahzab*, 33:14
2. *al-Ahzab*, 33:14
3. *Maryam*, 19:66

Forgiveness and Pardon

The Promised Messiah[as] gave some mail to his servant Hamid Ali[ra] to take to the post office. Hamid Ali[ra] misplaced this post. After a week's time, when the post was found laying in a heap of refuse and waste, the Promised Messiah[as] called Hamid Ali[ra], showed him the post and in a most gentle manner said: "Hamid Ali, you have become quite forgetful. You should do your work carefully."

A Dishonour to the Faith

The Promised Messiah[as] could not bear to see the sacred things of Allah dishonoured. In this relation, once the Promised Messiah[as] said: "It would be easier for me to see my property destroyed and my children cut to pieces before my eyes, than to see the Faith dishonoured and seen with contempt, and then for me to do nothing."

The Concealing of Virtue

On hearing the views of certain friends in relation to various expenses, the Promised Messiah[as] said: "Allah the Exalted knows well that I possess such tolerance as far as food is concerned that I can very easily eat twice a day on one paisa alone. Once, I was intrigued at heart to see the extent to which a human being can bear hunger. To test this, I ate nothing for six months—I would have a morsel or two every now and then. After six months, I estimated that I could extend this state of affairs to even six years. During this time, I continuously received my meals from home twice a day but I desired to keep this state of mine a secret. The difficulty that I bore in order to keep this secret was a burden that perhaps others could not bear due to hunger; I would distribute those two meals to two or three people in need. In this state, I would offer my five daily prayers in the mosque and none of the people who knew me could tell by any signs that I was eating nothing."

Appropriate Faculties

The Promised Messiah[as] states: "Whenever God Almighty has raised a person for a certain task, He has granted them with the appropriate faculties in order to prepare them and make available to them the necessary ingredients that enable the fulfilment of the goal or task at hand. Those people who do not truly possess the necessary qualities inherently by nature and then indulge in religious exercises, ultimately turn mad and lose their senses."

The Nature of the Descent of Revelation

In continuing the aforementioned discussion, the Promised Messiah[as] said: "Physicians associate certain natural factors with sleep. However, I observe that when it is the will of God Almighty to speak with me, at such a time, though I am in a state of complete wakefulness, God suddenly induces in me a state of drowsiness and light slumber, and pulls me out of this physical realm completely, so that I am able to relate to the spiritual realm. Then, after God has finished speaking, He returns my physical consciousness and senses so that I, as the recipient of revelation, may preserve it. Then, He casts a state of drowsiness over me again, whereafter He awakens me once again, so that I am able to memorise the revelation. In this manner, therefore, on certain occasions, this will happen even fifty times. This is the power of God. He is above and beyond the phenomenon of sleep as we observe in nature, and physicians and doctors cannot understand its deeper essence."

Restlessness for A Beggar

One day, when the Promised Messiah[as] was entering his home after offering the Prayer, a beggar asked to be given something, but due to the large number of people present at the time, his voice could not be heard clearly. The Promised Messiah[as] returned after entering his house and ran his servants here and there to call the beggar, but he could not be found. In the evening, the person returned again. When he made his request again, the Promised Messiah[as] took something out of his pocket and gave it to him. After a few days, on a certain occasion, the Promised Messiah[as] said: "The other day when that beggar could not be found, there was such a burden on my heart that I felt extreme unease. I was fearful that I had committed a sin by not paying attention to the beggar and by going into my home too soon. I am thankful to Allah the Exalted that he returned in the evening. If not, God knows how perturbed I would have been. I had also prayed to Allah Almighty so that He would bring the person back to me."[1]

---

[1] From a letter of Maulana Abdul-Karim Sahib[ra] recorded in *Al-Hakam*, vol. 4, no. 3, dated 24 January 1900, pp. 6-11

No Prescription is Definitive

1899—The Promised Messiah[as] said: "In our household, Mirza Sahib (referring to his revered father, the late Mirza Ghulam Murtaza Sahib) practiced medicine for fifty years. He was well-renowned in the art of medicine, but he would say that there was no such thing as infallible cure. In reality, he was right, because without the permission of Allah Almighty, not a single particle that enters a human being can have any efficacy at all."

Good Conduct Towards the Authorities and Relatives

An individual asked the Promised Messiah[as] about how one should act towards the authorities and relatives. The Promised Messiah[as] said: "Show good conduct towards everyone. It is an obligation upon every Muslim to obey and be loyal to the authorities. They protect us and have given us complete religious freedom. I deem it a betrayal if someone does not show sincere-hearted obedience and loyalty to the government.

A person owes rights to their relatives as well. One ought to treat them in a goodly manner also; however, one must remain apart from them in such matters as are against the pleasure of Allah Almighty. Our principle is that one should do good to everyone and show beneficence to all of God's creation."

Prayer and Divine Decree

The Promised Messiah[as] states: "When the grace of Allah Almighty draws near, He furnishes the means that are necessary for the acceptance of prayer. The heart develops a fervour, passion and emotion. However, when a prayer is not meant to be accepted, the heart is unable to feel contentment and inclination. No matter the extent that a person forces their disposition, one is unable to develop focus in prayer. The reason for this is because on certain occasions, God Almighty desires for us to submit to His decree, whilst on other occasions, He accepts our prayers. Therefore, until I perceive signs of God's permission, I have little expectation of a prayer being accepted. I become content with the decree of God and feel even more joy than that which is experienced on the acceptance of prayer, because the fruits and blessings that are received in being content with the will of God are far greater."

Pride in One's Ancestry Deprives One from Virtue

The Promised Messiah[as] states: "Allah the Exalted has no liking for the outer shell; it is spirituality and the essence that finds acceptance with Him. This is why God Almighty states:

$$لَنْ يَّنَالَ اللهَ لُحُوْمُهَا وَ لَا دِمَآؤُهَا وَلٰكِنْ يَّنَالُهُ التَّقْوٰى مِنْكُمْ ۚ^1$$

Their flesh reaches not Allah, nor does their blood, but
it is your righteousness that reaches Him.

In another instance, God Almighty states:

$$اِنَّمَا يَتَقَبَّلُ اللهُ مِنَ الْمُتَّقِيْنَ ^2$$

Allah accepts only from the righteous.

In actuality, this is a very delicate matter. Here, even if someone is the child of a Prophet, this is of no benefit. The Holy Prophet, peace and blessings of Allah be upon him, said a similar thing to Fatimah, may Allah be pleased with her. The Holy Quran also clearly states:

$$اِنَّ اَكْرَمَكُمْ عِنْدَ اللهِ اَتْقٰكُمْ ^3$$

Verily, the most honourable among you, in the sight of
Allah, is he who is the most righteous among you.

The Jews too are the progeny of Prophets. Did hundreds of Prophets not appear among the Jews? But what benefit did being the children of Prophets bring to them? If their deeds were good, why would they personify the following verse:

$$ضُرِبَتْ عَلَيْهِمُ الذِّلَّةُ وَالْمَسْكَنَةُ ^4$$

They were smitten with abasement and destitution.

God Almighty desires a pure transformation. On certain occasions, even pride in one's ancestry deprives one from acts of virtue and a person will surmise that they shall receive salvation due to their lineage alone, which is an utterly absurd notion. Kabir says: 'It is good that I was born in the home of the lower caste. O Kabir! It is good that we are among the lowly, for we greet everyone equally.'

---

1   *al-Hajj*, 22:38
2   *al-Ma'idah*, 5:28
3   *al-Hujurat*, 49:14
4   *al-Baqarah*, 2:62

God Almighty loves loyalty and sincerity, and desires good deeds. He cannot be pleased with boasting and bragging."

The Meaning of *Rafa*

The Promised Messiah[as] said: "The Holy Quran has come to remove dissension. If our opponents interpret the words رَافِعُكَ اِلَّ (*will exalt thee to Myself*) to mean that the Messiah ascended into heaven with his physical body, they ought to tell us: was this the matter the Jews denied? Did the Jews say that the Messiah had not ascended into the heaven? What the Jews alleged was that the Messiah was not exalted to Allah (i.e. that he was not the beloved of God). If the words رَافِعُكَ اِلَّ (*will exalt thee to Myself*) are not a refutation of this allegation, then our opponents ought to respond to this allegation of the Jews and show us where God Almighty has refuted them."

Residing in the Centre Must Be for a Religious Purpose

On one occasion, a friend submitted to the Promised Messiah[as] that they would like to come to Qadian for the purpose of business. On this, the Promised Messiah[as] said: "This very intention is corrupt. You should repent. One ought to come here for the sake of religion and should reside here with the intention of reforming their life to come. This should be the intention, and then, if along with this, a person engages in business as well to attain the objectives of their residing here, there is no harm. The actual intention must be religious and not worldly in nature. Are other cities not more well-suited to do business? The actual purpose in coming to Qadian should be nothing other than religious. After that, whatever you receive, consider it to be the grace of God."

Sympathy for Humanity

The Promised Messiah[as] states: "My state of affairs is that whilst engaged in Prayer if someone is in pain and their cry reaches my ears, I feel moved to go to their aid and give them sympathy insofar as possible, even if I am compelled to break my Prayer. It is against the principles of morality to not stand by a brother who is in pain and distress. If you can do nothing else, at least pray for them. What to talk of our own, I even say that you ought to show the same example of morality and sympathy to Hindus and others. One must not possess a thoughtless nature.

On one occasion, I was going out for a walk. A man named Abdul-Karim, who was a village registrar of lands, was also with me. He was somewhat ahead of me and I was walking at some distance behind. On the way, a frail, old lady of about seventy or seventy-five years of age met us. She gave a letter to Abdul-Karim and asked him to read it to her, but he scolded her and moved her away. This broke my heart. Then, the old lady gave me the letter. I took the letter and stopped. Then, I read the letter to her and explained its contents to her in detail. At this, Abdul-Karim was deeply ashamed, because he had to wait anyway, and was deprived of spiritual reward as well."

A Vision About the Future of the Community

The Promised Messiah[as] states: "It was disclosed to me by way of a true vision that kings too would enter this community. I was even shown these kings. They were mounted on horseback. Further, Allah the Exalted also stated: 'I shall bless you to such an extent that kings shall seek blessings from your garments.'

After a period in time, Allah the Exalted shall bring such people into the fold of our community, and with them, a multitude of people shall join us."[1]

1899

The Company of the Righteous

The Promised Messiah[as] states: "It is mentioned in the Holy Quran:

$$\text{قَدْ اَفْلَحَ مَنْ زَكّٰهَا}^2$$

Meaning, one who purifies their soul has found salvation. To purify one's soul, seek the company of the righteous, or fostering a relationship with those who are pious and virtuous is very beneficial. One ought to shun ignoble morals such as falsehood and the like, and seek guidance from one who already treads this path. One ought to correct their errors along the way. Just as one cannot improve their writing without identifying one's mistakes, so too morals cannot be rectified until one identifies their errors. Man is the sort of creature that remains on the right path only if he is purified continuously as he goes along, otherwise he will deviate."[3]

---

1 *Al-Hakam*, vol. 8, nos. 25-26, dated 31 July and 10 August 1904, p. 13
2 *ash-Shams*, 91:10-11
3 *Badr*, vol. 10, nos. 44-45, dated 5 October 1911, p. 9

1899

Fear of God

The Promised Messiah[as] said: "At night, when silence pervades in all directions, and I am alone, even then, my heart feels a constant sense of fear as I remember God, because He is Self-Sufficient."

Humility

The Promised Messiah[as] said: "When a person attains success, and a state of helplessness and difficulty no longer exists, a person who shows humility at such a time and remembers God is supreme.

چوں بدولت برسی مست نگردی مردی

*If you do not lose your senses even after finding
wealth, only then are you a true man."*

True Dreams Are a Proof of the Existence of God

Mufti Muhammad Sadiq Sahib[ra] alluded to a dream that he saw the previous night, which was fulfilled in the morning. At this, the Promised Messiah[as] said: "Allah the Exalted discloses things even before they exist and come into being. Why do atheists not reflect over this point?"

A Revelation

The Promised Messiah[as] said: "I received a revelation that the time has come for the prayers of the Governor General to be accepted." Then the Promised Messiah[as] said: "'Governor General' refers to a spiritual rank."[1]

6 January 1900

To Consort in Kindness

In the context of consorting with wives in kindness, the Promised Messiah[as] said: "With the exception of indecency, you ought to bear with patience all the other improprieties and discourteous behaviour of your wives."

---

[1]   *Badr*, vol. 10, nos. 46-47, dated 12 October 1911, p. 2

Then, the Promised Messiah[as] said: "I find it utterly shameful for a man to be in a state of conflict with a woman. God has made us men, and in reality, this is a completion of His favour upon us. The gratitude that we owe for this is to treat women with kindness and tenderness."

On a certain occasion, the harsh nature and foul tongue of a certain friend was mentioned to the Promised Messiah[as] and a complaint was made to him that the individual in question treats his wife in a harsh manner. His holiness was deeply grieved and said: "Our friends must not be as such." The Promised Messiah[as] continued to discuss how men should live lovingly with their wives. In the end he stated: "As for me, I once raised my voice to my wife. At the time I felt that this louder-than-normal voice of mine was mixed with sentiments of grief. Even though I had said no hurtful or harsh words, I later sought forgiveness from God continuously for a very long time. I offered voluntary Prayers with great humility and lowliness, and gave alms as well; for I felt that the sternness I had shown to my wife was due to some unconscious weakness in my obedience to God Almighty."

Forgiveness and Pardon

There is a certain incident that took place when Mahmud[1] was four years of age or so. His holiness was inside writing away as was his custom. He had placed his written copies aside. Miyan Mahmud had a matchstick and came with a crowd of children. Initially the children played and fought with each other as children do. Then, they did whatever their hearts desired and set these written drafts on fire, whereafter they began clapping in amusement. The Promised Messiah[as] was busy writing and did not raise his head to see what was happening. During this time, the fire died down and these valuable drafts were turned into a pile of ash. After this, the children began doing something else of interest. His holiness felt the need to consult his previously written pages to link the context of a certain passage. He asked one of them, but there was silence, then he asked another, but he too was afraid of being scolded. Finally, one child spoke up and said: "Miyan Sahib has burned the papers." The women, children and other members of the household were in shock and anxiously looked on to see what would happen now. The Promised Messiah[as] smiled and said: "Wonderful. In this must be great wisdom of Allah the Exalted. Now God Almighty desires to disclose upon me an

---

[1]   Hazrat Mirza Bashir-ud-Din Mahmud Ahmad, the Promised Reformer, may Allah be pleased with him.

even better exposition."

Similarly, on one occasion, Hazrat Maulvi Nur-ud-Din Sahib[ra] misplaced a treatise of the Promised Messiah[as] and in searching for this, he was worried immensely. When the Promised Messiah[as] was informed of this, he came and instead it was he who sought pardon from Maulvi Sahib for the anxiousness that he had felt for losing the papers. Then, the Promised Messiah[as] said: "I regret that you underwent such struggle and toil in search of these papers. It is my belief that Allah the Exalted will bestow upon me something better."

Forbearance

It so happened that on one occasion, the Promised Messiah[as] was experiencing a severe headache. The women and children around him were making noise and commotion nearby. Maulvi Abdul-Karim Sahib[ra] submitted: "Your holiness, this noise does not cause you pain, does it?" The Promised Messiah[as] said: "Yes, it gives me relief when they quiet down." Maulvi Sahib said: "Why does his holiness not instruct them then?" The Promised Messiah[as] responded: "You tell them in a gentle manner; I cannot."

Covering the Faults of Others

A maid was caught stealing rice from the home of the Promised Messiah[as]. All the people in the home began rebuking her. Coincidentally, the Promised Messiah[as] passed by while this was going on. When he was told what had happened, he said: "She is in need. Give her some rice and do not embarrass her. Follow God Almighty in the way that He covers up the faults of His servants."

Serving Humanity

One day, some village women came to the Promised Messiah[as] to obtain some medication for their children. The Promised Messiah[as] remained busy in attending to them and giving them medicine. Maulvi Abdul-Karim Sahib[ra] submitted: "Your holiness, this is a great inconvenience to you, and much of your valuable time is wasted." The Promised Messiah[as] said: "This too is religious work. These are people in need. There is no hospital nearby. It is for the sake of these people that I order and store all sorts of allopathic and Graeco-Arab medication, which proves beneficial when the time comes. This is a task that brings great spiritual reward. A believer must never show indolence and unconcern for such work."

Physically Reprimanding Children is to Associate Partners with God

On one occasion, a certain friend physically reprimanded his child. The Promised Messiah[as] was deeply affected by this and called the individual and delivered a heart-rending address. The Promised Messiah[as] said: "In my view, to strike a child in this manner is equivalent to associating partners with God. For the ill-natured perpetrator who hits a child arrogates themselves to a position of granting guidance, a position only held by God, and seeks to partake of God's station of providence. When an incensed man punishes someone for something, he will continue to grow in anger until he takes on the form of an enemy, and in proportion to the actual offence, he will overstep in punishment by miles. A person who is patient and does not lose the reins of self-control, and who is fully tolerant, forbearing, calm and composed, does have the right to punish or reprimand a child on an appropriate occasion. However, a short-tempered, intolerant and unreasonable person is not suitable at all for the training of children. Alas! If only parents would spend as much effort in prayer as they do in seeking to punish their children, and if only they made it a constant practice to supplicate for them with a burning heart. Indeed, the prayers of parents for their children are blessed with special acceptance."

A Few Prayers of the Promised Messiah[as]

The Promised Messiah[as] said: "I have made it compulsory upon myself to make certain prayers on a daily basis. Firstly, I pray for my own soul that the Merciful Lord may use me for such work by which His honour and glory is manifested, and may He enable me to act in a manner that fully pleases Him. Secondly, I pray for the members of my household that may Allah the Exalted grant me the delight of my eyes through them and that they may tread the path of His pleasure. Thirdly, I pray for my children that they may all become servants of the Faith. Fourthly, I then pray for my sincere friends by name. Then, fifthly, I pray for all those who are a part of this community, whether I know them personally or not."

The Upbringing of Children

The Promised Messiah[as] said: "It is unlawful for such a person to take the seat of a spiritual guide and leader,[1] who is negligent of his followers for even a moment."

The Promised Messiah[as] said: "Guidance and upbringing, in essence, is in the hands of God. Nagging incessantly and persisting on a matter beyond reasonable bounds, i.e. to prohibit and rebuke children on every little thing, demonstrates that we are, as if, the masters of guidance, and will be able to bring our children on the path that accords with our own will. This is a hidden form of associating partners with God. My community ought to refrain from such a practice."

The Promised Messiah[as] categorically said, and also gave instructions in writing, that any teacher in our school who has the habit of hitting children and does not refrain from this inappropriate action should be dismissed immediately.

The Promised Messiah[as] said: "I pray for my children, and see to it that they follow broad principles, etiquette and teachings; this is all, nothing more. Then, I place my entire trust in Allah the Exalted. The seed of goodness that is present in each of them, according to their nature, will flourish when the time comes."

To Refrain from Affectation

When the time came to build houses to meet the needs of guests, the Promised Messiah[as] emphasised again and again that it was useless to spend money on bricks and stone. Do what is sufficient to accommodate someone for a brief period. The carpenter was cleaning wooden panels and boards with a planer but the Promised Messiah[as] stopped him and said: "This is nothing but affectation. It is an unnecessary delay of time. Do what is necessary."

The Promised Messiah[as] said: "Allah the Exalted knows that I have no love for any property. I consider my properties to be the shared possession of my friends, and I desire greatly that we all come together and spend some time with one another." The Promised Messiah[as] said: "It would please me if there were a place where my friends occupied houses on all four sides and my house was situated in the middle, with an entrance leading to every home that surrounded my own, so that I could remain in constant contact and interaction with each and every one of them."

The Value of Time

His Holiness disliked wasting time in unnecessary formalities. In regards to this,

---

[1]   *Al-Hakam*, vol. 4, no. 2, dated 17 January 1900, pp. 1-11, Letter No. 6 of Maulana Abdul-Karim Sahib[ra]

the Promised Messiah[as] said: "My state is that I even feel regret when answering the call of nature, for all the time that is wasted. This time too could be better spent in some religious work." The Promised Messiah[as] also said: "When an important task of a religious nature arises, I deem food and drink, and sleep to be forbidden on me, until I have completed the task at hand." The Promised Messiah[as] further stated: "I am devoted to the cause of religion, in fact, I live for the sake of religion. Therefore, all I desire is that nothing obstructs my way in the path of religion."

Serving Others

On one occasion, there was a traditional indian-style bedstead *(charpoy)* in the new house on which Maulvi Abdul-Karim Sahib[ra] was sleeping. The Promised Messiah[as] was strolling there as well. After some time, when he awoke, the Promised Messiah[as] was lying down below the level of the *charpoy* on the ground. Maulvi Sahib stood up out of respect. The Promised Messiah[as] lovingly asked: "Why have you stood up?" Maulvi Sahib expressed that he had done so out of respect. On this, the Promised Messiah[as] said: "I was standing on guard for you. The boys would make noise and I would stop them so that your sleep would not be disturbed."

Humility

People enjoyed immense freedom in speaking to His Holiness and anyone could engage in a conversation with him without any hindrance whatsoever. In this relation, the Promised Messiah[as] states: "It is not my practice to sit in a fierce and frightful manner so that people should fear me as they are terrified of a carnivorous beast. I extremely detest the idea of sitting like an idol. I have come to abolish idol worship, not so that I should become an idol myself and people worship me. Allah the Exalted knows well that I do not give myself preference over others even in the slightest. In my opinion, there is no worse an idol-worshipper and no one more wicked than an arrogant person. An arrogant person does not worship any God at all; in fact, he only worships himself."

A Liking for Seclusion

His Holiness very much liked seclusion. In this regard, the Promised Messiah[as] states: "If God Almighty gave me a choice and asked whether I prefer seclusion or publicity, I swear by the Holy Being of God that I would choose seclusion. It was God Himself who pulled me out into the public sphere. Who can know more than God the pleasure that I attain in seclusion? I remained in solitude for almost twenty-five years, and never once, even for a moment, did I desire to be placed on a seat in the court of fame. I am naturally averse to sitting amongst a group of people, but I am bound by the Master's command." The Promised Messiah[as] also stated: "When I sit in public or go for a walk, and engage in discussions with others, I do all of this out of obedience to the command of Allah Almighty."

Only Servants of the Faith Are Truly Deserving of Our Prayers

If anyone took up the pen to support the cause of Allah or made any other effort for this purpose, the Promised Messiah[as] would look at this in high regard. In this relation, the Promised Messiah[as] said: "If an individual gives us even a single word in support of the Faith, I find it to be more valuable than a pouch of pearls and gold coins. A person who desires that I should love them, and that my humble and fervent prayers reach the heaven in their favour, must assure me that they are able to serve the Faith."

The Promised Messiah[as] has said on oath many times: "I love everything for the sake of God Almighty, whether it is my wife, my children, or my friends. My relationship with everyone is for the sake of Allah Almighty."

Consideration for the Vow of Friendship

The Promised Messiah[as] states: "It is my belief that any individual who makes a vow of friendship with me even once, I have such regard for this vow, that irrespective of their nature and no matter what they become, I cannot sever my ties with them. If the individual cuts off their ties with me themselves, in that case I am helpless. Otherwise, my belief is that if one of my friends had collapsed in the market after consuming alcohol and there was a crowd of people around him, I would pick him up and take him away without fear of reproach by any critic." The Promised Messiah[as] also said: "The bond of friendship is a most valuable gem. One must not waste it away easily. No matter how unpleasant a friend may be to you, one ought to forgive and forget."

10 January 1900

The Engagement of the Promised Messiah[as] During Ramadan

Seth Abdur-Rahman Sahib[ra] of Madras sought permission from the Promised Messiah[as] to return to Madras for some important work. He had also received a telegram to return. The Promised Messiah[as] said: "It is absolutely imperative for you to remain here during this blessed month." The Promised Messiah[as] also said: "I am ready to make such a prayer in your favour that would even move mountains." Then, he said: "During these days, I sit with my friends less than usual and remain in solitude for longer. This is truly to the benefit of my friends. I pray in seclusion with time and freedom, and spend a better part of the night in prayers."[1]

2 February 1900

Islam—a Pure Religion

On the occasion of Eid-ul-Fitr, the Promised Messiah[as] arranged for a gathering to take place to pray specifically for the success of the British in the Transvaal War, and to inform the Muslims about the rights they owe to the British government and about their obligations as citizens. In his Eid Sermon, the Promised Messiah[as] delivered the detailed discourse that follows. His Holiness said: "Muslims ought to be extremely thankful to God, Who has granted them a religion that is pure—both in theory and practice—of every form of corruption, abomination and defect.

It Is God Almighty Who Is Truly Worthy of Praise

If a person reflects closely and deeply, they will find that truly, it is Allah Almighty alone to whom all praise and quality belongs, and no human being or any other creation, in the true sense, is really worthy of praise and admiration. If an individual observes, pure of any vested motives, it shall become clearly evident to them that any individual who is declared worthy of praise can only be deserving if at some point in time, when nothing of existence or matter was to be found, they created those things. Another reason could be that in an era when nothing existed and when there was no knowledge of the means and elements that are required to bring a thing into existence, preserve it, safeguard its health and

---

[1]   *Al-Hakam*, vol. 4, no. 3, dated 24 January 1900, pp. 1-6

maintain its life, someone furnished all these necessary means. Or perhaps at a time, when this creation could have been prey to a multitude of afflictions, someone had mercy on it and protected it. Further still, someone could be worthy of praise if, for example, they saved from being wasted the effort of one who works and bestows the rights in full of those who labour. Although, apparently, fulfilling the rights of a labourer is nothing more than just recompense, such a person can be deemed a benefactor who also fulfils the rights of others in full. These are the noble attributes which make someone deserving of praise and admiration. Now if you are to reflect on this, you will see that in the truest sense, all of these praiseworthy qualities are due to Allah the Exalted alone, Who is the Possessor of these attributes to the highest level of perfection. No one else truly possesses these qualities.

Firstly, observe God's attribute of creation and providence. One could think that these attributes are to be found in mothers, fathers and other benefactors as well. However, if an individual reflects more deeply, they will come to know that a mother, father and other benefactors have certain aims and motives that move them to show favour. The proof of this, for example, is that if a healthy, beautiful and energetic baby is born, parents express joy, and if the baby is a boy, their joy is even greater; they rejoice and celebrate. However, if a girl is born, the home becomes a place of mourning as it were, and the day of the baby's birth becomes a day of sorrow; parents feel that they cannot even show their faces in shame. Often, certain foolish people will even kill their daughters through various contrivances or they will show less care in their upbringing. Then, if the child is born crippled, blind, or with some other disability, parents wish that the child would die, and on many occasions, unsurprisingly, they will even kill them with their own hands, considering the child to be a burden. I have read that the Greeks would intentionally kill such children; in fact, it was a royal mandate that any baby who was born handicapped, disabled or blind, etc., be put to death immediately. This manifestly demonstrates that although humans do possess the nature to care and support, their thoughts are adulterated with personal and selfish motives. However, Allah the Exalted has no selfish motive whatsoever in giving life to and nurturing His vast creation (which is so innumerable as is beyond one's ability to fathom, and difficult for the tongue to articulate, and which fills the heaven and earth). Unlike parents, God does not desire service and provision in return; in fact, He has given life to His creation due to the demands inherent in divine providence. Any person would accept that to plant a seed, water it, look after it and protect it until it grows into a fruitful tree, is an act of great benevolence. Hence, if one contemplates the nature of man, his state and the manner in which he was supported and maintained, you will see how great a favour God Almighty has done, by supporting man through countless transformations and changing stages of helplessness.

The second aspect that I have just alluded to relates to the full availability of such means as are necessary for human coexistence and the use of human faculties even before our coming into being. You can observe that even before we were born, God created the means necessary to support us. If the brilliant sun that is raised above us—owing to which there is light far and wide, and the day shines forth—did not exist, would we be able to see? How else would we reap the benefits and advantages that we are able to gain through light? If the sun and moon, and other forms of light did not exist, the faculty of sight would be futile. Although the eyes possess an ability to see, they are completely useless without outer and external light. So how great a favour is it that, in order to make use of our faculties, God has furnished the necessary means in advance, and how great a mercy is it that He has granted us such faculties and then vested them with inherent capacities that are absolutely imperative for the perfection of man and in reaching the ultimate objective? The qualities that have been vested in the brain, muscles and veins are put to use by man and he can perfect them. For at the same time, God Almighty has also created the means that perfect man's faculties. This is the state of the internal system whereby each and every faculty is geared to the objective and interest that results in man's prosperity. Even in the external respect, there is an established system whereby each and every individual who is skilled in an art has, at their disposal from the very beginning, the raw materials and tools that are required for their craft. For example, if there were no leather and thread, from where would a cobbler produce these things and how could he perfect his craft? Similarly, if there was no cloth, how would a tailor sew anything? This is the case with every human being. A physician, irrespective of how skilled and knowledgeable he may be, can do nothing if medicines were not available. He would write a prescription after extensive thought and reflection, but if the medicine was nowhere to be found in the shops, what would he do? What a great bounty it is that on the one hand, God has given us knowledge, and on the other hand, He created plants, minerals and other living organisms that are helpful to those suffering from illness, and has vested these creations with diverse properties and qualities that come to use in every era when unexpected needs arise.

Therefore, nothing that God Almighty has created is without benefit or useless—even ticks and lice are not without their benefit. It is written that if someone is unable to pass urine, on certain occasions, the insertion of lice into the urethra, can induce urination. Is it within anyone's power to even fathom the extent to which human beings benefit from these things?

Then, fourthly, there is the recompense of efforts. This too requires the grace of Allah. For example, just observe how much effort and toil man undertakes in agriculture. If it were not for the help of God Almighty, how could a farmer return home with harvested grain? It is by the grace and bounty of God that everything takes place at its appropriate time. As such, the people might well-nigh have perished in the recent dry season, but God sent down rain by His grace and saved a large part of His creation. Therefore, first and foremost, it is God Almighty Who intrinsically, more than anyone else, is supremely deserving of praise. In comparison to Him, no other being possesses any such inherent right.

Three Rights Mentioned in Surah An-Nas

If any other being does have a right to be praised, it is only through God's good graces. This too is a mercy of God Almighty that despite His being One and without Partner, as a gift, He has allowed certain others to be a part of His own praiseworthy qualities. As Allah the Exalted states:

قُلْ اَعُوْذُ بِرَبِّ النَّاسِ مَلِكِ النَّاسِ اِلٰهِ النَّاسِ مِنْ شَرِّ الْوَسْوَاسِ الْخَنَّاسِ الَّذِیْ یُوَسْوِسُ فِیْ صُدُوْرِ النَّاسِ مِنَ الْجِنَّةِ وَ النَّاسِ [1]

Say, 'I seek refuge in the Lord of mankind, the King of mankind, the God of mankind, from the evil of the sneaking whisperer, who whispers into the hearts of men, from among the Jinn and mankind.'

In this blessed chapter, along with that Being who is truly worthy of praise, Allah Almighty has also hinted at those who are worthy of praise in the partial sense. This is so that higher moral qualities may be perfected. As such, three kinds of rights have been alluded to in this chapter."

The Promised Messiah[as] said: "Seek refuge with Allah, who encompasses every

---

perfect quality, and Who is the Lord and King of mankind, the One Who is truly worthy of worship and sought by all. This chapter is such that although it retains the true essence of God's Oneness, along with this, it also indicates that one must not fail to fulfil the rights of other human beings either, who are a reflection, as it were, of these titles.

Two Manifestations of Divine Providence—
Parents and a Spiritual Guide

The Arabic word for 'Lord,' which is *rabb,* indicates that although it is God in reality who cares, nurtures and brings a thing to completion, in the partial sense, by way of reflection, there are two other beings as well who are manifestations of God's providence *(rububiyyat)*—one physically and the other spiritually. In the physical sense there are parents, and in the spiritual sense, a spiritual mentor and guide. In another instance, Allah the Exalted states in greater detail the following:

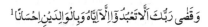

*Thy Lord has commanded, "Worship none but
Him, and show kindness to parents."*

Meaning, God desires that you worship no one else and treat your parents with kindness. Truly, what a remarkable sort of providence it is that when a human being is a child and has no power whatsoever, a mother renders invaluable service, and during this time, just observe how a father supports the efforts of the mother. It is merely out of His grace that God Almighty has created two agents to support His weak creation and has made them to reflect the light of His own love. However, it ought to be remembered that the love of parents is partial, while the love of God is true in essence. Until hearts are inspired by Allah the Exalted, no human being, not even a friend, neither equal nor a ruler, can love anyone; and it is a mystery of God's boundless providence that a mother and father love their children to such an extent that they will happily bear all sorts of pain to care for them. So much so that parents will not even hesitate in laying down their own lives to save their children. Hence, in order to perfect the higher morals of man, in the words *rabb-in-nas* (the Lord of Mankind), God Almighty has alluded to parents and spiritual guides, so that thankfulness for the system that is apparently

---

[1] *Bani Isra'il,* 17:24

observed in the figurative sense may lead a person to show gratitude to the True Lord and Guide. This is the key that unlocks the secret as to why this blessed chapter begins with *rabb-in-nas* (the Lord of Mankind), and not *ila-hin-nas* (the God of Mankind). Since a spiritual guide undertakes the spiritual upbringing of people in accordance with the will of God Almighty, and through the ability and guidance given by Him, a spiritual guide is also implied in these words.

The second part is *malik-in-nas* (the King of Mankind), i.e. seek refuge with God Who is your King. This is another hint that seeks to enlighten human beings about the principles of civil order, and that they themselves may become civilised. In essence, it is Allah Almighty Who is the true King, but this indicates that by way of reflection, there are kings on earth as well. It is for this reason that these words also imply that one must watch over the rights that are due to the ruler of the time. On this instance, no distinction is made between a king who is a disbeliever, idolator or a believer in God's Oneness; in fact, the statement is general— the king may be of any faith. Religion and belief are separate matters. In the Holy Quran, wherever God has alluded to a benefactor, He has made no stipulation of Muslim or monotheist, or of belonging to a certain order. As a matter of fact, God speaks of a benefactor in general terms without mentioning any religion. As Allah the Exalted states:

$$\text{هَلْ جَزَآءُ الْإِحْسَانِ إِلَّا الْإِحْسَانُ}^{1}$$

Meaning, can the recompense of goodness be anything other than goodness?

The Sikh Reign Was a Burning Furnace

Now I tell my community and all those who are listening to me clearly and openly that the British Empire is our benefactor. For it has done great favours upon us. Those who are sixty or seventy years of age would know well that we were once subjected to the rule of the Sikhs. The afflictions that plagued the Muslims at that time are not hidden. Even recalling them makes the body tremble and the heart begins to palpitate. At the time, Muslims were barred from observing their worship and religious obligations, which are more dear to them than their very lives. It was forbidden to loudly make the call to Prayer, which is a prelude to the Prayer. If ever by some mistake, the muezzin loudly called out the words *Allahu Akbar* (Allah is the Greatest), he would be killed. Similarly, there was needless

---

1   *ar-Rahman*, 25:61

interference in issues relating to what was lawful and unlawful for the Muslims. There was a case relating to a cow, where on one instance, 5,000 poor Muslims were executed. There is an incident that took place in Batala. There was a Syed who lived there. When he stepped out of his home, there was a herd of cows. He slightly moved one of the cows away with the tip of his sword and one of the cows sustained a minor scratch on its skin. The poor man was apprehended and pressure was exerted to kill him. Finally, after many requests, they settled on having his hand cut off. But now, observe the level of freedom that every people and religion enjoys. I shall speak of the Muslims alone. In fulfilling our religious obligations and forms of worship, the government has afforded complete freedom, and there is no hostility towards anyone, either in terms of their wealth, life or honour. This is in contrast to that perilous time, when everyone—no matter how clear their record—feared for their own life and wealth. Now if a person ruins their own behaviour themselves, and becomes worthy of punishment due to their own deformity and offence, then this is another matter. Also, if due to one's own misbelief or heedlessness a person is neglectful in worship, this is a separate issue. However, the government has granted complete freedom in every respect. At this time, a person can become as devoted a worshipper as they desire, for there is no hindrance whatsoever. Even the government itself guards the sanctity of religious places of worship and spends thousands of rupees to repair them etc. In the Sikh reign, the state of affairs, in contrast, was such that mosques were turned into places where *bhang*[1] was prepared and horses were stabled. Such examples are present even in Qadian and even in other major cities throughout the Punjab. To this day, there are many mosques that are still in the possession of the Sikhs. On the contrary, at present, the British government reveres these holy sites in every way by giving them the due honour they deserve, and deems it from among its obligations to show respect to these religious buildings, just as His Excellency, the Right Honourable Viceroy, Lord Curzon, recently demonstrated by his own practical example when on his recent visit, he voiced disapproval on entering the central mosque in Delhi with his shoes. He set a high moral example befitting of royalty that is worthy of being followed. It is also clearly evident from his speeches, which he has delivered from time to time on various occasions, that he holds places of religious significance in high regard. Then, you can see how the government has made no announcement banning the call to Prayer in a loud voice nor

---

[1]   An intoxicating drink made in India with milk and ground cannabis leaves. [Publisher]

does it forbid Muslims from fasting. In fact, the government has made available all forms of nourishment which were nowhere to be found in the awful reign of the Sikhs. They have made available things like ice, soda water, biscuits, bread, etc., and all other food items, and have provided to us every form of comfort. This is an indirect form of support that they have given to our Islamic practices. Now if someone does not fast themselves, this is another matter. It is regrettable that Muslims themselves dishonour the shariah. Therefore, observe that those who have fasted during these days have not become any thinner, and those who have taken this month lightly also have not put on any weight. Time has passed for both the former and the latter all the same. These were winter fasts. All that was required was a change in eating schedule. Instead of eating at seven or eight o'clock, everyone would eat at four or five o'clock in the morning. Despite such convenience, there were plenty who failed to honour the holy rites prescribed by God, and who looked at this revered guest of God Almighty—the month of Ramadan—with great contempt. The coming of Ramadan in these months of ease was a kind of touchstone as it were, and these fasts served as a measure to distinguish between the obedient and the sinner. God Almighty had granted ease, the government had given every kind of freedom, diverse fruits and other foods were available, there is no means of comfort and convenience that cannot be made available in this age. Then despite all this, what is the reason for the lack of concern prevalent in this respect? The reason is that hearts have lost faith in God. It is unfortunate that people do not even afford God the same regard that is given to a lowly sweeper. In a way, people think that they will never meet God, they will never be presented before Him and will never be made to stand in His court. Alas! If only the disbelievers would ponder and reflect over the proofs of the existence of God Almighty, which shine more brilliantly than the light of millions of suns. It is regrettable that on seeing a shoe it is accepted to a level of certainty that it has a maker. How unfortunate then is it that on observing the countless creations of God Almighty, people do not believe in Him, or if they do, their faith amounts to nothing. The favours of God Almighty upon us are countless and one of them is that He pulled us out from a burning furnace. The Sikh reign was like a flaming furnace and the arrival of the British heralded the dawn of mercy and blessing.

I have heard that when the British first arrived here, a muezzin made the call to Prayer loudly in Hoshiarpur. Since these were the early days of British rule, the Hindus and Sikhs thought that the British would also maintain a ban on the Muslim call to Prayer being made loudly, or like them, would cut off the hand of someone who injured a cow. Anyway, this muezzin who had loudly made the call to Prayer was apprehended. A large mob formed and the man was brought before the Deputy Commissioner. Distinguished chiefs and notables gathered and said: 'Sir, our food has become polluted and our utensils have been defiled.' When the Englishman heard these things, he was greatly astonished as to how a call to Prayer could be so potent as to contaminate food items. He told the head clerk to not move this case forward without a proper investigation. Hence, he instructed the muezzin to make the call to Prayer again, but the muezzin was fearful of committing a second offence. However, when he was assured, he sounded the call to prayer with the same vigour as before. The esteemed officer said: 'I, for one, have not been harmed in any way by this call to Prayer.' He asked the head clerk: 'Have you been harmed in any way?' 'Truly,' said the head clerk, 'I have not been harmed either.' In the end, the muezzin was released and he was told: 'You are free to make the call to Prayer as you wish.' Indeed! Allah is the greatest! What a shining example of freedom! What a grand favour of God Almighty! Now, after such goodness and favour any heart that still does not appreciate the kindness of this, the British government, is an ungrateful, treacherous heart that ought to be cut out of a person's chest and thrown away.

Religious Freedom

Even in my very own village where our mosque is situated, there used to be an area occupied by government officials. This was during my childhood days, but I have heard from credible sources that when the British assumed rule, for some days the old laws prevailed. A certain official was in the area and he was accompanied by a Muslim soldier who came to the mosque and told the muezzin to make the call to Prayer. The muezzin made the call for prayer in the same murmuring voice as he was accustomed, to which the soldier said: 'Is this how you make the call to Prayer?' 'Yes,' said the muezzin. 'No', the soldier responded, 'climb onto the roof of the mosque and make the call to Prayer in a loud voice; and do so in the loudest possible voice.' The muezzin was apprehensive, but then he finally made the call to Prayer in a resonating voice. All the Hindus got together and took hold of the *mullah*. The poor man was petrified and was worried that the officer would hang him. The soldier reassured him saying: 'I am with you.' Ultimately, the cruel, brutal Brahmans apprehended him, whereafter they took him to the official and said: 'Your honour! This man has corrupted us.' The official, of course, knew that rule had shifted and that the Sikh regime was no longer in power, yet he still inquired in somewhat of a soft tone: 'Why have you made the call to Prayer in a loud voice?' The soldier stepped forward and said: 'It was not him, but I who made the call to Prayer.' The official addressed the mob and said: 'You wretched people! What is all this uproar. In Lahore, the cow is now openly slaughtered without restrictions and you are wailing over the Muslim call to Prayer. Be gone and sit in peace.'

In short, my heart truly and honestly believes that it is a grave ingratitude and disloyalty to not acknowledge the favour of a people who have delivered us from the lowest depths.

The Facility of the Printing Press

In addition to this, ignorance was widely rampant. An old man by the name of Kammay Shah once related that he saw his teacher pray with great emotion so that he would be granted the opportunity to see a copy of *Sahih Bukhari* just once. On certain occasions, the thought that this was perhaps never possible would move him to weep bitterly in prayer. Now that very same *Bukhari* can be purchased in Amritsar and Lahore for a few rupees.

Then, there was a *maulvi* by the name of Sher Muhammad. He happened to find a few pages of *Ihya-ul-Ulum* from somewhere. And so after every Prayer, for quite some time, he would show the congregation with overwhelming joy and pride that this was the famous *Ihya-ul-Ulum*. It was his ardent desire to find the entire book from somewhere. Now, *Ihya-ul-Ulum* is available far and wide in printed form.

In short, the arrival of the British is a blessing that has opened the spiritual eyes of the people as well. God Almighty knows well the degree to which this govern-ment had aided the cause of religion—such as was impossible under any other government. Through the blessings of the printing press and the development of diverse stocks of paper, all sorts of books can be made available at low costs. Then, through the post office, these books can be sent far and wide from the comfort of our homes. In this way, the path for the propagation of religious truths has become easy and unobstructed.

The Benefits of Religious Freedom

Then, among the many blessings that we have received during the rule of this government and which have supported the cause of religion, one is the remarkable advancement of intellectual faculties and mental abilities. Since the administration has given each and every religion the freedom to preach their faith, in this way the people now have an opportunity to scrutinise and reflect over the principles and arguments of every faith. When the followers of various religions attacked Islam, the Muslims were pressed to ponder over their own religious texts in support of their religion and to prove its truthfulness, and in this way their intellectual faculties were refined.

It is a matter of principle that just as physical strengths improve with exercise, spiritual faculties also are developed and nurtured with exercise, just as a horse is disciplined by a trainer. Similarly, with the arrival of the British, people have received an opportunity to reflect over the principles of religion. Those who reflect have in turn become more firm and steadfast in Islam—the Religion of Truth. Further, wherever an opponent of the Holy Quran has put their finger to object, it is from that very place that those who contemplate have found a treasure of divine insight. Moreover, due to this freedom, the field of dialectics has also advanced a considerable degree, especially here. Now if someone from Turkey or Syria was to come here—no matter how knowledgeable and learned a scholar—they would not be able to sufficiently refute the objections raised by the Christians or Aryas, because that individual would not have been as able to receive such free and wide exposure to the principles of various religions so as to cross-examine between them.

Therefore, just as the country has found physical peace through the British government, so too we have attained spiritual peace as well. Since I am concerned with spiritual and religious affairs, I will speak mostly of those favours granted to us by the government, which have facilitated us in fulfilling our religious obligations.

The Conditions for the Observance of Worship

It ought to be remembered that a human being can only observe the various rites of worship with complete freedom and satisfaction when four conditions are met. They are as follows:

Firstly, there is health. If a person is so frail that they cannot get up from their bed, how can they adhere to the observance of Prayer and fasting? In the same way, such a one would be unable to act on many injunctions like the Hajj and Zakat, among others. One ought to think about the diverse means that this government has furnished to us by its good graces, in order to maintain our physical health. In every major city and town there is at least one hospital, where the sick are treated with immense sympathy and compassion; medicine, food and the like is given free of charge. Certain patients are kept in the hospital and treated, tended to and cared for in a manner that one could not be treated in such ease, facility and comfort even in their own home. A separate department exists to provide healthcare and millions of rupees are spent annually on this service. It has provided extraordinary resources to keep towns and cities clean. A dedicated system is in place for sewage and waste disposal. Then, a wide range of fast-acting medication has been produced and made available at such a low cost that anyone can purchase these medicines and keep them at home to treat themselves at a time of need. Large medical colleges have been established and medical training has been made available so widely that doctors can even be found in rural villages. Moreover, there are separate departments dedicated to deal with other harmful diseases like smallpox, cholera, plague and the like. The measures undertaken recently by the government in connection with the plague is truly worthy of gratitude. In short, the government has provided all the necessary means that are required in the context of health, and in doing so has furnished great support in fulfilling the primary condition for worship.

The second condition is faith. If a person does not even believe in God Almighty and His commandments and a person is plagued with the leprosy of disbelief and atheism from within, in this case also, one cannot fulfil the orders of God. There are many who say:

ایہہ جگ مٹھا تے اگلا کن ڈٹھا

It is this world that is delightful, who has ever seen the hereafter?

It is a shame. Before the law, a man can be hung on the testimony of two people, but despite the testimony of 124,000 Messengers and countless saints, there is still such widespread disbelief in the hearts of people. In every era, God Almighty declares through His powerful signs and miracles: اَنَا الۡمَوۡجُوۡد (*I am present*). But these unfortunate people do not lend an ear, despite having ears. Therefore, this is also a very important condition. So we ought to be thankful to the British government for this as well because wide-spread knowledge of religion was required in order to strengthen the faith and belief of the people, and religious education depends on the publication of religious books. It is due to the blessings of the printing press and the post office that religious books of all sorts can be obtained and newspapers provide an opportunity for people to exchange views. Good natured people have at their disposal ample opportunity to strengthen their faith and belief.

In addition to these points, another important and immensely crucial aspect that is necessary to strengthen faith is the signs of God Almighty, which are manifested at the hand of that individual who comes from God, commissioned by Him, and who revives lost truths and verities through his conduct. Hence, one ought to thank God that the person whom He has appointed to revive faith once again in this era, and whom He has sent to make people stronger in faith, has also appeared in the rule of this blessed government. Who is that person? It is the very same person who stands among you and addresses you now. It is an accepted fact that until man is complete in their faith, they cannot perform virtuous deeds to a level of perfection. The weaker an aspect or pillar of one's faith, the more indolent and weak one will be in practice. In this respect, a saint is a person whose every aspect of faith is complete and who is not defective in any respect, whose acts of worship are performed in a perfect and complete manner. Therefore, the second condition is soundness in faith.

The third condition is financial ability. The construction of mosques and the advancement of other such endeavours related to Islam depend on financial ability. Without this, civic life and the administration of affairs—particularly those relating to mosques—would become very difficult. Now look at the British government in this respect as well. The government has advanced all sorts of trade. Further, it has promoted education and has made employment available to the citizens of this land, even giving them high positions. By providing means for transport, it has made it possible for citizens to visit other countries and earn money. There are people working as doctors, pleaders, court officials, and also in the department of education etc., and through various means people are earning a substantial salary. Merchants involved in business and trade take their wide array of goods to England and other far-off lands, such as Africa and Australia etc., and return with abounding wealth. In short, the government has made employment available for everyone and has provided many avenues to earn an income.

The fourth condition is peace. This condition of peace is not within the power of any one individual. Since the creation of the world, this matter has depended chiefly on the ruling class. The more well-intentioned and sincere a ruling authority, the more this condition will be truly met. In the present era, this condition of peace is being met to the highest degree. I truly believe that even the bright days of Sikh reign are far darker than the dark nights of British rule. There is a village named Butr nearby. If ever a lady had to visit this village, she would go there weeping and crying thinking that perhaps she would never return. Now, the state of affairs is such that anyone can travel to the ends of this land without any danger whatsoever. Various modes of transport have been made so easy that every form of comfort is available. On the rail, one can travel anywhere they please, sitting or sleeping, as though they were at home. A large police department is in place to protect property and life. The courts are open to protect the rights of citizens and a person can pursue a case to the highest authority. How great are these favours which have resulted in freedom of practice. Therefore, in this state when our body and soul is receiving boundless beneficence, if we do not nurture within ourselves a sense of goodwill and gratitude, this would be strange indeed! One who is not thankful to human beings cannot show gratitude to God Almighty either. Why is this the case? It is because human beings too are the ambassadors of God and operate under His will.

In short, all of the points that I have mentioned compel a pure-hearted individual to feel a sense of gratitude towards such a benefactor. This is why I mention the favours of the British government again and again in my writings and speeches. For my heart is truly full of pleasure on account of these favours. Those foolish people who are ungrateful, judge my practice—which emanates from sincerity and morality—against their own hypocritical natures, and deem it to be false praise.

True Oneness of God

Now I return to my original subject and would like to elaborate that in this chapter, firstly, God Almighty says: *rabb-in-nas* (the Lord of Mankind), whereafter He proclaims: *malik-in-nas* (the King of Mankind). Finally, He declares *ila-hin-nas* (the God of Mankind), which refers to that Being Who is the true object sought by man. The word *ilah* refers to a thing that is desired, worshipped and sought after. The words لَا اِلٰهَ اِلَّا اللهُ *(There is none worthy of worship except Allah)* actually imply the following:

لَا مَعْبُوْدَ لِيْ وَلَا مَقْصُوْدَ لِيْ وَلَا مَطْلُوْبَ لِيْ اِلَّا اللهُ

I have no object of worship, or any being that I desire or seek, other than Allah.

This is true Unity of God, when one deems Allah the Exalted alone to be worthy of all praise and admiration.

Who Is *Khannas*?

Then Allah the Exalted states:

مِنْ شَرِّ الْوَسْوَاسِ الْخَنَّاسِ[1]

Meaning, seek refuge from the evil of the whisperings of *khannas* (the evil whisperer). In Arabic, the snake is called *khannas*, or *nahash* in Hebrew, on account of the sin that it committed in earlier times. Here, Allah Almighty does not use the name Iblis or Satan so that man is reminded of the trial he confronted in the very beginning, when Satan deceived his two ancestors. At that time, his name was *khannas*. Allah the Exalted employed this sequence so that man is reminded of past events and realises that just as Satan once deceived man, turning him away from obedience to God, he must not be allowed, in any future time, to make you rebel or turn away from obedience to the ruler of the time. In this way, man is moved to continuously scrutinise and judge the intentions and designs of the inner self to see the extent to which he is willing to obey their ruling king, and so that he continues to strive positively in this regard, and continues to supplicate before God Almighty that may Satan not infiltrate him by any avenue.

Hence, the commandment of obedience given in this chapter is obedience to God Almighty, for true obedience is due to Him. However, there is also an instruction to obey one's parents, a spiritual mentor or guide, and the ruler of the time, because it is God Almighty Himself who has instructed man to show obedience to these people as well. The benefit of obedience will be that one will be saved from the grip of *khannas*. Therefore, man has been taught to seek refuge from the evil whisperings of *khannas* because a believer is not bitten from the same hole twice. You must not fall prey to an affliction in which you have been

---

[1] *an-Nas*, 114:5

entangled before. So, there is a clear indication in this chapter to obey the ruler of the time.

The *khannas* (evil whisperer) has been invested with certain properties just as God Almighty has placed certain properties in trees, water, fire, and various other objects and elements. The Arabic word for 'element' is عنصر *(unsar)*, which is actually from عَنْ سِرّ (i.e. *an-sir*, literally meaning 'from secret'). In Arabic the letter س *(seen)* and ص *(saad)* are sometimes interchangeable, so the meaning of this word would be 'something from among the secrets of God.' In actuality, this word refers to a point where human investigations can go no further. In short, everything originates from God, whether they are single elements or compounds.

It is a fact that by sending such rulers, God has saved us from a thousand hardships and has transformed our state. We have been pulled out of a burning furnace and brought into a garden with delightful plants, and running streams in every direction, along with cool and pleasant winds. How ungrateful, therefore, would one be if one was to neglect these favours. My community—to which God has granted insight and which is free from duplicity—ought to be a paragon of gratitude, especially because its members have forged a relationship with a man who is free from hypocrisy.

The Insight in Faith of the Ahmadiyya Community

I am perfectly certain that my community is free from hypocrisy and in establishing a bond with me, their understanding has not erred. For in actuality, I am that very person who was destined to be accepted by those possessing insight in faith. God Almighty is a Witness and knows that I am the same truthful, trustworthy and promised one whose advent was foretold by the blessed tongue of our Chief and Master, the Truthful, the Honest, the Holy Prophet, peace and blessings of Allah be upon him. Those who have not forged a relationship with me are deprived of this bounty. Insight is something of a miracle. The word for 'insight' is فراست, which can be pronounced *'farasat*,' with the vowel sound 'a' denoted by a *fathah* over the letter 'f'; and can also be read *'firasat*,' with the vowel sound 'i' represented by the diacritic *kasrah* under the letter 'f'. With a *fathah* over the letter 'f', the word *farasat* means to mount a horse. A true believer mounts the steed of his inner self and tames it like an expert rider. Such a one finds their way by the light granted to them from God. It is for this reason that the Messenger of Allah, peace and blessings of Allah be upon him, said:

اِتَّـقُوْا فِرَاسَةَ الْمُؤْمِنِ فَاِنَّهٗ يَنْظُرُ بِنُوْرِ اللّٰهِ

Meaning, beware of the insight of a believer, for he sees with the light of Allah. Therefore, the greatest proof of the true insight of our community is that they have recognised the light of God.

Do Good to Those Who Do Good

In the same manner, I trust that my community will improve in their practical state. For they are not hypocrites and are absolutely free of the conduct of my opponents, who praise the officials when they meet them, but then call them disbelievers when they return home.

Take heed and remember that God does not like such behaviour. You who hold a relationship with me—and who do so only for the sake of God—ought to do good to those who do good and forgive those who do evil. No individual can be from among the Truthful until they become sincere. A person who is hypocritical and duplicitous is ultimately caught. There is a famous saying:

دروغ گورا حافظ نبا شد

A liar has no memory (i.e. a lie is quickly caught).

On this occasion, I would like to speak of another important point as well, which is that rulers are often required to embark on military campaigns. And these are also for the safety and protection of its citizens. As you have observed, our government has had to engage in wars on the Frontier. Although the people of the Frontier are Muslims, in my view they stand in the wrong. Their engaging in battle against the British is not justified in any religious aspect or regard, nor do these people actually fight for any religious purpose. These people ought to tell us whether the government has given Muslims freedom or not? Indeed they have; such freedom the like of which cannot be found anywhere in Kabul or in the surrounding regions. We do not hear favourable reports about the Amir of Kabul. Greed is the only reason for which these fanatic frontiersmen fight. A mere ten or twenty rupees is enough to drown their warrior spirit. These people are tyrants who mar the name of Islam.

The Rights of a Ruler and a Benefactor

Islam has established the rights due to the ruler of the time and a benefactor.

These ignoble people transgress the limits set by Allah out of greed. The fact that they will readily kill a human being for a piece of bread amply establishes their vile, foolish and bloodthirsty nature. At present, our government is at war with the small republic known as Transvaal. The republic is no larger than the Punjab and it is utterly foolish of it to have engaged in war with such a vast empire. Nonetheless, now that hostilities have begun, it is the duty of every Muslim to pray for the victory of the British. What have we to do with Transvaal? It is our responsibility to show support for those who have done us thousands of favours. A neighbour is due such rights that upon hearing of their suffering, one's heart bleeds. So now, do our hearts not ache when we read about the perils of the loyal soldiers of the British government? In my view, a person who does not deem the grief of the government to be their own is black-hearted.

Bear in mind that leprosy is of various kinds. One form of leprosy affects the body, while another form of leprosy afflicts the soul. There used to be a man who stayed here in the bazaar. If anyone became the subject of a lawsuit, he would ask how the case was proceeding. If he was informed that the accused had been exonerated or that the case was favourably promising, he would be taken aback and say no more. If on the other hand, someone told him that the person implicated had been charged, he would be overjoyed and would invite the person to sit with him and listen to the entire account. In short, the dispositions of certain men are so filled with a sense of spite that they are eager to hear bad news and enjoy the misfortune of others, because they are satanic in nature. Hence, it is wrong to bear ill will towards any individual, especially a benefactor. Therefore, I say to my community that they must not follow in the footsteps of such people. On the contrary, they ought to pray, with utmost sympathy and true goodwill, for the victory of the British government, and ought to demonstrate examples of loyalty even in practice.

Show Gratitude to a Benefactor

I do not make these statements out of a desire for reward or recompense. What do I care for reward, recompense and worldly titles? My intentions are well known to the All-Knowing God, and He is aware that my work is solely for His sake and in accordance with His command. It is He Who has taught us to be thankful to a benefactor. Therefore, in our gratitude we obey our Gracious Lord and it is Him from Whom we hope for a reward. Hence, you who are my community ought to hold your benevolent government in high regard. Now, it is my wish that we all pray for the Transvaal war."

After this, His Holiness raised his hands with immense fervour and sincerity to pray, and all those present—who numbered in excess of a thousand—joined with him in prayer.[1]

11 April 1900

Prayer on the Day of Arafat

On the morning of the day of Arafat, the Promised Messiah[as] wrote a letter to Hazrat Maulana Nur-ud-Din Sahib[ra] and informed him: "I would like to spend today and a part of the night in prayer for my friends. Therefore, those friends who are here at present should send me their names and place of residence, so that I remember them whilst I am engaged in prayer."

In accordance with these instructions, a list of friends was prepared and submitted to His Holiness. Afterwards, other friends arrived as well, who expressed a sense of restlessness to see the Promised Messiah[as] and seek his prayers, so they began to send in written notes. The Promised Messiah[as] sent word again and said: "Do not send me any further notes as this causes great disruption."

The Promised Messiah[as] emerged in the evening and the *Maghrib* and *Isha* Prayers were combined. After the Prayers had been offered, the Promised Messiah[as] said: "Since I have promised God Almighty that I would spend today and a part of the night in prayer, I now take your leave, so that I am not guilty of breaking my promise."

After this, His Holiness returned and engaged himself in prayer once again. The following morning, on the Eid day, Maulvi Abdul-Karim Sahib[ra] went in to see the Promised Messiah[as] and requested him especially to deliver an address. On this, His Holiness said: "God has ordered this Himself." Then he stated: "Last night, I received a revelation: 'Say a few sentences in Arabic to the congregation.' I thought this referred to some other congregation, but perhaps this is the one."[2]

The Sign of the Revealed Sermon

This sermon which the Promised Messiah[as] delivered in the Arabic language,

---

[1] *Al-Hakam*, vol. 4, no. 5, dated 10 February 1900,. pp. 3-10
[2] *Al-Hakam*, vol. 4, no. 13, dated 17 April 1900, p. 2

through divine inspiration and at divine behest, is a powerful and unparalleled sign from Allah, which was fulfilled before a large and illustrious gathering. The address was published under the name *Khutbah Ilhamiyyah* (The Revealed Sermon).

When His Holiness was ready to deliver his sermon in Arabic, he instructed Hazrat Maulvi Abdul-Karim Sahib[ra] and Hazrat Maulvi Nur-ud-Din Sahib[ra] to sit near him and transcribe the address. When the two esteemed scholars were ready, the Promised Messiah[as] began his sermon in Arabic with the words:

يَا عِبَادَ اللهِ

O servants of Allah!

At one point during the sermon, His Holiness also said: "Write this now because the words are fading away." When the Promised Messiah[as] had finished delivering his sermon and took a seat, at the request of a large part of the congregation, Maulana Maulvi Abdul-Karim Sahib[ra] stood up to present its translation. Before the esteemed scholar could begin presenting the translation, the Promised Messiah[as] said: "This sermon has been appointed to serve as a sign for the acceptance of those prayers which I made yesterday on the Day of Arafat and during the night preceding the Eid day, in that if I was able to deliver this sermon in the Arabic language extempore, all of my supplications would be deemed accepted by God. All praise belongs to Allah that all of those supplications have also been accepted by God Almighty in accordance with His promise."

A Prostration of Gratitude and Acceptance

Maulana Abdul-Karim Sahib[ra] was still presenting the translation of this sermon when the Promised Messiah[as] passionately and uncontrollably fell into prostration out of gratitude to God. Along with His Holiness, the entire gathering also fell into a prostration of gratitude. When the Promised Messiah[as] raised his head, he said: "I have just seen the word *Mubarak* (felicitations) written in red letters. This, is a sign of acceptance."[1]

---

[1] *Al-Hakam*, vol. 4, no. 16, dated 1 May 1900, p. 5

12 April 1900

A Heartfelt Desire of the Promised Messiah[as]

His Holiness, our Noble Leader, peace and blessings be upon him, always wishes and desires that our friends find the opportunity to visit Qadian, the Abode of Peace, time and again, so that by staying here, each and every individual may receive practical guidance to purify their mind, cleanse their inner self and polish their soul. In order to fulfil this objective, the Promised Messiah[as] has arranged for three gatherings to take place during the year: namely the two Eids and one gathering during the summer holidays. The proceedings of the gathering that took place on Eid-ul-Adha are presented hereafter.

The Relation of the Holy Prophet[sa] and the Promised Messiah[as] With Eid-ul-Adha

The Promised Messiah[as] said: "Today is the day of Eid-ul-Adha and this Eid arrives in a month which brings the Islamic months to a close. That is to say, after this month, the new year begins with Muharram. There is an underlying secret in the fact that this Eid comes in a month when an Islamic month or a specific period in time comes to an end. This indicates that our Noble Prophet, peace and blessings of Allah be upon him, and the awaited Messiah[as] held a very close resemblance with this occasion. What is that resemblance?

Firstly, our Noble Prophet, Muhammad, the Chosen One, peace and blessings of Allah be upon him, was a Prophet of the final age, and his blessed personage and era, represented the time of Eid-ul-Adha, as it were. As such, even Muslim children are well aware of the fact that the Holy Prophet[sa] was the Prophet of the latter days, and this month of Eid is also the last of months. Therefore, this month bears a resemblance with the life of the Holy Prophet[sa] and his era.

The second likeness to note is that as this month is the month of sacrifices, the Messenger of Allah, peace and blessings of Allah be upon him, also came to demonstrate a perfect example of true and sincere sacrifices in his own person. On this occasion, all of you slaughter goats, camels, cows and rams. Similarly, 1300 years ago there was a time when human beings were slaughtered in the cause of God Almighty. In the true sense, that earlier time was the real Eid-ul-Adha, and it was that time that was filled with the light of *duha* (the forenoon).

The Essence of Sacrifice

These physical sacrifices are not the essence, they are merely the shell; they are not the spirit, they are merely the body. In this era of ease and comfort, Eid is celebrated happily with joy. People believe that the ultimate purpose of this celebration is nothing but enjoyment and diverse forms of indulgence. It is on this day that women fully adorn themselves with jewellery and wear their most beautiful clothes. Men wear elegant attire and arrange for the finest foods. This day is considered to be such a happy and joyous occasion that even the greatest of misers will eat meat on this day. The Kashmiris especially devour goats without measure—though other people do no less. In short, for some, Eid is but a name for all sorts of amusement, enjoyment, mirth and merriment. It is regrettable, however, that the people do not realise this deeper essence at all.

The Essence of Eid-ul-Adha

The seed of sacrifice that was sown by Abraham[as] in a hidden manner was exhibited by the Holy Prophet, peace and blessings of Allah be upon him, in the form of flourishing crops—and this, in reality, is the great secret in this day. Abraham, peace be upon him, was even ready to slaughter his son to fulfil the commandment of God Almighty. This was a hidden indication of the fact that man ought to become wholly devoted to God; and one's own life, and the blood of one's children, and one's kith and kin, ought to appear insignificant in the face of God's command. Just observe the many great sacrifices that were offered in the era of the Messenger of Allah, peace and blessings of Allah be upon him, who perfectly exemplified each and every pure teaching. The wilderness was filled with blood. It was as though streams of blood began to flow forth. Fathers spilt the blood of their children and sons killed their fathers, and both were happy—in fact even elated—in laying down their lives and being hacked to pieces in the cause of Islam and God. But now reflect, except for fun and enjoyment, entertainment and amusement, what has remained of spirituality? This Eid-ul-Adha is greater than the Eid that precedes it, and people generally refer to this as the 'Greater Eid' as well, but reflect and do tell me, how many people, as a result of this Eid, are actually moved to purify their soul, cleanse their heart, partake of spirituality, and endeavour to absorb the radiance and light that is present in this *duha* (time of brightness)?

The Eid of Ramadan represents a struggle—a personal struggle—and the effort of the soul. But this Eid, also referred to as the 'Greater Eid', possesses a grand and magnificent spirit within itself. Alas! Due attention has not been given to this deeper reality. One immense favour of God Almighty—Whose mercy is manifested in many ways—upon the community of Muhammad, peace and blessings of Allah be upon him, is that this blessed community exhibited in itself the deeper essence of everything which existed in previous religious communities in the form of a shell or a husk.

The Holy Prophet^{sa} Alone Was the True Manifestation of God's Attributes

Four attributes of God Almighty have been mentioned in Surah *al-Fatihah*: *rabb-ul-alamin* (Lord of all the worlds), *rahman* (the Gracious), *rahim* (the Merciful) and *maliki yawm-id-din* (Master of the Day of Judgement). Although these attributes are manifested on earth in the general sense, in reality, they possess within themselves prophecies, to which people rarely direct their attention. The Holy Prophet, peace and blessings of Allah be upon him, displayed a manifestation of these four attributes in his person. For no deeper reality can be understood without an illustration of some sort. So how was the attribute of *rabb-ul-alamin* (Lord of all the worlds) manifested in the Holy Prophet, peace and blessings of Allah be upon him? The Holy Prophet^{sa} grew up in disadvantaged circumstances. There was no madrasa or school available from where the Holy Prophet^{sa} could develop and train his spiritual and religious faculties. He never had the opportunity to meet with an educated people; he had not even access to a basic education, nor was he able to study the deep and intricate sciences of philosophy. Now observe how despite not having had these opportunities, he was granted a blessing as great as the Holy Quran—no other knowledge even remotely compares to the sublime and true knowledge contained in this book. Any individual who reads the Holy Quran with even the slightest understanding and reflection will realise that every form of philosophy and all the sciences are worthless in comparison. It has left every sage and philosopher far behind. Prior to the Holy Prophet, peace and blessings of Allah be upon him, there have been two magnificent prophets. Firstly, Moses, peace be upon him, and secondly, Jesus, peace be upon him. Both of them, however, were able to obtain an education; no claim has ever been made that they were unlettered Prophets. This challenge and claim has only been made in respect of our Noble Prophet, peace and blessings of Allah be upon him. As such, God Almighty states:

مَا كُنْتَ تَدْرِىْ مَا الْكِتٰبُ وَ لَا الْاِيْمَانُ وَ لٰكِنْ جَعَلْنٰهُ نُوْرًا نَّهْدِىْ بِهٖ مَنْ نَّشَآءُ مِنْ عِبَادِنَا ١

And thus have We revealed to thee the Word by Our command. Thou didst not know what the Book was, nor what the faith. But We have made it (the revelation) a light, whereby We guide such of Our servants as We please.

Moses, peace be upon him, received a princely education, as it were, and was given a royal upbringing under the guardianship of the Pharaoh. Tutors were appointed for him because even in that era, such a custom was prevalent. If Moses, peace be upon him, had not taken up an ascetic life, he was next in line after the Pharoah. If it were not for God's grace, Moses[as] would have become a Pharoah as well, God forbid.

Bear in mind that the word 'Pharoah' is not evil in itself. In actuality, this was the title given to the Kings of Egypt, just as 'Caesar' and 'Chosroes' were the titles given to the rulers of Rome and Iran respectively, and how in this age, the Tsar of Russia and Ottoman Sultan have their own titles. My only purpose in mentioning this is to explain that if God Almighty had not prepared him for another office, it was certain that he would have ascended the throne. It is true that although the mother of Moses[as] felt pain and grief in casting an innocent soul into the river, what would have been the state of her extreme happiness and joy when God Almighty Himself promised to return the child to her? In short, Moses[as] was educated in the manner of royalty.

Jesus, peace be upon him, was also educated formally. I have a book by a Jewish writer, in which he has stated this point clearly and categorically. In fact, he has even mentioned the teacher of the Messiah[as] by name and then goes on to raise an objection. The author states that it was from his early days that Jesus[as] developed a liking for the subjects comprised in the Torah and the scriptures of the Prophets, and he also states that nothing in the Gospel is more than what has already been mentioned in the past scriptures of the Prophets. The author has also written that Jesus[as] was taught by the Jews for a long period in time. However, if you ask a Jew, Christian or anyone from India whether the Holy Prophet[sa] was educated anywhere, they will clearly reject such a notion. What a grand manifestation of divine providence!

---

[1]   *ash-Shura*, 42:53

When a child advances from infancy, before reaching an age of maturity, they are sent to school—this is the first step. However, the first step in the life of the Holy Prophet[sa] was something of a miracle! Since the Holy Prophet[sa] was the Seal of the Prophets, his person and every aspect of his life was miraculous in nature. His way of life was such that he did not receive even an elementary education, yet he brought a matchless bounty as great as the Quran and gave the Muslim community a magnificent miracle.

The Prophets of previous times appeared and after remaining on earth for some time, went on, after which their religion disappeared. In truth, God had destined for these religions to fade away but had determined to maintain the signs and imprints of this Faith. For no religion can remain without miracles. People can only believe in hearsay for a few days, then they begin to say:

یہہ جہاں مٹھاتے اگلا کن ڈٹھا

It is this world that is delightful, who has ever seen the next world?

This is why God has willed for a living miracle to accompany Islam.

A Sign of the Truth of Islam

A prophecy was made with immense strength, vigour and specificity—and through this prophecy, may the light of Islam shine brightly until the end of time. As such, in order to establish the truth of this ever-present divine light, even in our own era, it was foretold before the death of Lekhram that he would be killed within six years. One ought to reflect. Is it within the power of a human being to foretell the time, period and manner in which someone will die, and then for that person to die exactly as foretold?

When this prophecy was made, in a very short span of time, it gained fame amongst hundreds of thousands of people. Followers of every faith, whether Hindu, Muslim, Christian or Sikh, all came to know about my prophecy. This occurred to such an extent that everyone from the common man to government officials were aware of this prophecy. The Aryas themselves publicised this prophecy with great force and vigour. Even Lekhram himself would speak of this prophecy wherever he went and gave it publicity. When ultimately the prophecy was fulfilled, widespread uproar erupted. Even my home was searched—only to further establish the truthfulness of this prophecy and give it further publicity, and so that this sign left an indelible mark on the face of the earth. Then, as hearings in court were taking place, statements and other written documentation related to my prophecy were copied and included in the official records and case files.

In short, this was such a grand sign that no other nation can produce the like of it. Is it within human power and wisdom to foretell as to how and when a certain person will die, even a few days in advance? However, this prophecy was made six years before the occurrence and information was given as to the manner of death along with other details. Lekhram was a healthy young man of thirty, and he too prophesied that I would die of cholera within three years, and it ought to be noted that I was at the time far older and weaker, and almost constantly ill. But God Almighty displayed the brilliance of His hand, and dispatched Lekhram to set a seal on the truth of His true religion.

The Arya Samajists Are Deprived of Divine Cognisance

The fact is that the Arya Samajists fundamentally do not even know God. How then can they develop the strength to recognise, behold and show Him? They have erred at the very first step. In their estimation, life and death, being male or female, or becoming a goat or an ox, are all consequences of one's actions. Now when birth and everything else is the result of one's actions, then what is left of God? Why would there be anything in the way of new signs and miracles to prove the existence of God's being? In fact, what need would there be for them anyway? Their belief is that God is not the Creator, He is only an assembler, in the likeness of a builder or a potter. They suggest that matter was present from before and souls just happened to incidentally exist as well, and Parmeshwar whipped up his creation by joining and attaching things—God forbid.

I would ask, however, if souls and particles existed eternally, what argument could possibly establish that this phenomenon of joining and bonding could not have taken place without Parmeshwar? In fact, the natural argument that follows from this is that things are naturally pulled together by gravity. If this gravitational pull had not existed, neither could a brick be made, nor could a house remain grounded. Nothing else on earth would remain intact either. Therefore, in accordance with the belief of the Arya Samajists, if the soul and matter have existed since eternity, and there is evidence in physics for gravitational force, the Arya Samajists are free from Parmeshwar and owe no obligation to him whatsoever. Now what evidence and sign does an Arya Samajist possess in favour of the existence of Parmeshwar?

On the one hand, when these people are sullied by the impurity of not knowing God—how could one expect that they would be able to expound the ways in which to behold and manifest God? Then, on the other hand, what a grievous wrong they commit by suggesting that souls return in all creatures to pay for their actions, sometimes in the form of a pig, sometimes as a dog or a cat, etc.

Transmigration of Souls

In this context, an issue that arises is that if someone's mother passed away when they were still a child, and the mother was born again somewhere else, when both the child and mother reached an age of maturity, and if they were married for example, engaged in intercourse and then had children, this would be an utterly immodest thing, and lays the foundation for despicable indecency—this religion proves to be most shameless indeed.

Their Parmeshwar has given no catalogue that would indicate the signs by which one could recognise their own mother or sister. In truth, the Veda was responsible, that where on the one hand it invented this doctrine which cuts at the root of chastity and morality, if it had any common sense or insight, it ought to have outlined the signs by which a follower of the Arya faith would have the key in their hand, making it possible to refrain from such relations.

It was inevitable, however, that the Vedic teaching be scarred on its forehead by this flaw so that in every era, those who reflect could recognise its falsehood. On the one hand, these people are so extreme that they will not marry the relatives of their maternal grandmothers or even those of their grandmother's great grandmother. Yet, on the other hand, they have no argument for why they will marry their mother and sister. On the one hand they will stay thousands of miles away, yet on the other hand, they will bring home their own mother or sister in marriage. No religion is so sunk in darkness as this one. It is unfortunate that their Parmeshwar flung them into impurity and then did not care to give them a catalogue that would indicate which specific donkey or ox they should not use because a certain animal was a previous relative, or that a woman with such and such signs should not be married because she is actually a biological mother, or grandmother, aunt, sister, or niece who has been reborn and come again. In reality, the followers of the Arya faith are themselves excused, because it is Parmeshwar himself who is guilty of this entire injustice, as he failed to provide a catalogue of details.

Niyoga

Then, the third impurity that is the essence and flower of the Vedic teaching is *niyoga*. The details of this practice are that a woman can engage in intercourse with up to eleven men while her husband is still alive, right before him. If a husband and wife are young and after being married a few years have been unable to have children, a woman may have intercourse with another man so that she may impregnate herself with the sperm of another, because it is impossible for one to attain paradise without having children. Further, it is incumbent upon this wittol of a husband to provide excellent electuaries and fine tonics to the man who is giving the gift of his sperm, so that he does not tire or suffer from any weakness. Moreover, according to the Veda, the bedding, quilt and bed itself must be provided by the woman's husband. Then, the husband who sends his wife to sleep with another man must be the one to provide him with food, and he will then take half of the children that are born of his seed. Just reflect! What sort of a husband is this, who sits in one room as a cuckold, while his wedded wife is bringing shame upon herself in the room next door? The Arya Samajist listens to the sounds of their movements, and his heart is joyed at the thought that now the field of his hope will bloom and flourish with this 'water.' What a pitiful religion! Such injustice against God! Such injustice against honour and dignity. The Veda gives permission to indulge in such acts which even the most vile and impure of men would feel shame in committing.

Dyanand has written that this *shubh karam,* i.e. blessed deed, was abandoned as time went on, but now the Aryas of India will revive this practice because this deed results in spiritual reward. I have no need to further prolong this discussion. An individual may consult for themselves the religious texts of the Arya Samajists and their doctrines; in fact, simply ask their revered leaders. I trust they will go on about the merits of this strange action with great pride.

The Pure Teaching of Islam

When all of these religions are put before us and their teachings and doctrines are properly investigated, one realises the need for Islam and the honourable nature of this religion. One is left with no choice but to acknowledge the great bounty of God Almighty that He has kept Islam free from such corrupt doctrines and has demonstrated that every aspect of its teaching is a manifestation of perfection and possesses a miraculous nature.

In the teaching of Moses, peace be upon him, there was great emphasis on retribution—a tooth for a tooth, an ear for an ear, an eye for an eye. In the teaching of the Messiah, peace be upon him, emphasis was put on not resisting evil treatment. So, if someone were to slap a person on one cheek they were taught to turn the other as well; if someone compels a person to go one mile, one should go with them for two miles; if someone demands from a person their shirt, one should give them one's cloak as well, and so on and so forth. However, I would like to see whether any priest actually follows this teaching. Anyone can slap a priest on his face and see. Indeed, instead of turning the other cheek, the priest will drag the man to court, and think of any means—even by falsehood and deceit—to have the man punished. However, Islam has not given such a teaching; in fact, it has given a teaching that is the life of this world, and human beings naturally act upon it. This teaching is:

$$جَزٰٓؤُا۟ سَيِّئَةٍ سَيِّئَةٌ مِّثْلُهَاۖ فَمَنْ عَفَا وَاَصْلَحَ فَاَجْرُهٗ عَلَى اللّٰهِ ۚ^1$$

Meaning, the recompense of an evil is the like thereof, but if someone forgives when it is not inappropriate to do so, and the purpose of this forgiveness is reformation, then such a person will have their reward from Allah. For example, if a thief is released, he will only become bolder and then become a robber. Such a person deserves to be punished. Let us assume there were two servants. If one servant was such that a light reprimand was enough to embarrass them and move them to reform themselves, it would be inappropriate to punish such a person. If the other servant, however, was intentionally mischievous, forgiving him would only make him worse, and so he deserves to be punished. Now do tell us, is the more appropriate teaching the one taught by the Wise Quran, or the one put forth by the Gospel? What does the law of nature demand? It calls for differentiation and consideration that is appropriate in each individual case.

The teaching that forgiveness ought to be for the purpose of reformation is a matchless teaching indeed. It is this teaching that ultimately the civilised world must follow. It is by acting on this very teaching that man develops their faculty of rational judgement, reflection and insight. In other words, this teaching has in-

---

1 *ash-Shura*, 42:41

structed one to consider the evidence from every aspect and reflect with insight, and then if forgiveness is beneficial, to forgive; but if the individual in question is evil and mischievous, then one must act upon the following teaching:

$$جَزَاءُ سَيِّئَةٍ سَيِّئَةٌ مِّثْلُهَا^{1}$$

The recompense of an injury is an injury the like thereof.

This is the nature of the other pure teachings of Islam, which shine forth in every era like the mid-day sun. On certain occasions, even the sun is masked by clouds and apparently seems blurred. However, the countenance of Islam is free from this as well. The absence of divine insight has turned people blind and they see through the eye of malice. This is why their condition has deteriorated to an even greater extent than one who suffers from a cataract. How then can they make a proper judgement?

The Doctrines of Christianity

All of the religions that exist in the world are unblessed, deprived of light, dead, and utterly devoid of pure teachings. The Hindus have demonstrated the example that I have just mentioned. Similarly, the Christians have shown another example where they have turned a humble man into God—a man who was beaten at the hands of the Jews, which was a ruined nation themselves and a manifestation of the following:

$$وَضُرِبَتْ عَلَيْهِمُ الذِّلَّةُ وَالْمَسْكَنَةُ^{2}$$

And they were smitten with abasement and destitution.

Ultimately, this man was hung on the cross by the Jews and as per their belief, he became accursed and ultimately gave up his life crying: *'Eloi, eloi, lama sabachthani'* meaning, 'O God! O God! Why hast thou forsaken me?' Contemplate, can one possessing such attributes ever be God? Such a man cannot even be deemed a true worshipper of God, let alone God himself. Christians demonstrate by their belief that the prayer of Jesus[as], which was offered the entire night, went unheard. What could be more unblessed than this? How could one expect that such an individual could be an intercessor for others? I do not recall ever having had the opportunity to pray for two hours and then having had my prayer go unaccepted.

---

[1]   *ash-Shura*, 42:41
[2]   *al-Baqarah*, 2:62

In contrast, however, the condition of the son of God, rather, God himself (God forbid) is such that he himself prayed all night long, weeping, nay, wailing and screaming, while asking others to pray for him as well. He continued to say: 'O God! Nothing is impossible for you. If possible, do take away this cup,' but his prayer was simply not accepted.

If anyone were to suggest that Jesus[as] came for atonement and this is why his prayer was not accepted, I would say that when he knew that his purpose was to atone for the sins of man, then why such cowardice? If an official was sent on a duty to deal with an outbreak of plague, and he said that he was being sent in harm's way, and requested to be sent somewhere else, would not such a person be deemed foolish? Now when the Messiah knew that he had been sent only to atone for the sins of man, then what was the need for such lengthy supplications? Was the matter still under deliberation as to whether he would be required for atonement or was this matter already settled? Therefore, whether it is one blemish or two, or even countless blemishes, can such a one be God? Let alone God, such a person cannot even be considered a great individual.

Judaism

The poor Jews themselves are a manifestation of the following:

$$ضُرِبَتۡ عَلَيۡهِمُ الذِّلَّةَ^1$$

And they were smitten with abasement.

Their state of affairs could be described as in the following saying:

صورت .بيں حالش مپرس

Just look at his face, do not ask of his state.

They knew nothing but materialism. An Israelite here by the name of Muhammad Salman has converted to Islam, just ask him. The Jews have no other purpose but to eat and drink. It was God's decree that when the time came for ضُرِبَتۡ عَلَيۡهِمُ الذِّلَّةَ, i.e. for the Jews to suffer disgrace, it so happened that such actions took root in them which drew in and ultimately resulted in this disgrace. If they had repented, why would they become an illustration of this verse? This prophecy demonstrates that the consequences of their evil actions will forever remain as a collar around

---

1   *al-Baqarah*, 2:62

their necks. A righteous man is never disgraced or deprived of provision. One name of God is *Aziz* (Mighty). A person who lives a life that is devoted to God can never be disgraced. If the Jews were not living a life of impurity, why would they have suffered the consequences mentioned in the following verse:

$$ضُرِبَتْ عَلَيْهِمُ الذِّلَّةُ$$

And they were smitten with abasement.

Reflect on this closely. This possesses hidden secrets and one realises that the ways of the Jewish people would become corrupted.

Now, after casting a glance upon these religions, tell us sincerely, is there any other way that your heart may be satisfied? Can you gain any light from the Jews who are a manifestation of ضُرِبَتْ عَلَيْهِمُ الذِّلَّةُ *(those smitten with disgrace)*? Can the Christians, who deify a humble, weak, powerless unsuccessful man, give anyone success? What fruits can a man give to others who pray, when his own night-long prayers were useless and in vain? How can a man who says: *'Eloi, eloi, lama sabachthani,'* meaning, 'O God! O God! Why hast thou forsaken me?' and admits that God has abandoned him, join others with God?

Only Islam Possesses Living Blessings

Observe and listen closely! It is Islam alone which possesses blessings and does not let one fall into despair or failure. The proof is that I stand as an example of its blessings, life and truthfulness. No Christian can demonstrate that they hold a relationship with heaven. The hallmark of a believing Christian, as stated by Christianity, is that if a believer says unto a mountain, move from this place, it shall move. But what to speak of a mountain. There is not a single Christian who can flip over an overturned shoe.

On the other hand, I have demonstrated and clearly shown through my powerful signs that living blessings and living signs are the distinction of Islam alone. I have published innumerable announcements, and on one occasion I published 16,000 copies of an announcement. Now these people have nothing in their hands but to file fabricated cases against me in court, falsely implicate me in murder, and hatch conspiracies to disgrace me. But how can a servant of the Mighty God be disgraced by the means through which they have sought my dishonour? It was this very 'dishonour' which paved for me a way to honour.

ذٰلِكَ فَضۡلُ اللّٰهِ يُؤۡتِيۡهِ مَنۡ يَّشَآءُ[1]

That is Allah's grace; He bestows it on whom He pleases.

You see, if the Clarke case had not taken place, how would the revelation have been fulfilled, which foretold of my acquittal and which had been published to the knowledge of hundreds of people even before this case was contrived? It is Islam alone that is supported by miracles and evidence. Islam does not depend on any other source of light; it is a lamp in itself and its forms of evidence are so brilliant and clearly apparent that no likeness can be found in any other religion. Hence, there is no Islamic teaching for which a practical example does not exist.

The Holy Prophet[sa] Is a Manifestation of God's Attributes

I shall demonstrate how an illustration of each and every one of the the four attributes mentioned in *Surah al-Fatihah*—which is also known as the 'Mother of the Book' and the 'Oft-repeated' and which serves as a reflection and summary of the Holy Quran—could be seen exemplified in the Messenger of Allah, peace and blessings of Allah be upon him. In other words, these attributes held the value of a claim and the person of the Messenger of Allah, peace and blessings of Allah be upon him, served as evidence in their favour.

As such, what a strong proof of God's providence *(rububiyyat)* was given in the person of the Holy Prophet[sa]. Who was concerned with the upbringing of a child who wandered the Meccan wilderness perplexed and who went from place to place bewildered with apparently no avenues of opportunity? Who knew that Islam would spread to the ends of the earth and that that child would later go on to have 900 million followers? Now one may observe, however, that there is no inhabited land where Muslims cannot be found.

Then, reflect over God's attribute *ar-Rahman* (the Gracious), the purpose of which is to provide—without any prior action on the part of man—the means of success and other necessities. What immense graciousness of the Divine that even before the advent of the Holy Prophet[sa], God created the faculties and aptitudes that were needed. Umar, may Allah be pleased with him, played like normal children and Abu Bakr, may Allah be pleased with him, was born in the home of disbelievers. Yet both of them, along with other companions, joined the Holy Prophet[sa]. It is as though divine graciousness had already prepared these individu-

---

[1]   *al-Jumuah*, 62:5

als for the Holy Prophet[sa] well in advance. There are so many examples of God's graciousness in favour of Islam that I cannot even mention them in detail. However, the nature of being unlettered *(ummiyyat)* naturally attracts divine graciousness *(rahmaniyyat)*. Allah Almighty stated with regards to the Noble Prophet, peace and blessings of Allah be upon him:

$$هُوَ الَّذِىْ بَعَثَ فِى الْأُمِّيْنَ رَسُوْلًا١$$

He it is Who has raised among the Unlettered people a Messenger.

The objective of divine graciousness can be wonderfully understood by the following adage:

$$کر دے کرا دے اور اٹھانے والا ساتھ دے$$

*Tend to my affair, have my work done, and give
me someone to carry the burden.*

This happened at the very advent of Islam. Islam is a child in the lap of God, as it were. It is God Himself who tends to all of its needs and provides the necessities that it requires. Its neck is not burdened by the favour of any creature.

Then, *ar-Rahim* (the Merciful) is the attribute that does not allow efforts to go in vain. The opposite of this would be if someone remained occupied in efforts but still met failure. Now just observe how evidently divine mercy was manifested in favour of the Messenger of Allah, peace and blessings of Allah be upon him. There was no contest in which he did not triumph. Even small efforts brought forth immense fruit. His victories shone forth like flashes of lightening. Just look at the triumphs in Syria and Egypt. There is no human being on the face of the earth who attained success in the true sense, as did our Prophet, peace and blessings of Allah be upon him.

The Companions Attained Success in This World

Moving on, there is the divine attribute *maliki yawm-id-din*, i.e. master of reward and punishment, which refers to the giving of reward for deeds well done. Although this will fully be realised in the hereafter, and every nation states that reward and punishment will be given in the next life, but God has given a taste of this to the Muslims in this very world.

---

1   *al-Jumuah*, 62:3

Abu Bakr, may Allah be pleased with him, came forth to offer himself in the scorching afternoon sun, leaving behind his home, along with his wealth and possessions. He cast a glance on all his property and said: 'Let it perish, let it be lost.' He detached himself from everything and joined the Holy Prophet[sa]. He was bestowed the honour of becoming the first Caliph immediately after the Holy Prophet[sa]. Then, Hazrat Umar[ra] became so replete with faith and sincerity that he was bestowed the honour of becoming the second Caliph. In short, each and every companion of the Holy Prophet[sa] received great honour. The riches of the Caesar and Chosroes were handed over to them and they were married to their princesses. It is written that a companion of the Holy Prophet[sa] went to see the Chosroes in his royal court. The servants of the Chosroes arranged seats made of silver and gold before him in order to flaunt their pomp and splendour. The companion said, this wealth does not enamour us, for we have been promised that even the bangles of the Chosroes himself will come into our possession. As such, at a later time Hazrat Umar, may Allah be pleased with him, put these bangles on a certain companion so that the prophecy was fulfilled.

The Moderate Way of Islam

Since the religion of Islam follows a middle path, Allah the Exalted has instructed, therefore, to save ourselves from those who have incurred divine displeasure and those who have gone astray. A true Muslim can neither be one to incur the wrath of God, nor be among those who are astray. Those who have incurred the displeasure of God refers to a nation that has roused the wrath of God Almighty; since these people were wrathful themselves, they drew in the anger of God— these people are the Jews. The Christians are the ones termed as misguided.

The state of anger is provoked by the beastly faculty in man and misguidance is the result of man's faculty of imagination, and the faculty of imagination grows out of excessive love. Misplaced love causes a man to be misled.

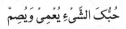

Your love for a thing makes you blind and deaf.

This state is caused by and describes the faculty of imagination. The example of one drowned in this state is that he will think that a sheet of cloth is an ox for example, or that a rope is a snake. This is why every poet has described their lover to be above and beyond those of others. The imagination of each and every one has conjured up their own unique image.

When the beastly faculty in man is stirred, a human being is derailed from the path of moderation. As such, in a state of anger, a beast is inflamed even more. For example, initially a dog will bark in a low voice, but when further provoked, it becomes very noisy. Ultimately, beasts will grow in their rage to the extent that they begin to claw and tear into flesh until they devour it.

In the same manner, the Jews also had developed within themselves evil habits of cruelty and oppression, and had grown in their rage to extreme levels. Finally, it was they themselves who became the recipients of wrath. When the imaginative faculty of man gains control of him, he will say that a rope is actually a snake and that a tree is really an elephant, and will provide no evidence for his assertion. This faculty is more predominant in women. This is why the Christian faith and idolatry depends heavily on women. In short, Islam has taught man to tread the path of moderation, which is known as *as-sirat-ul-mustaqim* (the straight path).

I shall now say a few words in Arabic because Allah the Exalted has instructed that I say a few sentences in Arabic to the gathering. Initially, I had thought that it was some other gathering in which this instruction of God would be fulfilled. However, may God Almighty give Maulvi Abdul-Karim Sahib[ra] a goodly reward for putting forth this proposal. It was this proposal of his which moved me to feel a powerful strength in my heart to do so. I trust that on this day, a promise and sign of Allah the Exalted has been fulfilled."

The Promised Messiah[as] was about to commence his address in Arabic when Maulana Abdul-Karim Sahib[ra] submitted: "Your Holiness! Please say a few words on mutual concord and love amongst the community." On this, His Holiness[as] made the address that follows.

Mutual Concord and Love

The Promised Messiah[as] said: "I have spoken many times before about the mutual concord and love that ought to prevail within our community. I have stated that you all ought to remain reconciled and united. This is the teaching that God Almighty gave to the Muslims that you must all remain as one being, or you will lose your stature. The reason that Muslims have been instructed to stand together in Prayer with their shoulders touching one another is to foster unity. The goodness in one person will flow into the next like an electric current. If you are divided and disunited, you shall be deprived.

The Messenger of Allah, peace and blessings of Allah be upon him, has said that you ought to love one another and pray for each other even without the other's knowledge. If an individual prays for someone without their knowledge, an angel says: 'May it be so for you as well.' What an outstanding thing indeed! If someone were to suggest that man's prayers are not heard, at least they will agree that the prayers of an angel are accepted. I would like to advise you and say that there should be no discord amongst you.

I have only brought you two teachings: firstly, to believe in the Oneness of God; secondly, to show one another love and sympathy. Show an example that serves as a miracle for others. This was what developed amongst the companions and it served as an argument to others. Allah the Exalted states:

$$كُنْتُمْ اَعْدَآءً فَاَلَّفَ بَيْنَ قُلُوبِكُمْ ^1$$

You were enemies and He united your hearts in love.

Remember! Unity is a miracle. Remember! Until each and every one of you likes for your brother what you prefer for yourselves, you are not from among my community. Such a one suffers misfortune and trial. He shall not meet a good end. I am about to prepare a book in which all those people who cannot control their emotions will be separated. People fight over trivial matters. For example, one person says that a certain performer jumped ten yards and another person will begin arguing on this point, and this then leads to malice.

Bear in mind that a sign of the Mahdi is that hatred would be dispelled. Now will this sign not be fulfilled? Indeed it will. So why do you not show forbearance? It is a fact in medicine that sometimes a disease cannot be cured until various other ailments are treated. Through my person, a righteous community will be established, God-willing.

What is the cause of mutual enmity? It is miserliness, pride, self-conceit, and emotional impulses. I have mentioned that I will soon write a book in which I shall remove all those from my community who do not have a grasp over their emotions, and who cannot coexist with mutual love and brotherhood. Those who act in this manner ought to remember that they are guests for a few days, unless they show an excellent example. I do not wish to be a target for objection on account of others. An individual who joins my community and does not act in

---

1 *Aal-e-Imran*, 3:104

line with my objective is a dry branch. If a gardener does not cut it off, what is he to do? A dry branch that is attached to a flourishing one sucks water but cannot become verdant itself. In fact, the dry branch causes the green branch to wither away as well. So have fear. One who does not cure themselves will not remain with me. Since I will provide a detailed explanation of all this in my book, now I shall say a few words in Arabic to fulfil my obligation."[1]

The Murder of Two Englishmen

During these days, a cruel Pathan murdered two innocent Englishmen in the region of Peshawar. On this, His Holiness[as] addressed a gathering and said: "This incident where two Englishmen have been murdered, is this Jihad? It is vile people like these who have given Islam a bad name. What this man ought to have done was care for these individuals and treat them in such an excellent manner so that they could have observed his morals and good conduct, and then become Muslims themselves. The duty of a believer is to crush his own ego.

It is written that Hazrat Ali, may Allah be pleased with him, was engaged in battle with a disbeliever. Hazrat Ali[ra] had subdued the man and just as he was about to bury his sword into the man, he spat on Hazrat Ali[ra]. On this, Hazrat Ali[ra] got up off of the man's chest. The man was surprised and asked: 'O Ali! What is the matter?' 'I was fighting you for the sake of God,' responded Hazrat Ali[ra], 'but now that you have spat on my face, my own ego has a part in this, so I have left you alone.' This act of Hazrat Ali[ra] had a deep effect on the man.

Whenever I hear such reports about these sorts of people, I am extremely grieved at the fact that they have become greatly distanced from the Holy Quran; they believe that the killing of innocent human beings results in spiritual reward.

Certain individuals from among the Muslim clergy call me 'Antichrist' because I have not deemed it permissible to wage war against the British. But what I find extremely regrettable is that these people call themselves *maulvis* (religious scholars) and then give Islam a bad name. Someone ought to ask them, what harm have the British done to them? What suffering have they caused them? It is a shame that a people whose arrival in this land has given us every kind of peace and comfort, and whose coming delivered us from the bloodthirsty claws of the Sikhs, and who provided us every opportunity and facility to propagate our religion, have been thanked for their favour with the killing of innocent British officials.

[1]   *Al-Hakam*, vol. 4, no. 14, dated 17 April 1900, pp. 2-9

I openly declare that those people who have no fear in spilling innocent blood and who do not fulfil the rights due to a benefactor are fully accountable before God Almighty. The task of the Muslim clergy ought to be to publicise this point with collective agreement and to admonish the uninformed and ignorant that they live their lives under the shade of the British government in security and freedom; thus, they are thereby obliged to the government, and owe it a debt of gratitude for its gifts. They ought to tell them that this blessed sovereignty is a true supporter in the dissemination of virtue and guidance. Therefore, any thought of waging war against this government is a terrible act of rebellion and is absolutely unlawful. The Muslim scholars ought to advise the ignorant both verbally and in writing and should not cause the world undue harm by defaming Islam. I consider the British government to be a heavenly blessing and deem it an obligation to value it.

It is a shame that the Muslim clergy have failed to undertake this task themselves, and when I endeavoured to dispel these ignorant notions from the hearts of people, they have called me an Antichrist—only because I am grateful to this kind government. But what harm can their opposition do to me? I have published scores of treatises on this subject in Arabic, Persian, Urdu and English, and have distributed thousands of announcements throughout various lands and cities, and not because I seek honour from the government. In fact, God Almighty knows well that I perform this task considering it to be an important obligation and even if I have to bear hardship to perform this service, I do not care in the least. For God has stated that the recompense of goodness is goodness the like thereof. Therefore, it is an obligation of the Muslims to show full obedience and loyalty to the British government."[1]

May 1900

The Passionate Sympathy of the Prophets

The Promised Messiah[as] states: "The coming of a Prophet is necessary. They come with a spiritual power and possess a fervour in their hearts which makes them restless due to their sympathy for mankind, their desire to do good to others and on account of their sentiments of universal goodwill. God Almighty states with regards to the Messenger of Allah, peace and blessings of Allah be upon him:

---

[1] *Al-Hakam*, vol. 4, no. 14, dated 17 April 1900, pp. 10-11

لَعَلَّكَ بَاخِعٌ نَّفْسَكَ اَلَّا يَكُوْنُوْا مُؤْمِنِيْنَ[1]

Meaning, will you grieve yourself to death because they do not believe? There are two aspects to this: firstly, it relates to the disbelievers and their not converting to Islam; secondly, this is also in relation to the Muslims and why they do not develop in themselves a spiritual power of the highest level—as was the case with the Holy Prophet[sa] himself. Since progress is attained gradually, the advances of the companions were also in stages. However, the hearts of the Prophets are an embodiment of sheer sympathy. Now, our Noble Prophet, peace and blessings of Allah be upon him, encompassed all the excellences of prophethood. The Holy Prophet[sa] thus possessed this sympathy to the highest degree. He would look at the companions and desire for them to attain the greatest heights, but this apex was destined to find fulfilment at a certain time. Ultimately, the companions attained that which the world had never received before and witnessed that which no one else had ever seen.

The Entire Foundation Rests on Struggle

The entire foundation rests on struggle. God Almighty states:

وَالَّذِيْنَ جَاهَدُوْا فِيْنَا لَنَهْدِيَنَّهُمْ سُبُلَنَا[2]

This means, those who strive in our way, we open to them all the avenues that lead to us. Nothing can happen without struggle. Those people who say that Syed Abdul-Qadir Jilani, may Allah have mercy on him, turned a robber into a saint, with a single glance, are deluded. It is statements like these which have ruined the people. People think that an individual can be transformed into a saint by incantations and spells.

Those who act hastily in the matter of God perish. Everything in the world progresses in stages. Spiritual advancement is no different and nothing can happen without struggle; and that struggle too must be in the way of God. One cannot make up their own futile ascetic practices and exercises like yogis. The very task for which I have been appointed by God is to demonstrate to the world how one can reach Allah the Exalted. This is the law of nature, neither do all people remain deprived, nor do all people receive guidance."[3]

---

[1]	*ash-Shu'ara*, 26:4
[2]	*al-Ankabut*, 29:70
[3]	*Al-Hakam*, vol. 4, no. 16, dated 1 May 1900, p. 6

14 May 1900

The Purpose for Remaining in the Company of the Righteous

The Promised Messiah[as] states: "The fact is that I look at the practice of seeking help from the dead with extreme disgust. It is a characteristic of those who are weak in faith to turn to the dead and flee from those who are alive. God Almighty states that during the life of Joseph, peace be upon him, the people rejected his prophethood, but the day that he passed away, they began to say that on this day prophethood has come to an end. Allah the Exalted has not instructed anywhere that we should turn to the dead; in fact, He gives the following commandment:

$$كُوْنُوْا مَعَ الصّٰدِقِيْنَ^{1}$$

Be with the truthful.

In doing so, God Almighty has instructed us to remain in the company of those who are living. This is precisely the reason that I encourage my friends emphatically to come here again and again. When I invite my friends to come and stay here with me, Allah the Exalted knows full well that I do so merely on account of my sympathy for their condition, as an expression of mercy upon them and out of my goodwill for them.

I truthfully say that faith cannot be rectified until a person remains in the company of one who possesses faith. This is because dispositions are diverse. A person who gives counsel cannot deliver a speech that addresses the state of every unique disposition at the same time. A time will arise when the discussions are in line with a person's understanding, way of thinking, and nature, and this brings beneficial results. However, if a man does not come here repeatedly and does not stay for a good number of days, it is possible that the discussion at that time (when the person is present here) may not accord with his nature. This in turn may dishearten the individual in question and push them away from thinking positively, ultimately leading them to ruin. Therefore, as per the the Holy Quran, it is the living in whose company we have been instructed to remain.

Only God Almighty Ought to Be Implored for Help

Moreover, as far as seeking assistance is concerned, it ought to be remembered

---

[1] *at-Tawbah*, 9:119

that in reality, it is Allah the Exalted alone who deserves to be implored for help. This is what the Holy Quran emphasises. As such, God Almighty states:

اِیَّاکَ نَعْبُدُ وَاِیَّاکَ نَسْتَعِیْنُ ¹

Thee alone do we worship and Thee alone do we implore for help.

Firstly, God Almighty states His attributes; *rabb* (Lord), *rahman* (Gracious), *rahim* (Merciful) and *maliki yawm-id-din* (Master of the Day of Judgement). Then He taught us the following:

اِیَّاکَ نَعْبُدُ وَاِیَّاکَ نَسْتَعِیْنُ ²

In other words, we worship Thee alone and it is from You that we seek assistance. From this we learn that the right to be implored for help is the sole prerogative of Allah the Exalted. No human being; no animal, whether beast or bird; no creation whatsoever, whether in the heaven or on earth, has this right. However, in the partial sense, as reflections of God, this right is given to saintly people and the holy men of God. We must not invent things of our own accord, rather we ought to remain within the boundaries of Allah's commandments and the Messenger of Allah, peace and blessings of Allah be upon him—this is the right path *(sirat-e-mustaqim)*. This point can also be understood from the following:

لَا اِلٰهَ اِلَّا اللهُ مُحَمَّدٌ رَّسُوْلُ اللهِ

There is none worthy of worship except Allah, and Muhammad[sa] is the Messenger of Allah.

The first part of this makes it clear that man ought to hold Allah the Exalted alone to be his beloved, worthy of worship and his objective.

The Deeper Reality of the Prophethood of Muhammad[sa]

The second part of the Muslim creed expresses the deeper reality of the prophethood of Muhammad, peace and blessings of Allah be upon him. It ought to be borne in mind that in prophethood there is an apparent aspect and a hidden aspect. For example, لَا اِلٰهَ اِلَّا اللهُ *(There is none worthy of worship except Allah)* is a phrase that the Holy Prophet[sa] conveyed to the people exactly in these words.

---

¹ *al-Fatihah*, 1:5
² *al-Fatihah*, 1:5

People are free to accept this or not; that is to say, the task of prophethood is merely to convey the message. However, this is the apparent meaning of prophethood. When we reflect more deeply and delve into the inner realms of this matter, we realise that the prophethood of the Messenger of Allah, peace and blessings of Allah be upon him, which is an inseparable part of لَا اِلٰهَ اِلَّا اللّٰه *(There is none worthy of worship except Allah)* is not limited to a mere conveyance of the message, but that the Holy Prophet, peace and blessings of Allah be upon him, through the force of his spiritual power, demonstrated an unparalleled example in making this propagation of the message truly influential.

The Motherly Benevolence of a Prophet

The Holy Quran also describes that degree of burning passion and anguish with which the Holy Prophet[sa] was consumed. As such, Allah the Exalted states:

$$لَعَلَّكَ بَاخِعٌ نَّفْسَكَ اَلَّا يَكُوْنُوْا مُؤْمِنِيْنَ ^1$$

Meaning, will you grieve yourself to death because they do not believe? It is a certain fact that every Prophet carries within themselves pain, emotion and anguish for the reformation of their people, and not just empty words. Moreover, this pain and perturbation is not artificial; rather it gushes forth naturally in a state of restlessness, just like a mother who remains absorbed in the upbringing of her child. Even if a king issued an order stating that a mother who did not give her child milk would not be responsible for her negligence, and that if even one or two of her children died because of this, she would be forgiven without question, would any mother be pleased by such an order? Of course not. Rather, she would curse the king. A mother simply cannot refrain from giving her child milk. This characteristic is naturally ingrained in her disposition and in giving her child milk, her object or motive is never to be admitted into paradise or to receive a reward. Rather, this fervour of hers is an inherent quality that is invested in her by nature. If this was not the case, then mothers in the animal kingdom, such as the mothers of goats, buffalos, cows and birds, ought to have turned away from the upbringing of their offspring. This is nature, it is a sense, a passion. It is nature's way for mothers to remain engaged in the upbringing of their young.

In the same manner, the divinely commissioned of God also possess a certain quality in their nature. What is that quality? It is their burning heart for God's

---

1 *Ash-Shu'ara*, 26:4

creation and their passionate benevolence for mankind. It is in their very nature to desire that the people may be guided and may be blessed with a life that is devoted to God.

Thus, this is the secret behind the second phrase in لَا اِلٰهَ اِلَّا اللّٰهُ مُحَمَّدٌ رَسُوْلُ اللّٰهِ *(There is none worthy of worship except Allah, and Muhammad*sa *is the Messenger of Allah)* which proclaims the prophethood of Muhammadsa. Those who convey a message often do so without caring about whether the recipient acts in accordance with the message or not. In other words, this conveyance of the message is limited only to the ears. Contrary to this, however, the divinely commissioned not only convey their message to the people's ears, but through the means and force of their spiritual power, they convey it to their hearts as well. Then, this magnetic attraction and firm resolve is given to an individual when they are cloaked in the mantle of God Almighty and become a reflection of Allah. It is then that they feel a restlessness within themselves for the sympathy and betterment of mankind. In this respect, our Noble Prophet, peace and blessings of Allah be upon him, was greater than all the other Prophets, peace be upon them. This is why he could not bear to see God's creatures in pain. As such, God Almighty states:

$$عَزِيْزٌ عَلَيْهِ مَا عَنِتُّمْ ^{1}$$

Meaning, this Messenger cannot bear to see you in pain, for this weighs down heavily on him. He is forever consumed and longs for you all to attain great and far-reaching rewards.

All of these points make it evident that first and foremost, it is God Almighty who helps us, and after Him come those who are commissioned by Allah, on account of the fervour that Allah the Almighty has placed in their hearts. It is due to the natural demands of this very fervour that they strive in every possible way for the betterment of mankind in the same manner that a mother gives her child milk—rather, even more so than her. For a mother is not appointed to purify, but a divinely commissioned one of God is responsible for purifying the people. It is these very people who have been referred to as the truthful in the following verse:

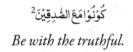

Be with the truthful.

The Class of Those Upon Whom Allah Has Bestowed His Blessings

I now wish to turn to *Surah Fatihah* and state that in the words: [1] اِهۡدِنَا الصِّرَاطَ الۡمُسۡتَقِیۡمَ
(Guide us in the right path) we seek the way of اَنۡعَمۡتَ عَلَیۡهِمۡ *(on whom Thou hast bestowed Thy blessings)*. I have stated many times that there are four classes of people referred to in اَنۡعَمۡتَ عَلَیۡهِمۡ *(on whom Thou hast bestowed Thy blessings)*— the Prophets, the Truthful, the Martyrs and the Righteous. Hence, when a believer offers this supplication, they actually make a request to be blessed with the morals, habits and knowledge of these classes. As a result of this prayer, if an individual does not develop the morals of these four classes of people, then this supplication would prove to be futile in his respect and the person who makes this entreaty is nothing more than an animal who utters lifeless words.

These four classes of people are those who have attained sublime knowledge and lofty ranks from God Almighty. The Prophets are those whose detachment from all else for the sake of God reaches such a state that they converse with God and receive revelation from Him. The Truthful are those who love truth. The greatest truth is لَاۤ اِلٰهَ اِلَّا اللّٰه *(There is none worthy of worship except Allah)* and the second truth is مُحَمَّدٌ رَّسُوۡلُ اللّٰهِ *(Muhammad[sa] is the Messenger of Allah)*. Such people hold dear all the avenues of truth and pursue nothing but the truth. Thirdly, there are those who are called the Martyrs who, as if, witness God. A Martyr is not merely one who is killed, or a person who dies in battle or by some epidemic. In fact, a Martyr is a person who is so strong in faith that they do not even hesitate in laying down their lives for the sake of God Almighty. The class of the Righteous are those who are purged from every inner corruption. For example, when a person is healthy, the taste of their tongue is also perfectly fine. In a state of complete equilibrium, such a one is deemed fully healthy and no disorder exists internally. In the same manner, the Righteous do not suffer from any form of spiritual illness from within and they are free from all elements of corruption. The pinnacle of this state is attained through a person's negation, whereas the excellence of a Martyr, the Truthful and a Prophet are in practical demonstration. A Martyr strengthens their faith to the extent that they behold God. Then, the Truthful actively love the truth and abstain from falsehood. Finally, the excellence of a Prophet is that he is cloaked in the mantle of Allah. Some people assert that these excellences cannot be attained by any other person. The Muslim clergy

---

[1] *al-Fatihah*, 1:6

and scholars say that a person ought to simply say the Muslim creed verbally, and adhere to the injunctions of Prayer and fasting, for beyond this there are no fruits or rewards in the observance of these commandments, nor do they possess any deeper reality. This is a grave error on their part and demonstrates a weakness of faith. Such people have misunderstood the very objective of prophethood.

The Purpose of the Divinely Commissioned

Does Allah the Exalted send those divinely commissioned by Him and His Messengers—who are sent for the guidance of humanity—so that the people will worship them? Nay, on the contrary, they are sent as an example. The example of this is like a king who gives the skilled workers of his country a sword. The purpose of this is obviously so that they too strive to forge a similar sword.

Allah the Exalted instils lofty morals and praiseworthy qualities in those whom He sends to the world in the form of His divinely commissioned ones and His Messengers, so that the common people may partake of their morals and excellences, and adopt similar manners and behaviours. For these holy men give benefit to the people for as long as they are alive. After their demise, they become physically detached from this world. This is why the Sufis say that a living cat is better than a dead lion. Allah the Exalted states in His Holy Word:

$$الٓرٰ كِتٰبٌ اُحْكِمَتْ اٰيٰتُهٗ^1$$

Alif Lam Ra. This is a Book whose verses have been made unchangeable and then they have been expounded in detail. It is from One Wise, and All-Aware.

The letter *alif* stands for Allah, the *lam* is for *Jibril* (Gabriel), and the letter *ra* stands for *rusul* (the Messengers). Since the subject of this chapter revolves around the necessary things that human beings require, for this reason God states:

$$كِتٰبٌ اُحْكِمَتْ اٰيٰتُهٗ^2$$

In other words, this is a Book whose verses are sound and firm.

The Solid Nature of the Holy Quran

Allah the Exalted has reinforced the teachings of the Holy Quran in many ways so that no doubt whatsoever remains. This is precisely the reason that He states

---

[1] *Hud,* 11:2
[2] *Hud,* 11:2

in the very beginning:

لَا رَيْبَ فِيْهِ¹

There is no doubt in it.

Allah the Exalted has strengthened the Holy Quran in many ways. Firstly, He has corroborated and reinforced the teachings of the Quran through the law of nature. Everything that is mentioned in the Holy Quran is supported by the law of nature. In other words, whatever is comprised in the Quran is exactly what we find in the hidden book of nature. This secret cannot be understood unless one follows the Prophets, peace be upon them. It is this very secret to which the following alludes:

لَا يَمَسُّهُ إِلَّا الْمُطَهَّرُوْنَ²

None shall touch it except those who are purified.

Therefore, firstly, the teaching of the Quran has been corroborated by the law of nature. For example, the Holy Quran states that an attribute of Allah the Exalted is that He is One and without partner. Now, when we reflect over the law of nature, one must accept that there is only one Creator and Master, and that He has no partner. This is what our heart tells us and this is what we find from the argumentation furnished by nature itself. For everything in the world possesses a spherical nature within it. For example if someone were to let a drop of water fall from their hand, it would be spherical in shape, and the spherical form necessitates oneness. It is for this reason that the Christian priests have had to concede that where the teachings of Trinity have not been conveyed, the inhabitants of such places would be judged by the concept of Divine Oneness. As such, Reverend Pfander has admitted this in his writings. This establishes that even if the Holy Quran had not existed in the world, even then worship of the One God would prevail. This also demonstrates that the words of the Holy Quran are true, because the imprint of these words is etched on the very nature and heart of man, and the argumentation furnished by nature also provides evidence of these words. On the contrary, no imprint of the Trinity proposed by the Gospel can be found in the heart, and nor is this concept supported by the law of nature. This is the meaning of the following words:

---

¹   *al-Baqarah*, 2:3
²   *al-Waqi'ah*, 56:80

كِتَبٌ اُحْكِمَتْ اٰيَتُهُ[1]

This is a Book whose verses have been made firm.

In other words, the teachings of the Holy Quran have been made so firm and sound that even idolators and Christians have had to admit that it is God's Oneness—the essence of man's nature—by which human beings will be questioned by Allah Almighty.

The second means by which the Holy Quran has been strengthened is through the signs of God Almighty. There is no Prophet or divinely commissioned man of God, who has not been supported by divine succour. The support and signs that accompanied our Noble Prophet, peace and blessings of Allah be upon him, are immensely magnificent and powerful. There were signs in the actions of the Holy Prophet[sa] and in his words. In other words, the very being of the Holy Prophet[sa] was a complete embodiment of divine signs.

The third means by which the Holy Quran was reinforced was the pure conduct and righteousness of the Holy Prophet[sa]. The wise also consider the trustworthy nature of an individual to constitute evidence of their truthfulness, and the aforementioned qualities are a part of this. For example, Hazrat Abu Bakr Siddiq[ra] accepted this to be a valid argument.

The fourth means by which the Holy Quran was corroborated, which is a powerful proof of its sound and firm nature is the spiritual power of the Prophet which shows its practical benefit. For example, a physician could make tall claims about his skill and ability, and may well know *Sadidi*[2] like the back of his hand, but if he cannot make his patients well, everyone will simply say that this physician is unable to cure people. In the same manner, the greatness and loftiness of a Prophet's grandeur is proportional to the degree that his spiritual power wields strength. In order to reinforce the teaching of the Holy Quran, this form of support is the greatest.

The Spiritual Power of the Holy Prophet[sa]

The spiritual power of the Prophet of God, peace and blessings of Allah be upon him, is at a level that if it was contrasted to any of the other Prophets, peace be upon them, it would appear that no other Prophet achieved anything in compari-

---

[1]   *Hud*, 11:2
[2]   A book of medicine. [Publisher]

son to him. The Jews are slaves of materialism. Then, look at the Christians and you will find that they have become distanced from the fountainhead of God's Oneness. There are some who worship Mary[as], there are others who consider the Messiah[as] to be God—the worship of this world has become the preoccupation and pursuit of the people. However, if one looks at the community prepared by the Holy Prophet, peace and blessings of Allah be upon him, it is apparent that they were wholly devoted to God and their practical lives had no match. The blessed and successful life of the Holy Prophet, peace and blessings of Allah be upon him, may be illustrated by an example. The Holy Prophet[sa] came to perform an assignment and he only left this world once he had completed it, in the likeness of officials who prepare their documents over a five-year period, then they appear to report one last time before returning home. This is exactly what we observe in the life of the Messenger of Allah, peace and blessings of Allah be upon him. If we cast a glance over his prophethood, from the beginning when he heard the call [1] قُمْ فَأَنْذِرْ (*arise and warn*) to the end when he was given the tidings of [2] إِذَاجَآءَنَصْرُاللّٰهِ (*when the help of Allah comes*) and [3] اَلْيَوْمَ اَكْمَلْتُ لَكُمْ دِيْنَكُمْ (*this day have I perfected your religion for you*), we are able to appreciate the unparalleled success of the Holy Prophet[sa]. These verses clearly demonstrate that the Holy Prophet[sa] was appointed for a special task. Moses[as] did not receive the success that was the ultimate objective of his prophethood. He was unable to see the Holy Land—the land that was promised to him—with his own eyes, and passed away on the journey. How would a disbeliever accept? Why would a faithless man bother listening to the reasons as to why Moses[as] died *en route* and was not able to reach the promised land? A disbeliever would say that if Moses[as] was divinely appointed, then why were these promises not fulfilled? In actuality, it was the Noble Prophet, peace and blessings of Allah be upon him, who saved the honour of all the other prophethoods of the past Prophets.

The Life of Christ

Similarly, if one observes the life of the Messiah it becomes clear that he spent the entire night praying himself and asked his friends to pray as well, but ultimately began to complain and said: '*Eloi, eloi, lama sabachthani*,' meaning, 'O God! O

---

1   *Al-Muddaththir*, 74:3
2   *an-Nasr*, 110:2
3   *al-Ma'idah*, 5:4

God! Why hast thou forsaken me?' Now who would look at this regretful state and say that he was commissioned by Allah? The image of Christ in his final state as put forth by the Christian priests consistently is one which causes utter despair.

These people make such tall claims that may heaven preserve us, yet Christ did not really achieve anything. Over the span of his entire life all he managed to do was to prepare a community of 120 people, and even these people were so foolish and ignorant that they could not even understand matters relating to the kingdom of God. Then, his greatest disciple, about whom Christ had declared that whatever you do on earth shall be done in heaven and in whose hand were the keys of the kingdom of heaven, was the first to curse Christ. Then, the man whom Christ had appointed as his treasurer and keeper, and in whom he took great pride, had him arrested for thirty pieces of silver. Now in such a state of affairs, who can say that the Messiah truly did justice to his divine appointment?

In contrast, the work of our Noble Prophet[sa] is of such standard that first he announced that he had come with a task at hand, and then he did not leave this world until he had finally heard the words:

$$اَلۡیَوۡمَ اَکۡمَلۡتُ لَکُمۡ دِیۡنَکُمۡ^1$$

This day have I perfected your religion for you.

The Holy Prophet[sa] claimed:

$$اِنِّیۡ رَسُوۡلُ اللّٰهِ اِلَیۡکُمۡ جَمِیۡعًا^2$$

Truly I am a Messenger to you all.

Now in view of this claim, it was necessary for the Holy Prophet[sa] to be opposed with all the schemes and conspiracies of the world. Just observe the resolve and courage with which the Holy Prophet[sa] proclaimed:

$$فَکِیۡدُوۡنِیۡ جَمِیۡعًا^3$$

In other words, leave no stone unturned, employ all the deceit and artifices that you can, hatch conspiracies to kill me, plot schemes to expel me or imprison me, but remember: $سَیُهۡزَمُ الۡجَمۡعُ وَ یُوَلُّوۡنَ الدُّبُرَ^4$, the final victory will be mine. All of your plans will be turned to dust. All your hosts will be scattered and dispersed; they

---

1　　al-Ma'idah, 5:4
2　　al-A'raf, 7:159
3　　Hud, 11:56
4　　al-Qamar, 54:46

will turn their backs and flee. No one made the magnificent proclamation:

اِنِّیۡ رَسُوۡلُ اللّٰهِ اِلَیۡکُمۡ جَمِیۡعًا [1]

Similarly, no one had the courage to say:

فَکِیۡدُوۡنِیۡ جَمِیۡعًا [2]

So devise plans against me, all of you.

In the same manner, no one declared:

سَیُهۡزَمُ الۡجَمۡعُ وَیُوَلُّوۡنَ الدُّبُرَ [3]

The hosts shall soon be routed and will turn their backs in flight.

This declaration was made only by the one who lay wrapped in the mantle of divinity, under the shadow of God Almighty.

In short, even if a stranger were to cast a glance upon these events, they would realise how clearly and evidently Allah Almighty has strengthened and reinforced the Book of Allah. When one studies the law of nature, one finds the word and action of God to be in harmony. Then, in respect of miracles, there are so many that they are beyond the scope of estimation. This is to such an extent that every statement, action, and movement of the Holy Prophet[sa] were miracles in themselves. Then, in the context of the spiritual power of the Holy Prophet[sa], the pure transformation of the noble companions is astonishing. Further, when one observes the success of the Holy Prophet[sa] it becomes evident that he was greater than all the Messengers and those who have been divinely commissioned.

In addition to the aforementioned aspects which reinforce the verses of the Holy Quran, there are many others as well. Of all these various elements, one small abbreviation alone الر *(alif laam raa)* alludes to an ongoing succession of Reformers and Messengers, which shall continue until the Day of Resurrection. Now the miracles, achievements and holy effects of the Reformers appearing in this community, among other things, are all factors that reinforce the verses of the Holy Quran, and which are beyond one's ability to count.

---

[1]   *al-A'raf,* 7:159
[2]   *Hud,* 11:56
[3]   *al-Qamar,* 54:46

The Success of Followers Is Actually the Success of Their Master

All of these miracles and successes which took place after the demise of the Messenger of Allah, peace and blessings of Allah be upon him, through his followers, and through Reformers, and which shall be attained until the Day of Resurrection, are actually the success of the Messenger of Allah, peace and blessings of Allah be upon him. In short, the coming of a Reformer *(Mujaddid)* at the head of every century clearly demonstrates that seeking help from the dead is contrary to the will of God Almighty. If help was to be sought from the dead, what need would there have been for the advent of the living? What significance would there have been in the many thousands of saints that have been born? Why would the institution of Reformers have been instituted by God? If Islam was to be handed over to the dead, then know for certain that all traces of it would have vanished already. The religion of the Jews was entrusted to the dead. What was the result? Do tell me, what did the Christians gain by worshipping the dead? They went on worshipping the dead until they themselves became dead. Neither has the spirit of life remained in their religion, nor do the followers of their religion possess any signs of life. From beginning to end, these people have become a horde of the dead.

The Self-Subsisting and All-Sustaining God of Islam

Islam is a living Faith. The God of Islam is a Self-Subsisting and All-Sustaining God. Why then would He love those who are dead? Time and again, that Self-Subsisting and All-Sustaining God gives a new life to the dead.

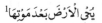

Allah is now quickening the earth after its death.[1]

Now does God do so by clinging to the dead? Nay, not at all. This Self-Subsisting and All-Sustaining God has taken it upon Himself to safeguard Islam and so He states:

We will be its Guardian.[2]

---

[1]   *al-Hadid*, 57:18
[2]   *al-Hijr*, 15:10

Hence, in every era, this religion receives life from those who possess life themselves, and revives the dead. Bear in mind that on every step it is those blessed with life who come to serve the Faith.

The Detail Expounded in the Holy Quran

Then, Allah the Exalted states in the Holy Quran:

Then they (i.e. the verses of the Quran) have been expounded in detail.

Firstly, there is the detail that is expounded in the Holy Quran; secondly, there is the continuous unveiling of divine insights and verities that shall extend until the Day of Resurrection. In every era, new insights and secrets are revealed. Philosophers expound them in their own way, physicians do so according to their own disposition and Sufis in their own manner. Moreover, this detail has been encapsulated in the Holy Quran by the All-Wise, All-Aware God. The attribute *Hakeem* (All-Wise) refers to a being who possesses perfect knowledge of what is required and whose actions are also perfect, such that He is able to put everything in its appropriate place. The meaning of *hikmat* (wisdom) is:

وَضْعُ الشَّىْءِ فِىْ مَحَلِّهٖ

To place a thing at its appropriate place.

Then, the attribute *Khabir* (All-Aware) is in the superlative form and refers to such vast knowledge that nothing is beyond His knowledge. Since Allah the Exalted has made the Holy Quran the Seal of the Books, and since this Book was to last until the Day of Resurrection, He knew full well the manner in which these teachings should be impressed on the mind; and it is in view of this that He has vested this Book with such detail. Further, God instituted a system of Reformers *(Mujaddidin)* who continue to appear in order to revive the Faith and expound the insights of the Book.

The Summary and Essence of the Holy Quran

Moving on from the aforementioned, a remarkable answer has been given to a natural question which arises in this context. One asks: what is the summary and

---

[1] *Hud*, 11:2

essence of this detail that has been expounded in the Holy Quran? And the answer is:

اَلَّا تَعْبُدُوٓا إِلَّا اللّٰهَ¹

This means, do not worship anyone except God Almighty in any circumstance. The fact of the matter is that the ultimate purpose in the birth of human beings is this very worship. In this respect, Allah the Exalted states in another instance:

وَمَا خَلَقْتُ الْجِنَّ وَالْإِنْسَ إِلَّا لِيَعْبُدُونِ²

And I have not created the Jinn and the men but that they may worship Me.

The Essence of Worship

The actual meaning of worship is for man to do away with all forms of hard-heartedness and crookedness and clear the tilth of their heart just as a farmer tills the land. The Arabs refer to a smooth and levelled path as *mawrun-mu'abbadun* and this may be likened to collyrium so refined that it can be applied to the eyes. Similarly, when the tilth of the heart is sifted of pebbles and stones and completely levelled, as it were, and when it becomes so pure that nothing but the soul and the soul alone remains, this is what would be referred to as worship *(ibadat)*. As such, if a mirror is purified and cleansed, one is able to see their own face reflected in it, and if the soil is purified and cleansed, it brings forth a diverse multitude of fruits. Hence, man has been created for worship and so, if he purifies his heart and clears it of all forms of crookedness, unevenness, pebbles and stones, one will see God in it. I reiterate that the trees of the love of Allah Almighty will take root in such a heart and they will grow and develop, until they begin to yield sweet and wholesome fruits that may be described as:

أُكُلُهَا دَآئِمٌ³

Its fruit is everlasting.

Bear in mind that this is the very station where the spiritual quest of the sufis comes to an end. When a seeker reaches this rank, all they can see is a manifestation of God, and God alone. The heart of such a one becomes the throne of God and Allah the Exalted descends upon it. All the stages of the spiritual quest reach

---

¹ *Hud*, 11:3
² *adh-Dhariyat*, 51:57
³ *ar-Ra'd*, 13:36

their end at the point where an individual becomes truly subservient to God. A spiritual garden begins to flourish in the heart of such a one and God can be seen reflected in it, just as a mirror reflects an image. It is at this very stage that an individual begins to experience a taste of paradise in this very world and it is at this very stage that they feel the pleasure and enjoyment in proclaiming:

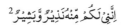

They will say: 'This is what was given us before,' and gifts mutually resembling shall be brought to them.

Therefore, when a person becomes truly subservient to God, this is true worship. Then, Allah the Exalted states:

اِنَّنِیْ لَكُمْ مِّنْهُ نَذِیْرٌ وَّبَشِیْرٌ ²

I am to you a Warner, and a bearer of glad tidings from Him

The fact is that man cannot accomplish the momentous task of becoming fully subservient to God without an excellent model, a perfect example and the full influence of a spiritual force. It is for this reason that the Messenger of Allah, peace and blessings of Allah be upon him, says that he has come as a warner and as a bearer of glad tidings from God. The Holy Prophet[sa] states that if one obeys him and accepts him, then there are great and magnificent glad tidings for such people, because he is a bearer of glad tidings; but if someone rejects him, then remember that he has also appeared as a warner, and one will have to face terrible forms of punishment and grief.

Paradise and Hell

The fact of the matter is that the life of paradise begins in this very world and a benighted life that is spent bearing no relationship with God Almighty and His Messenger is a life of hell. The paradise that one will receive after death is the true and complete manifestation of this very paradise. This is precisely the reason that the people of paradise, on experiencing the pleasure of the bounties of paradise, will declare:

---

1 *al-Baqarah,* 2:26
2 *Hud,* 11:3

هٰذَا الَّذِیْ رُزِقْنَا مِنْ قَبْلُ[1]

This is what was given us before.

The paradise that one is granted on earth is attained by acting on the following:

قَدْ اَفْلَحَ مَنْ زَكّٰھَا[2]

He indeed truly prospers who purifies the soul.

When an individual grasps the true spirit and essence of worship, they begin to receive a constant shower of God's favours and gifts. Those bounties which an individual will receive after death in the apparent, visible and tangible sense are received here in the spiritual sense. So remember, until a life of paradise begins in this life and a person experiences its pleasure in this world, one must not be satiated and satisfied, for one who attains nothing in this world but expects paradise in the hereafter, entertains a vain hope. Such an individual holds true to the following verse:

مَنْ كَانَ فِیْ هٰذِهٖ اَعْمٰی فَهُوَ فِی الْاٰخِرَةِ اَعْمٰی[3]

But whoso is blind in this world will be blind in the Hereafter.

Therefore, until you remove the pebbles and rocks of that which is besides Allah from the soil of your heart, and purify it in the likeness of a mirror and refine it in the nature of collyrium, do not rest.

The Need for A Perfect Guide

Indeed, it is true that one cannot traverse this stage of the spiritual quest without the support of a person who can purify his soul. It is for this objective and purpose that Allah the Exalted sent the Messenger of Allah, peace and blessings of Allah be upon him, as a perfect example. After this, God Almighty instituted a system of the coming of those who were true successors of the Holy Prophet[sa], so that the imprudent Brahmos would stand refuted. For example, it is a well established fact that a child with no background in farming would uproot the plant itself when weeding a patch of soil and softening it for cultivation. In the same manner, one cannot undertake this spiritual cultivation fully until they follow a

---

[1]   *al-Baqarah*, 2:26
[2]   *ash-Shams*, 91:10
[3]   *Bani Isra'il*, 17:73

perfect man who is experienced in all the stages in sowing the seed, watering the land and tilling the soil, as it were. This demonstrates that man is in need of a perfect guide. A person engaged in worship without a perfect guide to lead them is no different than a simple and uninformed child who sits in a field uprooting the actual plants in the field, all the while under the impression that they are weeding the soil. Do not surmise that you will learn how to worship God by yourselves. Nay, until the Messenger teaches you how, you cannot learn the ways of severing your ties from all else to the exclusion of God and of complete devotion to God.

Seeking Forgiveness from God and Repentance

Then, the question which naturally arises here is how this difficult task can be accomplished. Allah the Exalted has informed us of the remedy Himself:

$$اَنِ اسْتَغْفِرُوا رَبَّكُمْ ثُمَّ تُوْبُوَّا اِلَيْهِ^1$$

And that you seek forgiveness of your Lord, and then turn to Him.

Bear in mind that two things have been granted to this ummah: one which grants strength and the other which enables one to practically demonstrate the strength that they have attained. In order to build strength there is *istighfar* (seeking forgiveness from God), which may also be described as *istimdad* (seeking support) or *isti'anat* (seeking assistance). The sufis have written that just as meel clubs and lifting weights increase the strength and power of the body, similarly seeking forgiveness from God is a spiritual weight, which strengthens the soul and develops steadfastness in the heart. One who desires to develop strength ought to seek forgiveness or perform *istighfar*. The word *ghafrun* means to cover or suppress, and so, through *istighfar* a person seeks to cover and suppress those emotions and thoughts which stand between them and God. Therefore, the purpose in seeking forgiveness from God is so that man may overcome the venomous agents that attack him and seek to destroy him, and so that he may steer clear of the obstructions on the path of fulfilling the commandments of God Almighty, and so that he may act upon them in the practical sense.

It ought to be remembered also that Allah the Exalted has created man possessing two internal substances; one being a venom which is stimulated by Satan, and secondly, an antidote that lies within. When a person becomes arrogant

---

[1] *Hud*, 11:4

and grows conceited, and when he does not seek support from the elixir that is housed within, a person's infectious elements begin to dominate. However, when a person considers themselves to be lowly and insignificant, and feels an inner dependance on the support of Allah Almighty, a flowing spring takes form through the hand of Allah Almighty, by which a person's soul melts and begins to flow forth. This is the very meaning of *istighfar* (seeking forgiveness from God), or in other words, to gain this strength and overcome the poison that lies within.

Therefore, what this means is that one should remain firm in worship by firstly, obeying the Messenger, and secondly, by seeking assistance from God constantly. Of course, initially, one must seek assistance from the Lord, but when one receives strength, one must then turn to God.

Seeking Forgiveness from God Takes Precedence Over Repentance

Seeking forgiveness from God *(istighfar)* and repentance *(tawbah)* are two distinct things. However, in one respect, seeking forgiveness from God takes precedence over repentance. For seeking forgiveness from God means to seek help and strength from God, whereas repentance means to stand on one's own feet. The eternal way of Allah is that when a person seeks help from Him, He will grant them strength; and with this strength, a person will then be able to stand on their own feet and will develop the strength to perform good deeds, which is called 'turning to Allah' or 'repentance', as alluded to in the words: [1] تُوۡبُوۡۤا اِلَیۡهِ (*Turn to Him, i.e. God*). Therefore, in natural sequence, seeking forgiveness from God comes before repentance.

In short, the method that is prescribed for the seekers of God is that they must seek assistance from Him in every condition. Until a seeker is given strength from Allah the Exalted, what can they do? The strength to turn to God in repentance comes through seeking assistance from God, by begging for His forgiveness. If there were no seeking forgiveness from God, know for certain that the ability to turn to God in repentance would die as well. However, if you engage in seeking forgiveness from God, and then turn to him in repentance, the result will be as stated in the following verse:

---

[1]   *Hud*, 11:4

$$يُمَتِّعْكُمْ مَّتَاعًا حَسَنًا اِلَى اَجَلٍ مُّسَمًّى ^1$$

He will provide for you a goodly provision until an appointed term.

The way of God is that if you seek forgiveness from God and turn to Him in repentance, you will attain to lofty grades. Every individual has a scope of their own, within the bounds of which they advance in grades of progress. Everyone does not have it within them to be a Prophet and Messenger, or from among the Truthful and the Martyrs.

Hence, there is no doubt in the fact that the comparative greatness of ranks is a matter of truth. After this, Allah the Exalted states that a seeker who persistently remains engaged in these efforts shall progress in ranks and stations to the degree of their individual ability. This is precisely what is implied in:

$$وَيُؤْتِ كُلَّ ذِى فَضْلٍ فَضْلَهٗ ^2$$

And He will grant His grace to every one possessed of merit.

However, if a person is greater in capacity than others, then God Almighty will grant him more as well and the individual in question will receive the superiority to which they are naturally entitled. The distinction that God bestows is inherently His property, for He is the true Possessor of distinction. What this means is that God Almighty will never keep a person deprived of the distinction that they deserve. There are some who say: 'Sir! Are we out to become saints?' Those who say such a thing are mean-natured disbelievers. Man ought to strive in line with the law of nature.

Seeking Support from the Dead Is Forbidden

Now, the gist of this entire discourse is that God has nowhere stated that one should seek assistance from the dead; in fact, He has always spoken of those who are living. God Almighty has blessed us immensely by entrusting Islam to the living, for if He had left the Faith to those who were dead, who knows how catastrophic this would have been? Are the shrines of those gone by few and far between? Simply observe the number of shrines in Multan. There is a renowned saying about this place:

---

1 *Hud*, 11:4
2 *Hud*, 11:4

گردو گرما گدا و گورستان

Dust, heat, beggars and graveyards.

I also visited Multan once. Wherever one goes to visit a tomb, the attendants will surround a man for money. Just look at what goes on in Pakpattan thanks to the dead. Visit Ajmer and see what goes on there. Innovations in the faith and self-invented beliefs are rampant. In short, if one looks towards the dead, one will find nothing but innovations in the faith and forbidden practices. The right path *(sirat-e-mustaqim)* which Allah the Exalted has appointed for us is the way of the living, not the path of the dead. Therefore, one who desires to attain God—the Self-Subsisting and All-Sustaining God—must search for the living. For our God is a Living God, not dead. If those people whose God is dead and whose scripture is dead, seek blessings from the dead, this would not be surprising. It would be surprising, however, if a true Muslim, whose God is living, whose Prophet is living, whose Book is living, and whose religion has always welcomed the living; and for whom in every era, a living man has come to grant a living faith in the existence of God Almighty, turns their back to the living and remains lost in search of decayed bones and shrines.

Seek the Company of the Living

Hence, you ought to seek the company of those who are living and return time and again to sit with them. I would also say that once or twice is not enough to receive a full influence. The way of Allah is that progress is gradual, just as was the case with the community of the Messenger of Allah, peace and blessings of Allah be upon him. Therefore, the community which is to be established on the precepts of prophethood will also grow according to the law of gradual development.

Therefore, you ought to put aside your worldly affairs and return here, again and again, and remain in my company for good amounts of time, as the companions were accustomed in the time of the Holy Prophet[sa], so that you too can witness and find what Abu Bakr[ra], Umar[ra] and others, may Allah be pleased with all of them, attained. Someone rightly says:

یا توں لوڑ مقدمی یا توں اللہ نُوں لوڑ

You can either give precedence to your worldly
affairs or give precedence to Allah.

You know that when I take the oath of allegiance, I seek a declaration that you will give precedence to religion over worldly affairs. This is so that I may observe the degree to which the individual who takes the oath acts upon this declaration. If people are able to acquire even a small area of land, they will leave behind their homes and settle there; in fact, it is necessary for them to remain there so that this area of land may become inhabited. Even Muhammad Hussain has had to move out and settle on open farmland as well. Now when I am giving you a new land—a land which, if cultivated with purity and effort, can bring forth everlasting fruits—why do people not come here and build their houses on it? Then, if someone does accept this land, but does so with such a lack of concern that after swearing the oath of allegiance, they find it burdensome and difficult to come here and stay for even a few days, how can such a one expect that their crop would ripen and yield fruits? God Almighty refers to the heart as a 'land' as well.

$$\text{اِعْلَمُوٓا اَنَّ اللّٰهَ يُحْيِ الْاَرْضَ بَعْدَ مَوْتِهَا}^1$$

Know that Allah is now quickening the earth after its death.

Just observe the amount of struggle that a farmer must bear. A farmer will purchase an ox, plough the land, sow the seed and irrigate the soil. In short, a huge effort goes into this work, and until a farmer takes this work upon themselves, nothing can be achieved. It is written that a man once saw an inscription with the words: 'Agriculture is gold and nothing but gold.' So the individual took up farming, but delegated the work to servants. However, when it came time to calculate the earnings, far from making a profit, it turned out that he owed money instead. When he began to entertain doubts on this occasion, a wise person explained: 'The advice was true, but you were foolish. You must supervise everything yourself, only then will you make a profit.' The land of the heart is exactly the same in nature: one who shows it irreverence remains deprived of the grace and blessing of God Almighty. Remember that I have come for the reformation of humanity, and the one who comes to me shall inherit divine grace in accordance with their own individual capacity. However, I clearly state that a person who swears the oath of allegiance in a half-hearted manner and leaves, and then no one knows where he has gone and what he is engaged in, shall receive nothing. Such a one will leave empty-handed, just as he was empty-handed when he first came.

The divine grace and blessing of which I speak is received by remaining in

---

1   *al-Hadid*, 57:18

my company. The companions of the Messenger of Allah, peace and blessings of Allah be upon him, sat in his company. What was the ultimate result? The Messenger of Allah, peace and blessings of Allah be upon him, said:

$$ اَللهُ اَللهُ فِىْ اَصْحَابِىْ $$

Essentially, the companions became a reflection of God. They could not have attained such a rank if they remained afar from the Holy Prophet[sa]. This is a very important issue. Nearness to God is nearness to the servants of God. Further, God Almighty states:

$$ كُوْنُوْا مَعَ الصّٰدِقِيْنَ^1 $$

Be with the truthful.

This too is a testament to what I have just said. This is a secret that few are able to comprehend. It is never possible for a person who is appointed by God to say everything at once. In fact, he will diagnose the illnesses of his friends and cure them as appropriate with exhortation and advice, and every so often, he will remove their ailments. Just take today as an example—I cannot say everything now. It is possible that certain people may leave today after listening to the speech that I am delivering now, and perhaps some of the things that I will have said today may not suit their disposition or mindset, and so they will have left here deprived. However, an individual who stays here repeatedly, continues to foster a change within themselves and ultimately attains their objective. Every individual requires a sincere change. A person who is not transformed holds true to the following:

$$ مَنْ كَانَ فِىْ هٰذِهٖ آعْمٰى^2 $$

But whoso is blind in this world...

The Community Must Undergo a Pure Transformation

I constantly feel immense pain and grief so that a pure transformation may be brought about in my community. The vision in my heart for the transformation that I would like to see in my community has not been realised as of yet. And when I observe this, my condition is no different to the following:

---

1   *at-Tawbah*, 9:119
2   *Bani Isra'il*, 17:73

لَعَلَّكَ بَاخِعٌ نَّفْسَكَ أَلَّا يَكُوْنُوْا مُؤْمِنِيْنَ[1]

Haply thou wilt grieve thyself to death because they believe not.

When people take the oath of allegiance, I have no desire for them to repeat a few words in the likeness of a parrot. This can serve no benefit. Develop a knowledge of how one can purify one's soul, for this is what is needed. My objective is not for you to go around arguing and debating over the death or life of Jesus[as]—not at all. For this is a matter of lesser importance. This is not the main objective. This was an error that I have rectified. My actual task and prime objective is far from being realised, and that is for all of you to nurture a transformation within yourselves and become new individuals entirely. Therefore, it is incumbent on each and every one of you to grasp this secret and develop such a transformation within yourselves so that you can truly say: 'I have become a new person'. Indeed, I proclaim once again, that until and unless you remain in my company for such a period of time that you are transformed into an entirely new person, you have gained nothing.

If an individual develops a high degree of purity in their nature, and in their intellectual and emotional condition, then they have attained something, otherwise they have gained nothing. I do not suggest that you abandon your worldly occupations completely. God Almighty has deemed it permissible for one to engage in worldly occupations. For if not, man is tried by this avenue as well, and it is due to this very trial that an individual becomes a thief, a gambler, a fraud and a robber, and develops many other ill habits as well. However, everything has its limits. One ought to engage in worldly occupations to the extent that they furnish means to support you in the way of religion—the main objective ought to be religion alone. Therefore, I do not forbid you from engaging in worldly occupations, but neither do I say that you should become so engrossed, day and night, in worldly businesses and preoccupations so that you fill the place that is reserved for God with worldly affairs as well. Anyone who does so, only gives rise to means that will deprive them, and their tongue only makes an empty declaration. In short, remain in the company of those who are living so that you may behold a manifestation of the living God."[2]

---

[1]   *Ash-Shuʿarāʾ*, 26:4
[2]   *Al-Hakam*, vol. 6, no. 26, dated 24 July 1902, pp. 5-12

9 July 1900

Prayer Is the Best Form of Sympathy

The Promised Messiah[as] states: "Remember that sympathy is of three kinds: firstly, physical; secondly, financial; and the third form of sympathy is prayer, in which one is neither required to spend their wealth, nor undertake a physical effort. The grace of this third form of sympathy is extremely vast. An individual can only show sympathy physically if they possess the bodily strength to do so. For example, if there were a poor man who lay wounded in a helpless state, writhing in pain, how would a person who has no power and strength themselves be able to carry the man and help him? In the same manner, if someone were destitute, impoverished, poor and empty-handed, and they were suffering from hunger, until one possesses wealth, how can one show sympathy to such an individual? However, sympathy through prayer is a form of sympathy for which one neither requires wealth, nor physical strength. So long as an individual is a human being, they can pray for others and benefit them. The grace of this sympathy is immensely vast and if an individual does not show this form of sympathy, then know that such a one is a very unfortunate human being.

I have stated that in showing sympathy financially and physically, an individual is tied by constraints, but there are no constraints in showing sympathy with prayer. It is my belief that in prayer one should not exclude one's enemies either. The wider the scope of a person's prayer, the more beneficial this will be for the supplicant themselves. The more miserly a person is in their prayer, the more they will be distanced from Allah Almighty. In actuality, an individual who limits the favour of God—which is tremendously extensive—is also weak in faith.

The Recipe for a Long Life

Another magnificent benefit in praying for others is that one's own life is prolonged. Allah the Exalted has promised in the Holy Quran that those who benefit others and prove to be beneficial beings themselves, their lives are prolonged. As such, Allah the Exalted states:

$$\text{وَاَمَّا مَا يَنْفَعُ النَّاسَ فَيَمْكُثُ فِى الْاَرْضِ}^{1}$$

As to that which benefits men, it stays on the earth.

---

[1] *ar-Ra'd*, 13:18

Since the other forms of sympathy are subject to limitations, therefore, the perpetual aid that can especially be given, is the constantly flowing aid of prayer. When aid is beneficial to the people at large, we can derive the greatest benefit from this verse through prayer. It is absolutely true that the life of a person who is a source of benefit for the world is prolonged, and one who causes mischief is taken from this world quicker. It is said that Sher Singh would catch birds and roast them alive on a fire, and he was killed within two years of assuming power. Therefore, it is incumbent on man to reflect and contemplate on how they can hold true to the following:

$$ خَيْرُالنَّاسِ مَنْ يَّنْفَعُ النَّاسَ $$

The best of mankind is the one who benefits mankind.

Just as positive strategies are useful in medicine, it is the art of strategy that proves advantageous in the well-being and benefit of others. Therefore, it is necessary for human beings to constantly wait for opportunities and to continuously reflect as to the means by which others can be benefitted.

Do Not Rebuke a Beggar

Some people have the habit of becoming irritated when confronted by a beggar. Some, who have a clerical vein in them, will begin explaining the theological stance on begging instead of giving the person something, and will begin to impress their own scholarly prowess upon them, and sometimes they will even go so far as to call the beggar a useless sluggard. It is unfortunate that such people are bereft of the sense that is bestowed to pure-hearted individuals of sound nature. Such people fail to realise that even if a healthy person comes to them begging, it is the beggar who is guilty of sin. There is no sin in giving something to the beggar. In fact, the following words appear in a Hadith:

$$ لَوْ آتَاكَ رَاكِبًا $$

Meaning, even if a beggar comes to you riding on horseback, one ought to give him something. Furthermore, the Holy Quran instructs:

وَاَمَّاالسَّآئِلَ فَلَا تَنْهَرْ[1]

And him who seeks thy help, chide not.

Meaning, do not chide the beggar. This instruction does not distinguish and say that one should not rebuke a beggar of such and such nature, but ought to scold a beggar of such and such nature. So remember, you must not reprimand a beggar, because this, in a way, sows the seed of immorality. Morality demands that one is not quick to show displeasure to a beggar. Satan wishes for you to act in this way so that he may deprive you of virtue and make you the inheritors of evil.

One Virtue Gives Birth to Another

Reflect and you will see that one virtue gives birth to another, and in the same manner, one evil leads to the next. Just as one thing attracts another, similarly, God Almighty has established a phenomenon of attraction in the case of every action as well. Therefore, by being gentle to a beggar when a person gives the 'charity of good morals,' their state of spiritual contraction *(qabz)* will be removed and the person in question will be moved to perform another good deed as well, which is to give something to the beggar.

Good Morals Are the Key to Righteous Deeds

Morality is the key to other good deeds. Those who do not reform their morals gradually become lifeless. It is my belief that everything in the world serves a purpose. Even poison and filth has a use. Strychnine is useful as well and has an effect on the muscles. However, a human being who does not attain high morals and who is of no benefit to others, falls so low that they can be of no use whatsoever. Such a one becomes even worse than a dead animal, because the hide and bones of a dead animal can be used, but the skin of a dead man has no use whatsoever. It is at this state that a human being falls true to the following:

بَلْ هُمْ اَضَلُّ

They are even worse.

So remember that the reformation of one's morals is imperative, because good morals are the mother of righteous deeds.

---

[1] *ad-Duha*, 93:11

The first stage of goodness from which a person derives strength is through morals *(akhlaq)*. There are two words: firstly *khalq* and secondly *khulq*. The word *khalq* refers to physical birth and *khulq* implies inner birth. In the way that certain people are apparently beautiful and others are unattractive, so too certain people are beautiful and attractive as far as their inner birth is concerned, while others suffer an inner leprosy and vitiligo. However, since physical form can be seen apparently, everyone can perceive it as soon as they see it and are attracted to beauty; no one wishes for themselves to be unattractive or ugly. Since an individual can see physical beauty, they desire it for themselves. However, as *khulq* cannot be seen with the eyes, an individual remains unaware of its merit and does not desire it in the same way. Physical beauty or ugliness is all the same to a blind person. In the same manner, a person whose eye does not see the inner aspect is like the blind person I have just mentioned. Physical birth *(khalq)* is an apparent thing, but inner birth *(khulq)* is a conceptual matter. Only when a person comes to know about moral ills and their curse, will the deeper reality come to light.

In short, moral beauty is what ought to be deemed 'true beauty'. There are few who appreciate it. Good morals are the key to righteous deeds. For example, if there was a lock on the gate of a garden, one would see the fruits and trees from afar, but would not be able to enter the garden. However, if the lock was opened, one could enter the garden and the full reality would become apparent, and the heart and mind would derive pleasure and be refreshed. To attain good morals is to open this lock, as it were, and enter the garden.

The Very Abandoning of Good Morals Is Sin

No one has ever been granted moral strength and then not gone on to perform countless good deeds. The very abandoning of good morals is sin. For example, an individual who commits fornication with a woman is ignorant of the extreme pain that her husband will feel. Now if the sinner could feel the pain and grief of the husband, and if he possessed moral sense, he would not commit this evil deed. If this vile man knew of the grave dangers that this evil deed would bring for humanity at large, he would refrain from it. A thief—as wretched and cruel as he is—will rob someone, and not even leave behind enough for the victim to put food on the table that evening. It is often observed that a thief will ravage a poor man's efforts of many years and will take everything that they can get their hands on from the victim's home. What is the actual root at the heart of such despicable evil? It is the absence of moral strength. If a thief possessed mercy he would realise that the victim's children would wail in pain—screams that would even horrify enemies. A thief who stops to think that his victims have been hungry since last night and could not even find a few dry scraps to eat, would feel a deep sense of pain. Obviously, if a thief felt these conditions and was not blind to the moral state, why would he steal? Every other day, we read news reports of excruciating deaths, stating that some child was killed out of greed for jewellery or that such and such woman has been murdered. On one occasion, I myself served in a case as an assessor, and a man had murdered a child over a mere twelve annas or one and a quarter rupees. Now reflect and observe that if the people's moral state was good and healthy, why would these misfortunes have dawned upon us? How can a person not feel for their fellow human being on whom a misfortune has fallen?

The Characteristics of Cattle

The Holy Quran states:

$$\text{يَأْكُلُونَ كَمَا تَأْكُلُ الْأَنْعَامُ}^{1}$$

Meaning, they eat even as the cattle eat. This has various aspects. Firstly, cattle have no sense of quality and quantity, and go on consuming whatever comes before them no matter how much, just as dogs that eat and eat until they finally vomit. Secondly, cattle do not distinguish between that which is lawful and unlawful. An ox never thinks to itself that this is the neighbour's field and so I should stay out. Similarly, it does not make a distinction in the matter of food. A dog has no sense of uncleanliness and cleanliness. Cattle have no limits.

Those who break moral principles and show no concern in this regard, are not humans, as it were. Such was the indifference to distinguishing between that which is pure and that which is unclean that in Arabia, people would even eat dead dogs. The state of affairs is that in many countries even today rats, dogs and cats are eaten as delicacies. Filthy people, those of the lower castes and people who eat carrion exist today even in our own country. Then, people feel no reluctance or hesitance in devouring the wealth of orphans. For example, if the hay that belonged to an orphan was placed before a cow, it would eat the hay without a second thought, and this is also the condition of the people I have just described. The following refers to these very people:

---

1 *Muhammad*, 47:13

$$وَالنَّارُ مَثْوًى لَّهُمْ \,^{1}$$

Meaning, hell will be their resort. Therefore, remember that there are two aspects. Firstly, there is the greatness of Allah and one who rejects this goes against the dictates of good morals. Secondly, there is kindness towards the creation of Allah and a person who opposes humanity also stands against good morals. Alas! There are very few who reflect over these points, which are the true purpose and objective of man's life.

Self-Invented Invocations and Incantations

Renowned sufis and the successors of saints have deemed the height of their excellence to lie in long and enormous invocations, incantations and practices, which they have invented themselves. They have become engrossed in these practices and have lost the true essence of faith. Then, their greatest accomplishment, if anything, is that they will undertake forty-day retreats. They will take certain items along and appoint a person who will bring them milk or something else on a daily basis. These retreats are generally undertaken in dark, narrow and filthy rooms, or in a cave, and those who practice these exercises lay there in these rooms. God knows how they are able to remain in such places. Then when these people come out of the room, they emerge in a terrible state. This is what is left of Islam. I cannot understand how these retreats of seclusion benefit Islam, the Muslims or humanity at large, and how this improves a person's morals?

The Lofty Grandeur of the Holy Prophet[sa]

The honour of the Messenger of Allah, peace and blessings of Allah be upon him, is greater than the honour of all others, which has left its imprint on the entire Islamic world. It is the honour and indignation of the Holy Prophet[sa] that revived the world once again. Nothing had remained among the Arabs except for fornication, alcohol and war, and the rights due to God's creatures had been thrown away altogether. All traces of sympathy and welfare of humanity had vanished. While the rights of God's creatures had wasted away, the rights due to God had been obscured by darkness to even greater extent. The attributes of God had been ascribed to stones, plants and stars. Diverse forms of polytheism were rampant. The world was engaged in worshipping weak humans and even genitalia. If an

---

[1] *Muhammad*, 47:13

image of this loathsome state were to come before a pure-natured individual even momentarily, they would view it as a terrifying and horrible image of perilous gloom, tyranny and oppression. Paralysis seizes one side of the body, but this was a paralysis that had gripped both sides. Utter corruption had spread throughout the entire world. There was neither peace and security in the sea, nor tranquillity and comfort on land. Now in this era of darkness and destruction, we look to the Messenger of Allah, peace and blessings of Allah be upon him. It is remarkable how he set aright both sides of the scale and re-established the rights due to God and the rights due to His creation, and returned them to their original, perfect point of equilibrium. The perfection of the moral power of the Messenger of Allah, peace and blessings of Allah be upon him, can only be fathomed when one casts a glance upon the condition of that era. The pain that the adversaries of the Holy Prophet[sa] inflicted upon him and his followers, and in contrast, the manner in which the Holy Prophet[sa] treated them in return when he had complete power and authority over them, demonstrates his lofty grandeur.

What grief did Abu Jahl and his associates not give to the devoted followers of the Holy Prophet[sa]? Poor Muslim women were tied to camels that were made to run in opposite directions and torn apart, for the mere crime of believing in:

$$\text{لَا اِلٰهَ اِلَّا الله}$$

There is none worthy of worship except Allah.

However, the Holy Prophet[sa] bore all this with patience and tolerance, and when he gained victory over Mecca, he forgave these people and said:

$$\text{لَاتَثْرِيْبَ عَلَيْكُمُ الْيَوْمَ}^{1}$$

No blame shall lie on you this day.

How outstanding a moral excellence this is, which cannot be found in any other Prophet.

$$\text{اَللّٰهُمَّ صَلِّ عَلٰى مُحَمَّدٍ وَّعَلٰى اٰلِ مُحَمَّدٍ}$$

O Allah! Send salutations upon Muhammad[sa]
and upon the progeny of Muhammad[sa].

Therefore, the point is that you ought to develop sublime morals, for it is good

---

[1] *Yusuf,* 12:93

morals that are the key to righteous deeds."[1]

16 July 1900

Two Exquisite Couplets of the Promised Messiah[as]

هر که روشن شُدِ دل و جان و دَروں از حضرتش

کیمیا باشد بسر برون دے در محبتش

چیست دنیا چوں شبِ تار وزماں ابر سیاہ

آفتابِ رہنما یک ساعتی در غِذ متش

One whose heart and soul, and inner self has been illuminated by God;
Is one in whose company, a moment spent, is alchemy.

The world is a dark night and our present times are a black cloud;
The Sun of Guidance only stays in the world for a short while.

The Secret in Prophet Ezra[as] Coming Back to Life and the Death of Jesus[as]

The Promised Messiah[as] said: "Those who deny the death of Jesus, peace be upon him, present the issue relating to the life of Ezra[as] as one of their arguments and assert that he died for a hundred years and then came back to life. However, it ought to be remembered that this is a case of resurrection from the dead. There could be various forms of coming to life. The first could be if a person came back to life after death in a manner that their grave was ripped open and they returned to the world along with their possessions and necessities of life. The second could be if Allah the Exalted, through His bounty and grace, were to bestow another life—as he does with the people of God, for example, like the person who due to fear of God bequeathed that he should be cremated after death and his ash thrown into the wind. After this had been done, God Almighty brought the individual to life. When the ash had been gathered, the man was presented before God in the form of a body with a physical life. There is no question of gathering ash in the life that one receives after death. I would point out, however, that despite all this, one thing is for certain, and that is that the individual in question

---

[1] *Al-Hakam*, vol. 4, no. 25, dated 9 July 1900, pp. 1-5

did not return to his home on earth.

Maulvi Sahib stated that one convincing point which remains is that God says in relation to Jesus: 'We shall make thee a sign unto the people.'[1] I responded by saying that it is not necessary for the sign to be in accordance with the people's perception and expectation e.g. for a dead person's grave be torn open and for them to emerge therefrom—such a notion is preposterous indeed!

Certain men are referred to as a Proof of Allah; they are from among the Signs of God. Certain individuals are signs in themselves. There are some who leave behind signs. It was necessary to outline the underlying objective in this allegation. This objection is inconsistent with my stance on the matter. What our opponents believe in respect of the Messiah is that he ascended into the heavens alive and that he will return alive. Now what relevance or similarity does this have with the story of Ezra[as]? A similarity would exist if those who raise the allegation in question, held that the Messiah, peace be upon him, were to be resurrected from his grave. When they do not believe this, it is strange that they should present this example, because it is a false analogy.

These people hold the belief that some other individual who was given the appearance of the Messiah was hung while Jesus, peace be upon him, was raised into the heaven alive, with his physical body and earthly form. Then, they do not even tell us what he is doing sitting up in the heaven. What more could he do in paradise than to engage in carpentry and make furniture for those in paradise? Anyway, this does not concern me. In any case, what relation and similarity does the scenario that our opponents present have with the account of Ezra[as]?

Hence, in this context, to mix the case of the Messiah with the account of Ezra[as] is a false comparison. It is my belief that the account of Ezra[as] has nothing to do with whether the Messiah returns or not. Of course, if the nature of this question was different, and if it were asked, for example: 'How did Ezra[as] come back to life again?' then this would be another matter altogether. However, the fact is that I reject such resurrection; in fact, the entire Quran from beginning to end rejects such a notion.

Allah the Exalted has put in place a system for His servants who believe in Him, who believe in His angels, who believe in His books, etc., in connection with their passing away from this world. First, the angel of death comes and takes

---

[1]   Allah the Exalted states that He shall make Jesus a sign for the people. For example, refer to *Maryam* (19:22) and *az-Zukhruf* (43:62) of the Holy Quran. [Publisher]

the soul. Then, other events transpire. The angels Munkar and Nakeer arrive.
Deeds come forward. Then, a window is opened. Then, the Holy Quran says that
it is on the Day of Resurrection that the dead will be raised.

$$يَبْعَثُ اللّٰهُ الْمَوْتٰى$$

It is written in *Ma'alim* that the dead do not return.

An Important Point

There are two aspects of the Holy Quran. Certain discussions are in the form
of narratives whereas commandments are presented in the form of instructions.
Whatever the Holy Quran presents in the form of an instruction, it does so, so
that the people will accept it. For example, the Holy Quran states:

$$اَنْ تَصُوْمُوْا خَيْرٌ لَّكُمْ ^1$$

And fasting is good for you.

Now the Arabic word *'sawm'* refers to the dung of an ostrich, but obviously in the
verse just mentioned, this is not the meaning that is intended. The guidance of
the Holy Quran is always clear. In the same vein, therefore, the guidance that it
provides on the issue at hand is that first, the angel of death comes and then, a person is exalted. The Hadith supports this view. In one instance, the Holy Quran
states:

$$فَيُمْسِكُ الَّتِيْ قَضٰى عَلَيْهَا الْمَوْتَ ^2$$

Meaning, when He issues a decree of death against a soul, He does not allow it to
return. You see, this is the Word of God. The aforementioned statement is not in
the nature of a narrative; it is in the form of guidance.

Those who are unable to differentiate between narratives and points of guidance are forced to confront great difficulty; they only make it appear as though
the Holy Quran were riddled with contradiction and, for all intents and purposes, forsake the Holy Quran. For God Almighty states in relation to the Holy
Quran:

---

1   *al-Baqarah*, 2:185
2   *az-Zumar*, 39:43

لَوْ كَانَ مِنْ عِنْدِ غَيْرِ اللهِ لَوَجَدُوْا فِيْهِ اخْتِلَافًا كَثِيْرًا¹

*Had it been from anyone other than Allah, they would
surely have found therein much disagreement.*

The fact that the Holy Quran is free from contradiction has been put forth as an argument that it is from Allah. However, by failing to distinguish between narratives and points of guidance, these unwise people present the Holy Quran in a way so that it seems full of contradiction and appears that it is مِنْ عِنْدِ غَيْرِ اللهِ (*From someone other than Allah*). Their wisdom is pitiable indeed!

One ought to ask these people: do points of guidance take precedence or narratives? If a contradiction exists between the two, which shall be given preference? Allah the Exalted states again and again that those who die, do not return. There is a Hadith in *Tirmidhi* that a companion of the Holy Prophet[sa] was martyred. The companion submitted: 'O Lord! Send me back to the world.' On this, God Almighty responded, by saying:

قَدْ سَبَقَ الْقَوْلُ مِنِّیْ

My word has already gone forth.

حَرَّمٌ عَلٰی قَرْیَةٍ اَهْلَكْنٰهَآ اَنَّهُمْ لَا یَرْجِعُوْنَ²

*It is an inviolable law for a township which We
have destroyed that they shall not return.*

Now we have the Holy Quran and the clear words of the blessed Hadith are present in the form of a commentary. In comparison to this, what value can an imaginary and hypothetical tale possess in this respect? I ask, what more do the people want? I present the Quran and the Hadith. Furthermore, sound intellect and experience also supports my view. If I was presenting a self-invented idea, people could have put forth a narrative, but in this case, I am presenting a point of guidance from the Holy Quran and a Hadith in support. What more do the people seek?

فَمَاذَا بَعْدَ الْحَقِّ اِلَّا الضَّلٰلُ³

So what would you have after discarding the truth except error?

---

1   *an-Nisa*, 4:83
2   *al-Anbiya*, 21:96
3   *Yunus*, 10:33

It is not necessary for God Almighty to disclose to us the underlying facts in narratives. Just believe in them and leave the intricate details to God. In the case of fasting, the Arabs would ask about relevant details and many verses expound various aspects of this injunction. However, in the case of narratives, this is not necessary. For example, it is unnecessary for God Almighty to tell us about the appearance of the idols that belonged to the idolatrous opponents of Abraham[as]. To pursue such thoughts is disrespectful. In short, remember that it is improper for one to overdo an issue unnecessarily and raise absurd questions as to the details of narratives related in the Quran. A human being cannot follow an instruction until it is clear. Therefore, God Almighty states that He has made points of guidance simple, and in the same manner, Allah the Exalted has clearly explained that the dead do not return.

If our opponents possess a sense of honesty and fear of God, when they relate the narrative of Ezra[as], it is incumbent on them to not ignore those verses of the Holy Quran which state that the dead do not return.

Now, I will come down a degree for the sake of argument and provide another response. I have already mentioned that as far as narratives are concerned, a general belief in them is sufficient. However, since instructions are meant to be acted upon in the practical sense, therefore it is necessary for one to understand them. Now, it is written that Ezra[as] remained 'dead' for a hundred years and the Arabic word used for this is *amata*. It should be known that one definition of *amata* (to cause to die) is *anama* as well, which means 'to be put to sleep.' The word 'death' has also been used in the Holy Quran to describe a loss of strength in the faculties of growth and perception. In any case, we can also infer a meaning of sleep in this context, like the account of the Dwellers of the Cave. The difference between the account of the Dwellers of the Cave and that of Ezra[as] is that in the case of the Dwellers of the Cave, there was the dog, and in the case of Ezra[as] there is a donkey. The baser self is akin to both a dog and a donkey. God likened the Jews to a donkey and mentioned the dog in the context of Balaam. It is evident that the baser self does not let go of man. One who is unconscious will either be with 'a dog' or 'a donkey'.

Therefore, another aspect of this discussion is—as I have mentioned—that the Arabic word *amata*, which means 'to cause to die', is also defined as *anama* i.e. 'to put to sleep.' And I accept that one hundred years aside, a person may well sleep for two hundred thousand years—my contention is that once the soul is taken by the angel of death, it does not return to the world. In sleep, although the soul is seized as well, but the angel of death does not take it away.

Sleeping for an extended period of time is a matter that can, in no way, be objectionable. There are techniques written in Hindu books on holding one's breath. Moreover, holding one's breath is also practiced by yogis at various stages in meditation *(abhyas)*. Only a short time ago there was a report in newspapers that during the construction of a railway line, a small hut belonging to a Hindu ascetic was discovered. Similarly, there was a report circulating in the newspapers about a young boy who slept for twenty years. In short, it is no surprising matter for a person to remain asleep for a hundred years.

The Underlying Reality in the Food and Drink of Ezra[as] Being Preserved

Moving on, in the verse relating to Ezra[as], the words لَمْ يَتَسَنَّهْ [1] (*they have not rotted*) are worthy of contemplation. If one were to keep in view our present-day experience, no difficulty remains in comprehending the underlying reality in these words. A reliable person writes that he once ate some meat that had been cooked thirty years before his birth—the meat had been air-sealed.

Now, thousands, rather hundreds of thousands of bottles are brought here from foreign lands such as Europe and America which contain cooked foods that are preserved, or in other words: لَمْ يَتَسَنَّهْ (*they have not rotted*). This concept of لَمْ يَتَسَنَّهْ (*i.e. to remain free from decay and be preserved*) is applicable in the meditative practices of the Hindus and also reveals the underlying reality in today's intellectual advances. The Holy Quran had already mentioned this phenomenon long ago.

The fact of the matter is that just as a particular characteristic in air causes food to decay, the human body is affected in the same way. Now, if food can be preserved by guarding it from the effects of air through a specific method, what is so astonishing about this? It is possible that some time in the future, a method is discovered by which humans are able to undergo a process that is similar to preserved food. These are the sciences. There is no harm in being open to such possibilities.

Various investigations and scientific experiments have led to the development of such footwear by which a person can walk on water. Moreover, fire-repellant

---

[1]   *al-Baqarah*, 2:260

and bulletproof vests have been invented as well. In the same vein, if the underlying reality in ¹لَمْ يَتَسَنَّهْ (*they have not rotted*) as stated in the Holy Quran is proven at some point in terms of science, why should this be surprising? The effects of air cause food to decay and air has a significant effect on humans as well. There are two kinds of air. There is one form of air which when inhaled, revitalises, and another form, is exhaled through breathing, which is a burnt and foetid sort of air. In short, if the phenomenon alluded to in the words لَمْ يَتَسَنَّهْ (*they have not rotted*) was discovered, this would not harm us at all. In fact, the more and more that knowledge of the natural sciences spreads, the greatness and excellence of the Holy Quran will become all the more manifest.

I observe every other day that soups and meats cooked abroad are brought to India and they do not spoil. Foreign medicines come here from thousands of miles and are kept for months, even years, but they do not expire. A certain individual told me that if an egg is preserved in mustard oil, it does not spoil. The application of similar effects upon a person's youth and strengths could very well be a possibility. Certain Muslims have also made endeavours in holding their breath. In fact, a person even visited me and said that he only takes two breaths in one day. Practical evidence demonstrates that air has an effect in the process of decay. So if a human is isolated from such air and their life is prolonged, why should this be deemed an impossibility? What harm is there in accepting that lives can be prolonged in this way?

It is a matter of principle that innovations are developed and invented because God has granted scope for them in the law of nature, or because the system of various elements found in the natural world can accommodate them. My belief is that the more the natural sciences progress and practically come to the fore, the more the greatness of the Holy Quran will become clear to the world."²

17 August 1900

A Sermon of Maulana Abdul-Karim[ra] and Praise from His Holiness[as]

His Holiness, the Promised Messiah[as], praised the sermon that was delivered by Maulana Abdul-Karim Sahib[ra] on 17 August 1900. Maulana Sahib wrote out this sermon again with his own hand and said: "If only I could know whether these words that have sprung from my heart will be accepted. Yesterday, before the call

---

¹ al-Baqarah, 2:260
² Al-Hakam, vol. 4, no. 26, dated 16 July 1900, pp. 1-4

for the morning prayer, I saw that there were many telephones on my right ear, and I am hearing voices of various friends from various places who are saying: 'We understand well whatever you say about our Promised Messiah[as].' I believe that I also heard someone say: 'We accept this.'

I also deem it necessary to narrate—in order to share the favour of God—that after the Friday prayer service, I went in to say something to His Holiness. After I had finished discussing other matters, I asked the Promised Messiah[as] about the sermon. The Promised Messiah[as] said: 'What you have said is precisely my view as well.' He went on to say: 'It is the grace of God Almighty that in expounding divine insights, you now stand on a towering cliff, as it were.'"[1]

The Night Between 25 and 26 August 1900

A Prelude to A Magnificent Sign

On Friday, a throng of people who held differing religious views, and who had come to drink from the same fountain of malice, as it were, gathered at Lahore station. Once they had seen off Pir Sahib of Golarha, they strutted through the city as though they were dissenters, beating their chests, and rebuking the holy. Falsehood became as glaring as it was on the day when the Chief of both worlds, the Holy Prophet[sa] was exiled from Mecca, and the disbelievers of Mecca celebrated a false hope. Today, the truth is being called 'falsehood' and righteousness is being trampled underfoot and many wretched people are coming forth from all directions. On this day, that revelation of the Promised Messiah[as] which was published some time ago has been fulfilled.

The Promised Messiah[as] said: "They seek to portray this House of Truth as though it were a House of Falsehood." At night, His Holiness, the Prophet of Allah, the Promised Messiah, on whom be peace, spoke on this for quite some time. He said: "How can I be awed by such clamour? All of this tumult seems a precursor to me for the coming of the succour of God Almighty, which for a long time had been deferred. The way of God has always been that when rejection reaches its extreme, the jealousy of God begins to surge forth to support His beloved in equal degree. The Atham affair caused an uproar, and I was rejected and dishonoured, but the jealousy of God Almighty showed the sign of Lekhram in a most swift manner. Similarly, I strongly believe that the current noise of op-

---

[1]   *Al-Hakam*, vol. 4, no. 30, dated 24 August 1900, p. 12

position is a precursor to some magnificent sign. An unfortunate individual may possibly be awed by this tumult and leave us, but what remedy can I give to such a person? For this is the way of Allah."[1]

August 1900

The True Bestower of Benefit Is God Almighty Alone

The Promised Messiah[as] states: "The people of this world will go to great lengths in flattering officials and other individuals on the basis of an imaginary hope that they will be able to derive a certain benefit from them. In fact, even ordinary workers and attendants must be appeased. However, even if the official is pleased and made content, one can hope to gain benefit from them either on a particular occasion or for a few days at best. On this fanciful hope a person will flatter an official's attendants to such an extent that even the thought of such sycophancy makes me tremble. My heart is filled with grief over the fact that foolish people flatter other human beings, who are no different than them, over fanciful and unreal hopes, yet they give no importance to the true Bestower, who has blessed them with countless forms of bounty without any desire for return and without their asking. The fact is, even if a human being desired to be of benefit to another person, then what? I truthfully say that no benefit can be attained except through God Almighty. It is possible that even before a person is able to secure their interest, the individual from whom they expect this benefit or even they themselves, depart this world, or they are gripped by some terrible disease, whereby they are no longer able to reap any personal benefit or advantage from the individual in question.

Therefore, without the grace and mercy of Allah Almighty a person can derive no benefit from any other human being. Now when it is Allah the Exalted who is the true Bestower of benefit, how shameless is it for man to beg and knock at the doors of other human beings. The honour of a God-fearing believer could never bear to flatter another human just like themselves, when they do not command this right. Allah Almighty takes it upon Himself to open avenues for a righteous person; and they are granted provision from where no one else could know. Allah Almighty Himself becomes the Friend and Nurturer of such a one. Allah the Exalted shows kindness and love to those of His servants who give precedence to

---

1   *Al-Hakam*, vol. 10, no. 35, dated 10 October 1906, p. 8

the Faith over this world. As such, Allah the Exalted Himself states:

اَللّٰهُ رَءُوْفٌ بِالْعِبَادِ[1]

Allah is Compassionate to His servants.

Who Are the Servants of God Almighty?

The servants of God are those who dedicate the lives which they have been grant-ed by Allah Almighty in His cause, and who sacrifice their lives in the way of God. They consider it a blessing of God and their own good fortune to be able to spend their wealth in His cause. However, those who deem the wealth and property of this world to be their ultimate objective, being unaware, misjudge the true significance of religion. However, this is not the way of a true believer and a genuine Muslim. True Islam is for one to dedicate all of one's strengths and facul-ties in the way of Allah Almighty, until one's last breath, so that he may receive a pure life. Therefore, Allah Almighty Himself alludes to this dedication in the cause of Allah in the following words:

مَنْ اَسْلَمَ وَجْهَهُ لِلّٰهِ وَهُوَ مُحْسِنٌ فَلَهُ اَجْرُهُ عِنْدَ رَبِّهِ وَلَا خَوْفٌ عَلَيْهِمْ وَلَا هُمْ يَحْزَنُوْنَ[2]

Whoever submits himself completely to Allah, and is the
doer of good, shall have his reward with his Lord. No fear
shall come upon such, neither shall they grieve.

The meaning in this instance is that one must don the garb of self-effacement and humility and fall at the threshold of God, and dedicate one's life, wealth and honour—everything that one possesses—for the sake of God, and one must turn the world and all that belongs to it into a means of serving the Faith.

In Pursuing Worldly Affairs the Ultimate Objective Must Be Religion

No one must think that the aforementioned implies that an individual should have no relation whatsoever with worldly affairs. This is not what I mean, nor does Allah Almighty forbid a man to engage in worldly matters. In fact, what Islam does forbid, is asceticism. This is the way of cowards. The more diverse a believer's worldly associations, the more they advance in higher ranks, because their prime objective is religion, and the world along with its wealth and honour

---

[1]   *al-Baqarah*, 2:208
[2]   *al-Baqarah*, 2:113

serves the Faith.

Hence, the fundamental point is that the world must not be one's ultimate objective. As a matter of fact, in pursuing worldly affairs, the primary purpose must be religion, and the world ought to be pursued in a manner that serves the Faith. For example, when a person travels from one place to another, they will take a mount and pack their provisions. They do this because their actual purpose is to reach their final destination, not because they seek the mount itself or the provisions for the journey. In the same manner, one ought to strive in the world, but only so that this may serve the Faith.

Allah the Exalted has taught us the following prayer:

$$رَبَّنَآ اٰتِنَا فِي الدُّنْيَا حَسَنَةً وَّفِي الْاٰخِرَةِ حَسَنَةً وَّقِنَا عَذَابَ النَّارِ ^1$$

Our Lord, grant us good in this world as well as good in the
world to come, and protect us from the torment of the Fire.

In this prayer, the world has been given precedence, but what 'world' exactly? It is the good of this world *(hasanatud-dunya)* which becomes a means by which to reap good in the hereafter. The fact that we have been taught this prayer clearly demonstrates that in attaining the world, a believer ought to have in view the good of the hereafter. The words *hasanatud-dunya* as mentioned here encompass all the best means by which a Muslim believer ought to pursue the world. Pursue the world in every such way that leads to benefit and goodness, not in a manner that causes pain to another human being, nor in a manner that is disgraceful or ignoble amongst the people. Engaging in the world in such a manner would definitely enable one to reap the good of the hereafter *(hasanatul-akhirah)*.

Be Not Indolent

Therefore, bear in mind that an individual who dedicates their life for the sake of God is never left in a helpless state. Nay, not at all. In fact, religion and devoting oneself to the cause of Allah makes an individual vigilant and active. Indolence and sloth can come nowhere near such a person. In a narration it is related by Ammar ibn Khuzaymah[ra] that Hazrat Umar[ra] said to his father: 'What has held you back from planting trees on your land?' My father responded: 'I am an old man, I will die soon.' Hazrat Umar[ra] responded by saying: 'You must do this task.'

---

1   *al-Baqarah*, 2:202

After this, I saw Hazrat Umar[ra] himself planting trees with my father on our land. Our Noble Messenger, peace and blessings of Allah be upon him, would always pray to seek refuge from helplessness and sloth.

I reiterate, do not be indolent. Allah the Exalted does not forbid you from pursuing worldly objectives; rather, He teaches us to pray for the good of this world *(hasanatud-dunya)*. Allah the Exalted does not desire that a person sit hand on hand helplessly; in fact, He states clearly:

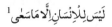
لَيۡسَ لِلۡاِنۡسَانِ اِلَّا مَاسَعٰى [1]

Man will have nothing but what he strives for;

Therefore, it is incumbent on a believer to strive with effort, but insofar as is possible for me, I shall repeat again and again that you must not turn this world into your ultimate objective. In fact, make religion your ultimate objective, and let worldly endeavours serve as a vehicle to this end. Often, the rich are able to do things that the poor and indigent cannot. In the time of the Messenger of Allah, peace and blessings of Allah be upon him, the first Caliph, who was a very skilled merchant, offered invaluable support when he became a Muslim, and he received the rank of the Truthful *(Siddiq)*; he was the closest companion of the Holy Prophet[sa] and became his first Caliph.

The Faith of Hazrat Abu Bakr[ra]

It is written that Hazrat Abu Bakr[ra] met someone as he was returning from a trade expedition, before he had reached Mecca. He asked the man for any current news. The man said: 'There is nothing else worthy of mention, but one new development is that your friend has claimed to be a Prophet.' Abu Bakr[ra] said there and then: 'If he has made this claim, then he is truthful.' As such, when he returned to Mecca, Hazrat Abu Bakr[ra] met the Messenger of Allah, peace and blessings of Allah be upon him, and inquired: 'Have you really claimed to be a Prophet?' 'Yes,' said the Holy Prophet[sa] and Hazrat Abu Bakr[ra] received the honour of accepting Islam immediately.[2] Hazrat Abu Bakr Siddiq[ra] had no need to witness a miracle in order to accept Islam. Only those people want to be shown a miracle who do not personally know the claimant. However, an individual who knows the claimant at a personal level has no need or desire to be shown miracles. This is pre-

---

[1]   *an-Najm*, 53:40
[2]   *Al-Hakam*, vol. 4, no. 29, dated 16 August 1900, pp. 3-4

cisely the reason that Hazrat Abu Bakr Siddiq[ra] did not ask for a miracle, for he was well aware of his disposition, and he knew more than anyone that the Holy Prophet[sa] was truthful and honest, not a liar and a cheat. He knew that when the Holy Prophet[sa] was never disingenuous in his interactions with other people, how could he possibly have the audacity to forge a lie against Allah Almighty.

Hence, it ought to be remembered that a sign is asked for only when a person apprehends that the claimant perhaps may have told a lie. However, when it becomes clearly evident that the claimant is truthful and honest, there remains no need for a person to witness a sign. It should also be borne in mind that those people who are desirous of witnessing a sign and who insist on this, are not strong in faith; in fact, they are forever in a state of danger. Such people do not receive the fruits of believing in the unseen, because when a person believes in the unseen, this encompasses another good deed as well, which is to think well of others. The hasty who lay emphasis on being shown a sign are deprived of this good deed.

The disciples of the Messiah, on whom be peace, insisted that a table spread with food be sent down from heaven. God Almighty rebuked them and said that We shall send down a table spread with food, but after We do, anyone who disbelieves shall be punished severely. The benefit of mentioning this story in the Holy Quran is to tell us about the sort of faith that is best. The fact is that the signs of Allah Almighty are clear and manifest, but on the other hand, they are meant to serve as a final argument against the disbelievers and also as a trial for the believing community. At times, this is why these signs possess a certain trial within them. It is a matter of principle that those who demand a sign are hasty and do not think well of others, and their dispositions possess an element that gives rise to doubt and suspicion. After all, this is why they ask for a sign. And then, this is also the reason that when they see the sign, they begin to interpret it in absurd ways, or they will claim that this is magic, or describe it in some other way. In short, their sceptical nature distances them from the truth. Therefore, I advise you to develop the faith of Abu Bakr, may Allah Almighty be pleased with him, and the faith of the companions, may Allah be pleased with them, because such faith is characterised by thinking well of others and patience, and is the result of many blessings and fruits. To accept after one has been shown a sign is a conditional faith—such faith is weak and generally not fruitful. However, when a person believes with a favourable view (without entertaining doubt), Allah the Exalted shows a believer of this nature a sign which increases their faith and opens their heart. In fact, God turns such people into Signs of Allah themselves. This is exactly the reason that no Prophet has shown a sign as per the people's demand. A truthful believer must never let their faith be hinged upon the fact that they are shown a sign.

The Importance of Spending in the Way of Allah

I now return to the actual subject and reiterate that the wealthy and affluent can serve the Faith very well. This is why God Almighty has declared that one aspect of what characterises the righteous is as follows:

مِمَّا رَزَقْنٰهُمْ يُنْفِقُوْنَ ¹

They spend out of what We have provided for them.

Here, there is no distinction of wealth alone. Whatever Allah the Exalted has given to a person, they ought to spend in the way of Allah. The purpose in this is for one to show sympathy and give support to humanity. The shariah of Allah Almighty is based on two things alone: to honour the commandments of Allah and to show compassion to the creation of Allah. Therefore, it is compassion for the creation of God that has been taught in the following:

مِمَّا رَزَقْنٰهُمْ يُنْفِقُوْنَ ²

They spend out of what We have provided for them.

The affluent receive great opportunities to offer services in the cause of faith.

On one occasion, our Noble Prophet, peace and blessings of Allah be upon him, made a financial appeal and Hazrat Abu Bakr, may Allah be pleased with him, brought everything that he had in his home, and presented himself before the Holy Prophet[sa]. The Holy Prophet[sa] asked: 'Abu Bakr! What have you left at home?' Hazrat Abu Bakr[ra] responded: 'I have left behind the name of Allah and His Messenger.' Hazrat Umar[ra] brought half of all his property. The Holy Prophet[sa] asked: 'Umar! What have you left at home?' He responded by saying: 'Half.' The Messenger of Allah, peace and blessings of Allah be upon him, said: 'The difference in the actions of Abu Bakr and Umar, is the difference between them in rank.'

In the world, we see that people have an immense love for wealth. This is why it

---

1   *al-Baqarah*, 2:4
2   *al-Baqarah*, 2:4

is written in books on the science of the interpretation of dreams that if someone sees that they have taken out their liver and given it to someone, this implies wealth. This is why in order to attain true righteousness and faith, Allah the Exalted states:

$$لَنْ تَنَالُوا الْبِرَّ حَتّٰى تُنْفِقُوْا مِمَّا تُحِبُّوْنَ^1$$

Meaning, never shall you attain to true righteousness unless you spend what you most love, because sympathy and good treatment towards the creation of God depends to a large extent on the spending of wealth. Sympathy towards humanity and God's creation at large is the second aspect of faith, without which one's faith cannot be complete and firm. Until a person sacrifices for others, how can they give them benefit? Sacrifice is necessary in benefiting others and showing them sympathy. It is this very teaching of sacrifice which has been given in the following:

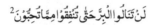

$$لَنْ تَنَالُوا الْبِرَّ حَتّٰى تُنْفِقُوْا مِمَّا تُحِبُّوْنَ^2$$

Never shall you attain to true righteousness
unless you spend what you most love.

Therefore, spending wealth in the cause of Allah Almighty is also a criterion and touchstone by which to judge the good nature and righteousness of an individual. In the case of Abu Bakr, may Allah be pleased with him, the extent and level to which his life was devoted to God was that the Messenger of Allah, peace and blessings of Allah be upon him, expressed a need and he came with everything that he owned.

Why the Prophets Are Faced with Needs

Here, I would like to explain an important point about the reason that Prophets, peace be upon them, are faced with various needs. Allah the Exalted has the power to ensure that they are never put in a situation where they lack what is required, but they are confronted with such needs so that examples may be set of dedication to God—so that the dedicated life of Abu Bakr[ra] could be brought to light for example; so that belief in the existence of a Powerful God would develop on earth; so that such people who dedicate their lives for God could serve

---

1   *Aal-e-Imran*, 3:93
2   *Aal-e-Imran*, 3:93

as a Sign of Allah before the world. Moreover, this is necessary so that the people learn about that hidden love and pleasure in the face of which even a beloved and preferable thing, such as the wealth and property of this world, can be easily and gladly sacrificed. Furthermore, this is necessary so that after an individual spends their wealth and property, they develop the strength and courage where they do not hesitate in even giving up a thing as dear as their own life for the sake of God Almighty, in order to crown their dedication to Allah.

In short, the fundamental purpose for which the Prophets, peace be upon them, are faced with various needs is so that the people can be taught to turn away from their hollow love for the transient things of this world, so that they may develop a delightful faith in the existence of Allah Almighty and so that they develop the strength that is needed to offer sacrifice for the betterment and benefit of mankind. Thus, this holy class of people advances in the supervision of that Master Who owns the خَزَآئِنُ السَّمٰوٰتِ وَالْأَرْضِ (*treasures of the heavens and earth*). Could such people ever really need anything? The sort of needs that they are faced with are to perfect religious teaching and firmly instil morals and faith in the people."[1]

The Level of Perfect Certainty

The Promised Messiah[as] said: "Allah the Exalted states:

$$وَاعْبُدْ رَبَّكَ حَتّٰى يَأْتِيَكَ الْيَقِيْنُ^2$$

And continue worshipping thy Lord, till death comes to thee.

Commentators state that the word *yaqin* here implies 'death.' However, this death is in the spiritual sense. The ultimate objective that a person ought to seek as indicated and alluded to in this verse is obvious. I would say, however, that irrespective of whether death is implied here in the spiritual sense, or whether your life is dedicated to the service of God, a believer must not tire or fall slow in worship until this illusion of a life is turned to ash, and until a new life, which is everlasting and comforting, takes its place and begins to flourish. Further, until one's burning and fire for the life of this temporary world dies down and a pleasure is felt in faith, and until the soul develops a sense of tranquility and comfort, know for certain that one's faith is not sound and complete. Therefore, in the aforementioned verse, Allah the Exalted states that one ought to continue in worship

---

[1]   *Al-Hakam*, vol. 4, no. 30, dated 24 August 1900, pp. 3-4
[2]   *al-Hijr*, 15:100

until one attains a level of perfect certainty. An individual must continue until every obstruction and veil of darkness is moved aside and until they perceive that now they are not what they once were; in fact, now they are in a new country, a new land, a new sky, and even they themselves are a new creation altogether. This second life is what the sufis term as *baqa* (subsistence). When a person reaches this stage, the spirit of Allah Almighty is breathed into them and the angels descend upon them. This is the secret in the Prophet of God, peace and blessings of Allah be upon him, saying that if anyone wished to see a walking corpse, they could look at Abu Bakr[ra]. The rank of Abu Bakr[ra] was not only due to his apparent deeds, but because of what was in his heart.

Faith Is a Secret

Bear in mind that faith is a secret between a believer and Allah Almighty—it is a secret of which no one from the rest of mankind, except for the believer themselves, can be aware. This is the deeper essence of the following:

$$أَنَا عِنْدَ ظَنِّ عَبْدِیْ بِیْ$$

I am to my servant what he thinks of me.

On certain occasions, those people who are bereft of true knowledge and divine verities, due to their being unaware of the ties that a certain believer holds with Allah Almighty, are surprised or astonished as regards their circumstances—those which relate to their finances and livelihood, for example. At times, this astonishment of theirs will even take them to ill-thinking and lead them astray, because their sight is limited to their own limited means. Such people are unaware of the secret and mysterious nature of the relationship between that person and Allah the Exalted. It is my desire that my friends make their hidden relationship with God on the pattern of the honourable companions of the Holy Prophet[sa].

Dedicate Your Lives in the Way of Allah Almighty

My purpose is that people must dedicate their lives in the way of Allah Almighty. I have read in certain newspapers that such and such person has dedicated their life for the cause of the Arya Samaj and so and so priest has given over their life to the mission. It surprises me as to why Muslims do not dedicate their lives for the service of Islam and in the way of God. If such people looked at the blessed era of the Messenger of Allah, peace and blessings of Allah be upon him, they would come to know how lives are dedicated for the life of Islam.

Remember! This is not an unprofitable bargain, in fact it is a bargain of unfathomable gain. If only the Muslims were informed of this, and if only they realised the benefits and profits of this bargain. Does a person who dedicates their life for the sake of religion waste away their life? Not at all. Allah the Exalted states:

$$فَلَهُمْ أَجْرُهُمْ عِنْدَ رَبِّهِمْ وَلَا خَوْفٌ عَلَيْهِمْ وَلَا هُمْ يَحْزَنُوْنَ ^1$$

Meaning, their Lord is the one who shall give them the reward of this dedication in the cause of Allah. This dedication grants a person deliverance and salvation from all forms of sorrow and grief.

It astonishes me that everyone naturally desires peace and comfort, and seeks deliverance from grief and sorrow, and from agonies and worries, but when a tried and tested prescription is given to them for this ailment, they pay no heed whatsoever. Has dedication in the way of God not proven successful over the last 1300 years? Did the esteemed companions of the Holy Prophet[sa] not inherit holy lives and prove worthy of being conferred everlasting lives due to this very dedication? Then what reason is there now that people should desist from reaping the benefit of this efficacious remedy? The fact is that people are unaware of its reality and are oblivious of the pleasure that is derived after one makes this dedication. Otherwise, if people had caught a whiff of the pleasure and comfort of which I speak, they would enter this field with countless hopes and aspirations.

The Personal Experience of the Promised Messiah[as] and His Advice

I am myself experienced in this way and have felt this pleasure and delight merely by the grace and bounty of Allah Almighty. My desire is such that if the price of dedicating my life for the sake of Allah the Exalted be that I die, and then come back to life, only to die once more and come back to life again, each time my passion would only increase with pleasure.

Therefore, I am myself experienced in this and have felt these effects. Allah the Exalted has instilled such fervour in me for this dedication that even if I was told that there would be no spiritual reward and benefit in this dedication, and there would only be pain and grief, I could still not refrain from this service to Islam. Therefore, I consider it an obligation to advise my community and convey this

---
1   *al-Baqarah*, 2:113

message to them. Hereafter, everyone is free to heed my words or ignore them. Any one of you who desires salvation and seeks a pure or everlasting life ought to dedicate their life for the sake of Allah. Let each and every one of you strive and anxiously endeavour to reach the stage and rank where they can say that their life, their death, their sacrifices, their Prayers, are for Allah alone; and in the likeness of Abraham[as], let their soul proclaim:

$$اَسْلَمْتُ لِرَبِّ الْعَلَمِيْنَ^1$$

I have submitted to the Lord of the worlds.

Until an individual is lost in God, and does not give up their life in God's way, they cannot be granted a new life. All of you who hold a relationship with me see for yourselves that I consider the dedication of my life for the sake of Allah to be the fundamental purpose of my existence. Now all of you ought to delve into yourselves and see how many of you prefer this action of mine for yourselves and hold dear the dedication of their lives in the way of God.[2]

Allah the Exalted states:

$$وَلَقَدْ ذَرَأْنَا لِجَهَنَّمَ كَثِيْرًا مِّنَ الْجِنِّ وَالْاِنْسِ^3$$

Verily, We have created many of the Jinn and men whose end shall be Hell.

An individual who does not dedicate their life for the sake of Allah Almighty ought to remember that Allah the Exalted has prepared hell for such people. Certain people who are unwise and entertain vain notions believe that each and every person must enter hell. This verse evidently demonstrates that this is false. There is no doubt, nonetheless, that there are few who are saved completely from the punishment of hell, but this is no surprising matter. Allah the Exalted states:

$$قَلِيْلٌ مِّنْ عِبَادِيَ الشَّكُوْرُ^4$$

Few of My servants are grateful.

The Reality of Hell

Now, one ought to understand what hell is exactly. One hell is that which Allah

---

1   *al-Baqarah*, 2:132
2   *Al-Hakam*, vol. 4, no. 31, dated 31 August 1900, pp. 3-4
3   *al-A'raf*, 7:180
4   *as-Saba*, 34:14

Almighty has promised after death. Secondly, this life also, if not devoted to God Almighty, is also a hell. Allah the Exalted does not concern Himself to save such people from pain and give them comfort. Do not think that a large share of worldly riches, authority, wealth, honour and children can give a person any pleasure, comfort and tranquillity, and that these things constitute an early paradise in this world. Not at all. That comfort, that satisfaction, and that tranquillity which are from among the rewards of paradise cannot be attained through such means. This can only be attained by living and dying in complete devotion to God. The Prophets, peace be upon them, and especially Abraham and Jacob, may Allah be pleased with both of them, left behind the bequest that:

$$\text{لَا تَمُوْتُنَّ اِلَّا وَاَنْتُمْ مُّسْلِمُوْنَ}^1$$

Let not death overtake you except when you are in a state of submission.

The pleasures of this world only spawn a filthy greed which further increases one's desire and thirst. The thirst of such a person can never be quenched, like someone suffering from polydipsia who eventually dies. Therefore, the fire of these unnecessary desires and longings is also from the fires of hell, which do not let a person's heart feel peace and comfort, but rather causes them to writhe in anxiety and restlessness. Therefore, my friends must never lose sight of the fact that man should not lose himself and become intoxicated in the love and passion of wealth and riches, or in a woman or son, to the extent that they become a screen between him and God Almighty. This is why wealth and children have been termed a 'trial.' These too can lead a person to hell; and when a person is separated from them, man displays extreme anxiety and restlessness. In this state of affairs, the following do not remain words alone:

$$\text{نَارُ اللهِ الْمُوْقَدَةُ الَّتِيْ تَطَّلِعُ عَلَى الْاَفْئِدَةِ}^2$$

It is Allah's kindled fire, which rises over the hearts.

In fact, these words take on an apparent form. Hence, this fire, which burns the human heart and makes it even darker and blacker than coal, is this love of anything that is besides Allah.

When two things come together or are rubbed against one another, this creates a heat. In the same way, the friction of man's love and the love of this world along

---

1   *al-Baqarah*, 2:133
2   *al-Humazah*, 104:7-8

with the love of materialistic things burns down the love of God, and the heart grows dark and becomes distanced from God; and then it becomes prey to all sorts of restlessness. However, if a person has a relationship with God as people have with the things of this world, and if a person loves the blessings of this world out of love for God, this mutual friction burns down the love of all that is besides Allah, and a radiance and light is filled in its place. At such a time, the will of God becomes their will, and their will becomes the object of God's will. When one reaches this stage, the love of God assumes the place of life itself for such a person. Just as there are necessities which help to sustain life, all that is needed to sustain the sort of person I have just mentioned is God and nothing but God. In other words, one could say that the joy and comfort of such a person lies in God alone. Then, even if such an individual is given grief or pain by the people of the world, the fact is that in this grief and pain as well, the individual in question derives a divine pleasure with satisfaction and comfort, which is not enjoyed by even the most care-free person in the eyes of a worldly individual. Any state between man and God which is contrary to what I have just described is a hell. In other words, a life that is spent without God Almighty is also a hell.

Then, we also learn from the Hadith that a fever also is from the heat of hell. The various sorts of disease and misfortune that afflict man are also a sample of hell and this is so that people can witness to an extent the world of the hereafter, so that this may serve as proof of the underlying reality in the concept of divine reward and punishment, and to refute the absurd concept of atonement. Just take the example of leprosy, where the limbs begin to decompose and emit a liquid substance. A person loses their voice. This itself is a hell, but then the people grow averse as well and stay away from such a person. Even the most loving of wives, sons and parents turn their backs on such a person. Then, some people turn blind and deaf, while some fall prey to various other ailments. People develop stones and some develop tumours in their stomach. In short, all of these afflictions befall man because he lives his life distanced from God, and acts insolently and rudely in God's presence, and because he gives no regard to the instructions of Allah Almighty—in this state, a hell is born.

I now return to my actual subject. God Almighty states: 'We have created many men and Jinn whose end shall be hell.' Then God states that they themselves have created this hell, even though, in reality, they are called to paradise. A pure-hearted individual listens with a sense of purity, but a person of impure thoughts acts in accordance with their own benighted sense. Hence, where such people will be met with hell in the hereafter, they shall not be free and safe from the hell of this world either. For the hell of this world only serves as an argument and proof in favour of the hell that is to come.[1]

The Duty of Preaching

The unworthy and vile do not have it within them to lend an ear to a word of truth, rectitude and wisdom. Whenever divine insight or a point of wisdom is put before them, they do not pay attention; in fact they ignore it with no concern.

There is no doubt that those who speak the truth are also few and far between. Those who preach the truth purely for the sake of Allah Almighty are very few in number—as though there was no one at all. Generally, there are preachers who exhort others, but their actual purpose and objective is nothing but to receive from others and earn the world. When this motive is mixed with their counsel, the truth and divine nature of their words is overshadowed by the darkness of their vested interest, and the fragrance of that pleasure and insight which reaches the heart and mind on hearing the Word of God, and which perfumes the soul, is suppressed by the stench of selfishness and materialism. Even in the very same gathering, people will say: 'Sir! All these words are for nothing more than to earn you bread and butter.'

There is no doubt that many people have turned the enjoining of good and the forbidding of evil into a means of livelihood, but everyone is not of this nature. There are pure-hearted individuals as well who convey the words of God and His Messenger, peace and blessings of Allah be upon him, to the people only because they are commissioned to enjoin goodness and forbid evil, and they consider this task to be an obligation, and through this they desire to seek the pleasure of Allah Almighty. The duty of preaching is a position of lofty stature, and as it were, possesses within it the nature and grandeur of prophethood, provided that one does not neglect the fear of God.

A person who exhorts others receives an opportunity to particularly reform their own selves as well, because in the least, it is necessary for a person to show others that they practice what they preach. In any case, if an individual enjoins good, even if it comes from a vested interest or motive, a person should not turn away from it, just because the individual who exhorts them does so for some

---

[1]   *Al-Hakam*, vol. 4, no. 33, dated 16 September 1900, pp. 6-7

selfish purpose. The point that the individual conveys is good in and of itself. Therefore, it is incumbent on the pure-hearted to reflect on what the individual enjoins. There is no need for one to debate over the objectives and purposes in view of which the individual exhorts them. How excellent indeed, is the following verse of Sa'di:

مرد باید که گیرد اندر گوش   گر نوشت است پند بر دیوار

A man ought to put into his ear;
a piece of advice, even if written on a wall.

Look At What is Being Said and Not Who Says It

It is absolutely true that one ought to focus on what is being said, and not on the person who makes the statement. For if not, a person can be left deprived of accepting the truth, and the seed of arrogance and pride begins to germinate from within. For if an individual genuinely seeks the truth, what need have they to find fault in others?

A preacher may have their own vested interest in admonishing the people, but why should you care? Your fundamental purpose is to seek the truth. There is no doubt that these people begin speaking about irrelevant matters, without consideration for time or place, and when they advise and counsel, they do not address issues that the present time demands, nor do they keep in view the sorts of ailments by which their addressees are afflicted. In fact, they only come to beg in various manners.

The Manner of Speech Employed by the Messenger of Allah[sa]

If such people had closely observed the manner of speech employed by the Messenger of Allah, peace and blessings of Allah be upon him, they would learn the art of admonishing others as well. A certain individual came to the Messenger of Allah, peace and blessings of Allah be upon him, and inquired: 'What is the greatest virtue?' The Holy Prophet[sa] responded: 'Generosity.' A second person came and asked the same question and the Holy Prophet[sa] said: 'The service of your mother and father.' A third person came and he received a different response altogether. Here we have the same question, but different answers.

Many people have stumbled in the face of such Hadith and even the Christians have levelled forceful allegations against such Hadith. However, these asinine individuals have not thought about the beneficial and blessed manner of response employed by the Messenger of Allah, peace and blessings of Allah be upon him, in such instances. The secret is that the Noble Messenger, peace and blessings of Allah be upon him, would prescribe a cure that accorded with the individual requirements of the patient that came to him. For example, there could be no greater virtue for a habitual miser than for them to forsake this habit. An individual who did not serve their parents, and who in fact, treated them harshly, needed to be taught to serve their mother and father.

Advice for the Community

Just as it is necessary for a physician to diagnose a patient in the best possible manner, similarly, the position of admonishing others demands that before a person exhorts and admonishes, they must keep in view the diseases by which their addressees are afflicted. However, this is very difficult in itself. Unless one is a godly preacher, they receive very little share of this insight and knowledge. This is the very reason that although hundreds and thousands of preachers wander this country, the practical state of the people continues to deteriorate day after day. All sorts of error and weakness in doctrine, faith and morality continue to produce their effects. This is because admonitions are devoid of truth and spirit. All of this is prevalent; however, at this time, I would like to tell my friends that by the grace of Allah Almighty, as they have felt a thirst in their hearts to seek the truth, they must not hesitate in accepting truth and righteousness when they see it. Though a preacher may ask to be given something indirectly in various ways, this one reason alone should not move you to ignore the actual underlying wisdom in their address. After all, the individual who looks at such people with an eye of contempt on account of their solicitation is also guilty. Could anyone throw away a ruby or a rare jewel just because it is wrapped in a foetid and filthy, tattered rag? Of course not. Therefore, if a preacher asks to be given something, you must know that you for your part have been instructed:

And him who seeks thy help, chide not.

Even if a beggar comes to you mounted on horseback, it is not permissible for

---

[1]   *ad-Duha,* 93:11

you to turn him away. You have been instructed to not rebuke the one who begs of you. Indeed, God has instructed the other person as well to refrain from begging, but such people will receive their punishment from God for their misdeed. It does not behove you, however, to disobey a commandment of God Almighty that ought to be honoured. Therefore, if you are able, then give something to such preachers, and if you have nothing, then tell them gently.[1]

Ill-Thinking

Conflict begins when a person begins to harbour corrupt thoughts and doubts. If a person thinks well of others, they will be enabled to give them something as well. If one errs at the very first stage, how can one reach their intended destination? Ill-thinking is a most vicious thing and it deprives an individual of many a virtue. This then grows until the condition reaches a state where a person begins to think ill of God.

If the disease of ill-thinking had not grown, then do tell me on what basis do the Muslim clerics declare me a disbeliever and reject me? For they have left no stone unturned or spared any expense in declaring me a disbeliever and inflicting grief upon me. I have proclaimed loudly and sworn by God Almighty again and again that I am a Muslim. I have said that I believe in the Holy Quran as the Seal of the Books, and the Messenger of Allah, peace and blessings of Allah be upon him, as the Seal of the Prophets. I declare that Islam is a living Faith and is the true means of salvation. I believe in the decrees of God Almighty and in the Day of Resurrection. I face the same Qiblah to offer my Prayers, and I offer the same number of Prayers. I keep all of the fasts in the month of Ramadan. Then what have they found to be so odd in me for which they considered it necessary to label me a disbeliever. This is extremely unjust. These people do not reflect upon their own impure deeds and lives. They fail to reflect and ponder over the heaven and earth in order to come to the understanding that all of these creations have a Creator. What benefit did the Muslim clerics derive from the sign of Lekhram?

The Sign of Atham

What benefit did the Muslim clerics derive from the sign of Atham? Goodness gracious! How clearly was it fulfilled and yet attempts were made to discredit

---

[1]   *Al-Hakam*, vol. 4, no. 34, dated 24 September 1900, pp. 4-5

the prophecy. In fact, if any objection remains in this respect, then it lies with Atham, who set a seal on the truth of this prophecy, by holding his peace and not responding to my requests. When this prophecy clearly stipulated a condition, even a man of legal bent would view it in two ways—in the case that the condition was met, Atham would be saved, and if not, Atham would die. Now in the case that he was saved, the point that a believer ought to determine is whether Atham met the condition or not.

It ought to be borne in mind that in this prophecy there was a clear and evident condition that stipulated 'in the case that he does not incline to the truth.' However, there are certain prophecies of divine punishment which do not apparently state a condition, yet even they, in reality, are conditional. The incident of Prophet Jonah[as] is clearly before us. One may consult the commentaries and see what is written. Despite the fact that such a precedent exists in the Holy Quran and in all the past scriptures, but with regards to me, due to this very ill-thinking of which I speak, these people have gone so far as to ignore a determined law of Allah the Exalted. My prophecy contained a clear condition. The fact that Atham survived and was saved is proof of the fact that he benefited from the condition stipulated in the prophecy. In fact, I have even more arguments in support of the fact that Atham benefited from the condition in the prophecy, which even an obtuse individual would be able to comprehend. I repeatedly published announcement after announcement and invited him to take an oath; and I even said that if he took a false oath, and subsequently did not die within a period of one year as a punishment, I would consider myself a liar. I even offered to give him a reward of 4,000 rupees to take this oath. I even proved to him that it was not a sin as per the Bible to swear an oath of this nature, but rather, it was more of a sin to refuse. I also said that if I was false, then he should bring legal action against me. The Christian priests instigated and encouraged him as well to file suit against me, but despite such an effort, Atham did not come forth; and in doing so, by his silence, and by abstaining from his criticism of Islam and publishing writings against Islam, he demonstrated that in reality, he benefited from the condition stipulated in the prophecy.

The very condition in this prophecy was a prophecy in itself. If Atham was not going to benefit from the condition, why would this prophecy be conditional? Now, an honest and God-fearing person ought to reflect over whether Atham benefited from the condition of 'inclining to the truth' or not. Moreover, if swearing an oath was contrary to the religious law, did Clark and Premdas, among other Christians, take an oath or not? In addition to this, I also proved and demonstrated that in order to bring about a true verdict, it is actually incumbent upon a Christian to take an oath.

In short, this prophecy was conditional. Atham remained fearful and would wander from city to city. If he had complete faith and trust in his Lord Jesus, then why did he feel such anxiety? However, as soon as he began to hide the truth and sought to mislead the people—as hiding the truth was a rock that could have lead the uninformed to stumble—Allah the Exalted, in accordance with His true promise, took him from this world within seven months of my last announcement. Ultimately, the death that Atham feared and fled from, caught up with him.

I cannot understand what difficulty the people could have in the matter of Atham. Such solid evidence is present, yet they reject it! If evidence is solid, the courts will issue a verdict of 'death by hanging' against a criminal. In short, the Atham affair was a grand sign. A revelation has been recorded in *Barahin-e-Ahmadiyyah* about this trial in clear and explicit words.

The Sign of the Conference of Great Religions

Then, the sign of the Conference of Religions was also a great sign. Khawaja Kamal-ud-Din Sahib and many other friends are a witness, and they can swear on oath that they had been informed in advance, and an announcement had been published and distributed as well, that 'the paper has been declared supreme'. This sign was fulfilled before thousands of people, exactly as the prophecy had been made. Both English and Urdu newspapers unanimously declared that my paper stood above all the others.

The Sign of Acquittal

Then, there was the case of attempted murder that was filed against me, in which people like Dr Clark were involved as well. Maulvi Muhammad Husain also went to give testimony against me and the well-known Arya, Ram Bhajat—the lawyer—came to pursue the case as well. There are many hundreds of people present who could testify to the manner in which all the details and circumstances of this trial were foretold in advance. Finally, a prophecy of my acquittal was also made through the revelation: ابرا, i.e. to exonerate.

These are God's matters of the unseen. Is it within the power of man to make a prophecy in this way? Is it possible for a human being to provide an entire illustration of what would transpire at a time when there were no signs and traces of this case?

The Sign of Lekhram

Moving on, the sign of Lekhram could be likened to an unsheathed sword. Five years in advance, announcements were published by the parties involved in which a prophecy was made. Even Lekhram himself would relate the prophecy wherever he went. This prophecy contained no condition and was perfectly straightforward. If Lekhram had lived, undoubtedly, an uproar would have erupted. But this could only happen if what I had said was not from God; in which case, the end would have spelled humiliation for me. Would Muhammad Husain have remained silent? Even now, when this sign has been fulfilled and hundreds and thousands of people have accepted the truth of this prophecy, he states that some member of my community probably murdered him. It is a pity that such people fail to understand that what sort of a blind follower could continue to believe in a spiritual leader who encourages them to commit murder? How could people believe in a spiritual leader who claims that his prophecies are a criterion for his truthfulness, but at the same time he instructs his followers to employ unlawful means to fulfil his own prophecies? Shameful indeed are such notions.

Those people who entertain such an idea, in essence, seek to disgrace our good-natured, just and vigilant government as well. The government left no stone unturned in this matter and led a full-scale inquiry into the matter of Lekhram, but the mantle of my community and I were proven completely free and clean from the stain of this blood.

Such people do not understand: did Lekhram murder my father or grandfather? He did not inflict any sort of harm or injury upon my own person directly. He did, however, make insolent attacks against the holy personage of the Noble Messenger, peace and blessings of Allah be upon him, and dishonoured him in such ways that my heart began to palpitate and I was extremely grieved. I presented his disrespects and impertinences before God with a broken heart, and as a recompense for Lekhram's insolence and disrespect, God conferred upon me a prophecy about him. In the very same prophecy, his death, the time of his death and the manner in which he would die—among other details—were explicitly stated. In the context of this prophecy there is an illustration of a hand. Then, in the same connection, the following words are mentioned:

بترس از تیغِ بُرّانِ محمدؐ

Fear the sharp sword of Muhammad[sa].

All this is clearly recorded. Now someone ought to tell me whether it is within human design and power to foretell of such a happening five years in advance, when Lekhram was a young man of merely twenty-four or twenty-five years of age? Of course not. This is an act of God Almighty. This is far beyond and above human power, or human understanding and comprehension.[1]

The Need for Signs

Now tell me, do these signs require any other external evidence to demonstrate and establish their truth? Jesus, peace be upon him, has said that even one miracle is enough. As such, when a sign was demanded from him, he would always say that no sign, except for the sign of Prophet Jonah[as], would be given to the people.

I have already stated that those people who are informed of a claimant's personal circumstances, have no real need for signs. It is only out of His mercy that Allah the Exalted manifests signs so that such people may receive further satisfaction and so that they develop a stronger belief in God's existence. My astonishment knows no bounds and I am utterly surprised that these people accept that the saints of Allah manifested miracles, and will relate such miracles for which there is neither any proof, nor any rational or written evidence. They are nothing but legends and tales that gained publicity in an era long after their demise.

If, for example, one was to ask a Shia to relate a miracle of Hazrat Ali, may Allah be pleased with him, they will narrate so many that a person would tire just counting them. But if they were asked for evidence, they have nothing. The miracles of Syed Abdul-Qadir Jilani, may Allah have mercy on him, are related abundantly, but none of them are recorded in any of his books. Now, people ought to fear God and tell us after reflection: how can those events which were recorded hundreds of years after their assumed occurrence be held as true, while those signs which are being witnessed before the very eyes of the people be rejected? It is a

---

[1] *Al-Hakam*, vol. 4, no. 35, dated 1 October 1900, pp. 2-3

pity that such people do not realise that a report cannot be equal to one's own observation. A story that is narrated cannot compare to a true and established event. Therefore, those who witness my signs and reject them do not reject me, they reject established events; in fact, this is a denial of Allah Almighty Himself.

Bear in mind that this affliction has befallen the people because righteousness and purity has vanished. It is the law of God that when fear and awe of Allah Almighty disappears, when hearts lose their emotion, and when souls no longer melt with passion, at such a time, signs of warning are manifested. At this juncture, people ought to have been fearful. Yet, it is a shame that these people have become blind and deaf, and have ignored these divine signs (which could have resulted in tearful supplication and humility, and which could have breathed new life into their faith) and they have passed on as صُمٌّ بُكْمٌ *(those who are deaf and dumb)*. What can I say of such people, for the verdict of God Almighty in their relation is:

$$صُمٌّ بُكْمٌ عُمْيٌ فَهُمْ لَا يَرْجِعُوْنَ^1$$

They are deaf, dumb and blind; so they will not return.

A Duty of My Community

It is the duty of my community, however, that has recognised me to not let these signs of Allah Almighty go stale. These signs develop a strength in certainty. Therefore, our community must not let these signs remain hidden, and those of you who have witnessed them must inform those who are not present so that they may be saved from evils and so that they may develop a revitalised faith in God. Present these signs by decorating and adorning them with excellent arguments. Remember! Those who do not view with attention the arguments and proofs of God are blind and cannot see the truth; they do not have ears with which to listen. Such people are no less than cattle; in fact, they are worse, and God does not support such people. God Almighty is responsible for the life of a righteous person and a believer. Allah the Exalted states:

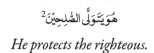

$$هُوَ يَتَوَلَّى الصّٰلِحِيْنَ^2$$

He protects the righteous.

---

1   *al-Baqarah*, 2:19
2   *al-Aʿraf*, 7:197

God is not a Guardian of those who are distanced from His path and who resemble cattle. After all, do tell me, do human beings sit and weep over goats when they are slaughtered? Then, why would anyone care for the lives of such people who are even worse than goats?

Just observe the lives of animals. They are used for labour and slaughtered. As such, there remains no guarantee for the life of an individual who severs their ties with God Almighty. Hence, Allah the Exalted states:

$$ قُلۡ مَا یَعۡبَؤُا بِکُمۡ رَبِّیۡ لَوۡ لَا دُعَآؤُکُمۡ ^1 $$

Meaning, if you do not supplicate to Allah, my Lord would not care for you. Remember, Allah Almighty does not care whatsoever for those who worship Him for the world or who do not have a relationship with Him."[2]

---

[1] *al-Furqan*, 25:78

[2] *Al-Hakam*, vol. 4, no. 36, dated 10 October 1900, p. 3

Glossary

Many of the Arabic terms used in this translation are found in *The Oxford English Dictionary*, including, Islam, Quran, Hadith, Sunnah, etc. Such words have not been italicised in the text, and generally, are not glossed here. In various places, the Promised Messiah[as] has explained various words in a linguistic context or expounded their deeper spiritual meaning, as is the case, for example, with *ilah, ansar, laqq, aws,* among others. Such words, though italicised in the text, have not been included in the glossary. Similarly, foreign terms which can adequately be translated into English—though given in the text on certain occasions—have not been elaborated here. Therefore, please note that only such terms are included in this glossary which require an explanation above and beyond a simple translation in English.

alhamdulillah literally, 'all praise belongs to Allah', which is an expression in Islam for showing gratitude to God.

Asr the third of the five daily prayers, which is offered in the late afternoon.

aqiqah a tradition of the Holy Prophet[sa] observed by Muslims on the birth of a baby, in which the newborn's head is shaved, charity is given to the poor, and animal sacrifice is made. The *aqiqah* is performed on the seventh day after the child's birth.

Badr the second official organ of the Ahmadiyya Muslim Community established on 31 October 1902. This weekly newspaper was published from Qadian, District Gurdaspur, in the Urdu language.

bast or 'expansion' refers to a state in which the seeker experiences a high in their spiritual condition and communion with God.

baqa literally, 'subsistence' or 'life.' See *fana.*

Bukhari also referred to as *Sahih Bukhari* is the most authentic book of Hadith tradition among the *sihah sittah* i.e. the six authentic books of Hadith.

dhikr-e-arra literally, the 'invocation of the saw'. A Sufi invocation, commonly found among the Yasavi order and others. The sound that comes from the throat of those performing this chant aloud resemble the grinding of a saw and is symbolic for the Sufi 'sawing their desires.'

Eid-ul-Adha literally, 'the festival of sacrifices' is celebrated by Muslims to mark the end of the annual pilgrimage to Mecca on the tenth day of Dhul-Hijjah. Animals are slaughtered throughout the Muslim world in remembrance of the sacrifice of Abraham[as], and this meat is distributed amongst the poor. It is also referred to as 'the Greater Eid.'

Eid-ul-Fitr a festival celebrated at the end of Ramadan with the sighting of the new moon, to offer gratitude to Allah for the blessings of Ramadan.

Fajr the first of the five daily prayers, which is offered at dawn before sunrise.

fana literally, 'annihilation' or 'to cease to exist'. The Sufis speak of three stages in man's spiritual journey to God. The first stage is *fana,* or the complete denial of the self and the realisation that only when a person imposes a death upon their own soul can they be truly united with God. The second stage is *baqa* (subsistence or life) and the third stage is *liqa* (meeting), which is the state of union with God. The state of *fana fillah* means to be lost or absorbed completely in the love of Allah.

fayj-e-a'waj literally, 'a crooked group' refers to a dark period destined to dawn upon the Muslims after the first three golden centuries of Islam. According to the prophecies of the Holy Prophet[sa], this would be an era in which the Muslims would lose their spirituality and be misguided.

Futuhat refers to *Al-Futuhat-ul-Makkiyyah* (The Meccan Openings) is a well-known book in the field of Islamic mysticism by Abu Abdullah Muhammad ibn Ali ibn Muhammad ibn Arabi.

Gulistan literally, 'The Garden' is a famous work of Persian literature by the renowned poet Sheikh Sa'di comprising deep points of wisdom and insight.

Al-Hakam the first official organ of the Ahmadiyya Muslim Community established on 8 October 1897. The first editor of *Al-Hakam* was Hazrat Sheikh Yaqub Ali Irfani[ra]. This weekly newspaper was published from Qadian, District Gurdaspur.

halalah a practice among certain Muslims in which a female divorcee marries another man, consumates the marriage, and then gets a divorce, so that it becomes permissible for her to remarry a previous husband. Such pre-planned marriages of convenience are forbidden in Islam and the Holy Prophet[sa] has sent curse on those who engage in this unlawful practice.

ihsan a favour, but in the context of worship, the Holy Prophet[sa] has expounded that *ihsan* means to worship God as though one can see Him, and if this is not possible, then at least to stand before Him in worship knowing that He can see you.

Ihya-ul-Ulum refers to *Ihya Ulum-ud-Din* (The Revival of the Religious Sciences) by Abu Hamid Muhammad ibn Muhammad Al-Ghazali. It is widely regarded by Muslims as a major work in religious philosophy and spirituality.

Isha the last of the five daily prayers, which is offered in the evening, shortly after nightfall.

Ishraq is an optional Prayer consisting of two phases: two *rak'ats* are offered when the sun has risen for a while but not enough to have heated up the environment. Once the latter has occurred, this is the second phase, in which one may offer four or eight *rak'ats*. The first phase is known as *salat-ul-ishraq* and the second *salat-ud-duha*. It has been named *salat-ul-awwabin* as well. In some Traditions, however, the Prayer offered between Maghrib and Isha consisting of six *rak'ats* is called *salat-ul-awwabin*.

khatm-e-nubuwwat is a term in Islamic literature that refers to the rank of the Holy Prophet Muhammad[sa] as the Seal of Prophets. Please see 'Seal of Prophets' for further details.

Maghrib the fourth of the five daily prayers and offered right after sunset.

Mahdi literally 'the guided one' and also refers to the Imam Mahdi—a title meaning 'Guided Leader', given to the Reformer of the Latter Days prophesied by the Holy Prophet Muhammad[sa].

Malfuzat written records of sayings, discourses and audiences of pious men, Sufis and religious divines.

maulvi a Muslim cleric

mi'raj literally, 'the ascension' was a spiritual experience of the Holy Prophet[sa] in which he travelled into the heavens, met various Prophets and ultimately Allah Himself.

Munkar and Nakeer are the names of the two angels appointed by Allah the Exalted to question a person in their grave after death. Those who are able to answer correctly will rest in ease, while those who are not will suffer until they are raised from their grave by Allah Almighty.

nafi-o-asbat a meditative practice among the Sufis, in which they recite, as a formula, the Muslim creed *la ilaha illallahu muhammadur-rasulullah,* and direct the energy of these words throughout their body, whilst holding their breath. First they recite *la ilaha* (there is no God) and this constitutes a negation *(nafi)* of all that is besides God. Then they recite *illallah,* (except for Allah) which is an affirmation *(asbat)* of the One True God.

Nakir see Munkar.

Nusherwan surnamed Adil or the Just ascended the throne on the death of his father Qubad as the Chosroes or king of Persia in 531 AD. He died after a reign of 48 years and was succeeded by his son Hurmuz IV in 579 AD. Nusherwan was famed for his exemplary adherence to principles of equity and justice irrespective of religion or creed.

qabz or 'contraction' refers to a state in which the seeker experiences a low ebb in their spiritual condition.

qawwali a style of music employed by certain sufi sects within Islam as a form of devotion and worship.

qiblah the direction in which a Muslim should face when observing the formal Islamic Prayer. The *qiblah* of the Muslims is the Holy Ka'bah in Mecca.

rak'at a single unit in the formal Islamic Prayer, consisting of the standing and bowing positions, as well as two prostrations.

salahiyyat a higher level of virtue. Please see *muttaqi* and *salih.*

sati a Hindu tradition in which a widow would burn herself to death on her husband's pyre as an expression of loyalty to her to him. This was done by the widow voluntarily and, as if, demonstrated that she was a dutiful wife who followed her husband to the afterlife.

Seal of the Prophets is *Khatam-un-Nabiyyin* in Arabic. The Arabic word *khatam* means, a signet ring, a seal, a stamp or a mark; the end or last part or portion and result or issue of a thing. The word also signifies embellishment or ornament; the best and most perfect. Therefore, the expression *Khatam-un-Nabiyyin* or Seal of the Prophets would mean, the best and most perfect of the Prophets; the embellishment, ornament or crown of the Prophets. It also means the 'last' of the law-bearing Prophets.

Seal of the Books is *Khatam-ul-Kutub* in Arabic and refers to the Holy Quran, which is the best and most perfect book of all divine scriptures. It is also the last of all divine laws revealed by Allah the Exalted. See 'Seal of the Prophets.'

Seal of the Book or *Khatam-ul-Kitab* is one of the names of Surah Fatihah, the first chapter of the Holy Quran. This chapter encompasses, all the divine insights and verities expounded in the Holy Quran and is the best of all prayers.

Shaykhayn literally, 'The Two Chiefs' is a title of honour that refers to Hazrat Abu Bakr[ra] and Hazrat Umar[ra], the first and second Caliphs of the Holy Prophet[sa] respectively.

Syed a descendant of the Holy Prophet Muhammad[sa].

Tahajjud the voluntary prayer offered in the middle of the night, before the obligatory Prayer at dawn.

Tirmidhi also referred to as *Jami at-Tirmidhi* is the fourth authentic compilation of Hadith tradition among the *sihah sittah* i.e. the six authentic books of Hadith.

wahdat-ul-wujud literally, 'Oneness of Being' is a Sufi doctrine generally attributed to Ibni Arabi, which suggests that God and His creation are one in the same thing. Those who believe in this doctrine are referred to as Wujudis.

Zuhr the second of the five daily prayers, which is offered in the afternoon after the sun begins to decline from its zenith

Index

Index of Verses of the Holy Quran

Index of Subject Matter

W

Y